10 0418648 7

Dodin and the
Maly Drama Theatre

DATE DUE FOR RETURN

This book may be recalled

D1494585

This is the   company, the M   din.
   Maria S   ctorial
processes a   thods,
which she   ctions.
Dodin and   w the
impact of   l gives
the reader
   Includir   Maly,
Dodin and t   model
for actor t   idio to
stage.

Maria Sh   of Post-
graduate S   -editor
of *New Th*   tledge,
2005).

Dodin and the Maly Drama Theatre

Process to performance

Maria Shevtsova

Routledge
Taylor & Francis Group

LONDON AND NEW YORK

NOTTINGHAM UNIVERSITY LIBRARY

1004186457

First published 2004 by Routledge
11 New Fetter Lane, London EC4P 4EE

Simultaneously published in the USA and Canada by Taylor & Francis Inc
29 West 35th Street, New York, NY 10001

Routledge is an imprint of the Taylor & Francis Group

© 2004 Maria Shevtsova

Typeset in Baskerville by The Running Head Limited, Cambridge
Printed and bound in Great Britain by MPG Books Ltd, Bodmin

All rights reserved. No part of this book may be reprinted or
reproduced or utilised in any form or by any electronic,
mechanical, or other means, now known or hereafter
invented, including photocopying and recording, or in any
information storage or retrieval system, without permission in
writing from the publishers.

Every effort has been made to ensure that the advice and information
in this book is true and accurate at the time of going to press. However,
neither the publisher nor the authors can accept any legal responsibility
or liability for any errors or omissions that may be made.

British Library Cataloguing in Publication Data
A catalogue record for this book is available from the British Library.

Library of Congress Cataloging in Publication Data
Shevtsova, Maria, 1945–
    Dodin and the Maly Drama Theatre process to performance / Maria
Shevtsova.
    p. cm.
    Includes bibliographical references and index.
    1. Akademicheskiæi maliæi dramaticheiæi teatr (Saint Petersburg,
    Russia)–History. 2. Theater–Russia–Saint Petersburg–History–20th
    century. 3. Dodin, Lev, 1944–Criticism and interpretation. I. Title.
    PN2726.S252M3 2004
    792.02'33'092–dc22   20030181

ISBN 0–415–33461–6 (hbk)
ISBN 0–415–33462–4 (pbk)

To the memory of my parents Lyudmila and Semyon, and for my daughter Sasha

Contents

Figures

Foreword

Simon Callow

In the summer of 1988, I was rehearsing the part of Faust in David Freeman's version of Goethe's play. We were doing it more or less in its entirety, an epic undertaking, with a suitably lengthy rehearsal period (three months). Freeman, noted for his innovatory opera productions, was exploring the work with great freedom. It was hard work, but we were definitely getting somewhere with it. One evening, shortly before we opened, I thought it would be useful to take the night off and see someone else's work. The play I chose was *Stars in the Morning Sky*, performed by the Maly company at the Riverside Studios. I had heard rumours of their excellence, but I had read nothing about them; this was the first preview, before any notices had appeared.

It is scarcely possible for me to exaggerate the impact that evening had on me. It's an interesting play, and the physical production was striking. What lifted it into another realm altogether, however, was the acting. Each performance was audacious, powerfully expressive, rhythmically exhilarating. One seemed to be taken through layer after layer to the heart of the characters, and beyond that, to their very essences. This group of riff-raff, tarts and nutcases was transfigured into a vision of the human condition as piercing as the greatest painting, the most searing music, could offer. But the achievement was a collective one, like the playing of a great orchestra. What was exceptional was the *melos*, the underlying sense of the whole. More extraordinary, even, than the individual performances or the interplay between the characters, was the corporate life manifested on the stage. The connectivity of the actors was almost tangible, an organic tissue which made them breathe as one and move with a profound awareness of everything that was going on within the group.

I was overwhelmed. I had never seen a group like it and never had a comparable experience in a theatre. Everyone in the theatre that night felt the same, unmistakably. There was a very specific reason that I was so particularly shaken by it, however. It was everything for which my training (at the Drama Centre in London) had been a preparation, namely, the ideal of the true ensemble, but which I had never seen. It had been a central tenet of our work as students that the highest form of theatrical endeavour was to belong to such a group, committed to each other for many years, in perpetual evolution, who would grow by working together closely over a long period of time, creating levels of confidence and courage which would enable them to take on the greatest challenges of the repertory with an unprecedented level of depth across the board: every player a star, one day carrying the play, the next day a spear. The actors would be in perpetual training, spurred on by voice and movement teachers; by exploratory workshop sessions requiring a degree of openness and commitment only available to people who have learned to trust each other and risk making fools of themselves without embarrassment, by directors who monitored the actors closely, noting their strengths and weaknesses, shaping the repertory and the distribution of roles according to a graph of personal development.

By the time I saw the Maly, I had come to believe that this was not so much an ideal as a myth. Even the great companies I had seen – the Moscow Art Theatre, the Berliner Ensemble, the Schaubühne – had either ossified or disbanded, and the noble British attempts at it in the 1960s, by Peter Hall at the RSC and Laurence Olivier at the National Theatre, had by the mid-1970s moved towards the model of the repertory theatre with a group of players hired for a season or two to perform specific plays. There were smaller groups like Mike Alfred's Shared Experience and Declan Donnellan's Cheek by Jowl whose actors and directors experimented together over some years with stimulating results, but the concept of the ensemble demands a scale of organisation which was simply not available to what were essentially touring outfits, woefully underfunded and overworked. It must be said, too, that the notion of an unending training is deeply inimical to most British actors who feel that three years at drama school is quite enough of a good thing, thank you very much. The vision began to fade.

Now here I was, suddenly, in the presence of the Holy Grail. My first reaction was one of humility, almost of shame. How shallow, obvious and meretricious an actor I felt myself to be in the face of what every single one of these actors was achieving. In a few days, our production of *Faust* would open. Rehearsing it, I had dimly thought that virtually every scene merited a month's rehearsal, instead of the day we were able to give it. Serious and exploratory though Freeman's work was, and dedicated and hard-working though we actors were, we were attempting to stage two plays which together amounted to seven hours of pulverisingly dense text. Quick decisions had to be made, linear logic identified, effective solutions found. We attempted to tell the story with clarity, to find a physical metaphor for the play, to create credible characters. On the whole we succeeded in all these things, and the lumbering *Meisterwerk* was brought to a public which was for the most part very appreciative. But (and here of course I speak only for myself) we could have done so much better. The work, complex and elusive though it often is, deserved so much better. I was conscious, as Faust, of getting through the role, using my skills to paper over the cracks. It was partly a matter of time, but that was not all. The company, most of whom had never worked together before, were committed and democratic, but came from diverse backgrounds, with different trainings, or no training at all, and despite group warm-ups and sessions of collective music-making, had no shared view of the work and were thus essentially executants rather than interpreters. The actors of the Maly had somehow fused themselves into a single body without having lost their individuality.

How had they done it? I had to find out. Whenever the Maly came to Britain, I went out of my way to see their work: *The Cherry Orchard*, light and swift, but so emotionally communicative that I never stopped weeping from beginning to end, even – especially – when it was at its funniest. The party scene in Act II was a miracle both of staging and acting: every character, every unnamed guest at the party was a universe unto him- or herself, as they wove across the stage, sweeping up the other characters, cutting through and across scenes, not disrupting but enhancing the movement of the play. This was not a text staged, but a world in which movement, language, character were all part of a stream of human life which passed before us, eddying, flowing, now babbling, now murmuring, sometimes torrential, sometimes placid. *The Devils* started monumentally with the entire ensemble singing Russian Orthodox chants, and proceeded with relentless casuistical energy to lay bare the whole malaise of the nineteenth-century Russian soul; *Gaudeamus*, a wild slapstick performed with reckless physical daring and sudden shafts of surreal pain; *A Play With No Name*, their version of the text generally known in English as *Platonov*, for me perhaps the greatest of their achievements, where the physical realisation of the play and its emotional cross-currents was of such audacity – most of the action was played in a deep pool of water; at regular intervals the company, playing a variety of instruments, would strike up a classical piece or some mad jazz riff – that the stage seemed entirely liberated from its confines, though within all this highly projected life were scenes of the most scrupulous naturalism and exercises of skill (as when a drunken character dances on the table while the servants slowly and imperturbably remove the remains of supper, including the table-cloth), breathtaking in their observed accuracy.

Curiously, though the design of each show is remarkable, and the staging itself is prodigiously brilliant, it is not of the director or the designer that one thinks while watching the show. One doesn't even particularly think of the writer. It is the actors who hold you absolutely, not simply as performers, nor even as individuals, but as some kind of collective conduit for the life-force. A Maly production is contained within the actors' bodies, brains, hearts and souls; it is the sum total of their work, their relationship with each other, their relationship to the world. The experience of the production, no matter how stylised the conception, is always deeply human. There is nothing *out there*, no objective artistic statement, simply the sum total of the artists' contribution, both as people and as players. Dodin is clearly a visionary of the highest order, but in no sense are the actors merely enacting his masterplan: they are its living matter, shaping the production as much as shaped by it.

How this extraordinary phenomenon has come about is described by Maria Shevtsova in the probing and highly evocative pages that follow. For those, like me, who believe in the supremacy of the ensemble as a means of taking the theatrical arts to the highest level of which they are capable, it is a moving and inspiring account; for those to whom the idea has yet to appeal, it may finally convince them of its urgent necessity. It will have served its purpose even if it merely records that such a company exists, that such things are possible. It is fervently to be hoped otherwise, but it is possible that economic circumstances may threaten the Maly's existence. Such a company is not, let us be realistic, commercially viable; moreover, it demands absolute commitment over a long period of time from its participants. To exist at all it requires enlightened support from government sources, and necessitates the abandonment by the company of other professional possibilities. It is not for all actors or directors. But surely somewhere, somehow in the English-speaking world it is possible to truly honour the art of the theatre – to which so much lip-service is paid – by investing in an organisation comparable to the Maly; the template, so precisely and so acutely described by Maria Shevtsova, is here for all to behold. I can think of no more important book for the theatre at the beginning of this uncertain century.

Preface

This is a dedicated study of the work of Lev Dodin with the Maly Drama Theatre of St Petersburg. It includes a discussion of his productions of opera on the international stage, without which a sense of his achievements as a director would not be complete. His opera productions, while independent of the Maly, nevertheless sharpen perception of his theatre process with his own company. My book is analytical and informative rather than critical. It is motivated by a desire to show how and why the productions are made, and its detailed analysis of them is an attempt to capture that most ephemeral of arts which is the art of performance. I do not for a moment labour under the illusion that an account of performances can be objective, since a subjective eye is always involved in the act of emotional understanding. This having been said, while spectators' viewpoints vary, there is something like the basic foundations of a production, or its 'drawing', as Dodin would say, that does not shift altogether. I have seen the productions discussed here numerous times, some over a span of several years. My analysis is a compound of them, and any significant shifts in the production over time are noted, especially because a work of the theatre is, for Dodin, an organism that grows and changes with those who make it.

My book details the Maly's working processes and the various steps its virtual productions take before they are shown to the public and/or subsequently re-edited by Dodin. There is so much talk in theatre studies about 'process', about recording working methods and their articulation in performances, but this area of research is fraught with many difficulties and has remained, as a result, largely unexplored. I am privileged to have been allowed to observe the every-day work, devising and rehearsals of a remarkable group of actors and their no less remarkable director. This opportunity has enabled me to record aspects of the rehearsal process as well as of its results in public performance, some of which I interweave with my study of individual productions. Dodin's direction of *The Queen of Spades*, the subject of my last chapter, condensed the rehearsal time, by contrast with the long rehearsal periods of the Maly, allowing me to receive the full impact of his working process in a singularly immediate way. The company, not least its teachers and administrators, generously shared their professional and personal experiences with me, treating me as one of their own. In my text, I include their voices to create polyphonic discourse. Their remarks, whether indirectly reported or quoted, are indicated by a date in brackets so as to fix the fleeting word.

Where my narrative permits, I include critical reviews to suggest the impact of the Maly's work in Russia and the many countries where they have built their formidable international reputation; also to suggest from what different cultural perspectives this work is viewed. While I situate Dodin and the Maly in their Russian context, sociopolitical and theatrical, it will be clear to my reader that their outlook is not insular and that Dodin is both a Russian and a European director.

A note on transliteration

I have opted for a user-friendly transliteration from the Cyrillic alphabet, intended for readers with no Russian. Thus I have deleted soft and hard signs. The terminals u and ŭ are given as y, as is ы; я is given as ya; ю as yu. I have retained such familiar spellings as Meyerhold, Dostoevsky, Tchaikovsky and Gergiev, and Charlotta instead of Sharlotta in *The Cherry Orchard*. All translations from Russian, French, Italian and German are my own, except for the one indicated in chapter 4.

Acknowledgements

Every book is written with the support of others and this one is no exception. I am indebted to the British Academy for a Research Leave Grant; to Lancaster University for honouring it in kind and helping with my travel expenses; to the Arts and Humanities Research Board for its generous travel grant and to Goldsmiths College, University of London, for allowing me a sabbatical of two months when I really needed it.

My deepest thanks go, above all, to Lev Dodin and the Maly actors, many of whom I quote in my book. All gave me their time, energy and attention, patiently answered my questions and discreetly ignored my presence when it might have been easier not to have me there. I am grateful to the numerous members of this company in their various capacities, but must especially thank Mikhaïl Stronin and Dina Dodina for their consistent attention, as well as Roman Malkin, Natalya Kolotova, Aleksandra Golybina and Yelena Aleksandrova, the Maly's archivist, whose exemplary courtesy and efficiency facilitated my research; the Maly teachers Valery Galendeyev, Mikhaïl Aleksandrov, Yevgeny Davydov, Yelena Lapina, Valery Zvezdochkin, Yury Vasilkov and Yury Khomutyansky; also the designers Eduard Kochergin, Aleksey Poray-Koshits and David Borovsky. I wish also to thank Chloé Obolensky and Declan Donnellan.

My research could not have been completed without the help of several institutions and key people in them: the Academy of Theatre Arts, St Petersburg; La Scala, Milan; Maggio Musicale Teatro Comunale, Florence and especially Susanna Colombo and Lara Colzi; the Opéra National de Paris-Bastille and especially Catherine Heuls; De Nederlandse Opera, Amsterdam, whose staff showed me great kindness, especially Tia Schutrups; the Barbican Centre in London, whose staff always helped, especially Griselda Yorke and David Jays; the Newcastle Playhouse and Alan Lyddiard. To the boundless hospitality of Yelena Levshina in St Petersburg I owe devoted thanks, and to Michelle and Marc Bonet-Maury in Paris. Wendy Cobcroft, who has always been a supportive friend, is the best proof-reader I know; any errors left in this book are entirely my responsibility. My daughter Sasha is glad to see the last of it. Thank you, Lisa Cagnacci, for providing me with hands when I needed them.

The section on *A Play With No Name* in chapter 5 developed from my article

'Drowning in Dixie: The Maly Drama Theatre Plays Chekhov Untitled', *Theatre-Forum* 13, pp. 46–53. My section on *Mazepa* in chapter 6 derives from an earlier version, 'War and Ash at La Scala: Lev Dodin Rehearses *Mazepa*', *TheatreForum* 16, pp. 95–104.

Photographs courtesy of the Archive of the Maly Drama Theatre of St Petersburg for plates 1, 2, 3, 4, 5, 7, 15. Photograph courtesy of Teatro alla Scala, Archivio Fotografico, for plate 16. Photographs courtesy of Ken Reynolds for plates 6, 8, 9, 10, 13, 14. Photographs courtesy of Marc Enguerand for plates 11, 12. Photographs courtesy of Hans van den Bogaard for plates 17, 18, 19. Photograph courtesy of Eric Mahoudeau for plate 20.

Part I
The Maly in context

1 From Leningrad to St Petersburg

Dodin and the Maly: journeys to the future

The uncommon story of the Maly Drama Theatre unfolds in the city built by Peter I as a 'window to Europe' on the swamps of the River Neva. It was St Petersburg from 1703, Petrograd during the First World War and the Revolution, Leningrad after 1924, and St Petersburg, again, in September 1991. St Petersburg's last transformation took place three months before the USSR was dissolved and the Russian Federation became 'Russia' once again, a country faced with the enormous task of reinventing itself as best it could in circumstances far from propitious for renewal and growth. Peter the Great had made St Petersburg a European city in appearance, culture and outlook. The Soviet Union aimed to make it neither European nor Russian. It was to be Soviet, a transnational phenomenon meant to supersede the relativities of time, space and history for the sake not of a particular socialism, but of world Socialism. Today, St Petersburg has returned to its Russian roots and European aspirations in order to reclaim an identity that would not be narrowly national or inward-looking, nor, on the other hand, subordinate to an allegedly globalised world. This is the difficult act which the Maly Drama Theatre also aimed to accomplish at the dawn of the new millennium.

'Maly' means 'small', which describes quite adequately the 35-seat theatre that was founded in May 1944 to 'service' the outlying region of the city of Leningrad; and the term 'service', which was used without any prevarication at the time, indicates the populist intentions behind the enterprise. No one could ever have imagined that this theatre, designated for local communities, would radically alter direction and become, in the last decade of the twentieth century, a star player on the international stage. When the Maly was founded, the Leningrad blockade of 900 days and countless terrors had recently come to an end, as soon would the Second World War. Nearly a million people had died from starvation, disease and cold during the blockade; its survivors were nothing less than monuments to the city's awesome heroism.[1] Most theatres had been evacuated fairly early on, with the notable exception of the theatre named after the actress Vera Komissarzhevskaya, which worked right through those fearsome years. The Maly Drama Theatre was created to help bring life back to normal. This also meant performing for the troops at the battlefront in the region until the war came completely to an end. Like all theatres in the Soviet

period, it was established by governmental decree, and, like them, was super-
vised by the Ministry of Culture and various committees answerable to the
Communist Party. It performed in all sorts of makeshift venues, in factories,
halls and clubs, to fulfil its mission of making theatre performances available, as
well as culturally accessible, to people unable to see them in the everyday course
of their lives. By and large, its purposes were similar to those of its people's-
theatre and popular-theatre counterparts endorsed by governments after the
war in western Europe and beyond, of which the salient example might well be
Jean Vilar's Théâtre National Populaire.[2] When in Leningrad, the Maly Drama
Theatre was located in its dedicated space in a building that had been constructed at the end of the nineteenth century as a variety theatre by its owner
for his dancer wife. Here, in a corner of this Petersburg folly, it usually performed to some 30 spectators. The term 'drama' is used in Russia to distinguish
this type of theatre from lyrical theatre, opera or musical theatre.

The theatre lived on in a hand-to-mouth sort of way until 1973, when
Roman Malkin became its managing director and Efim Padve its artistic director. Padve already enjoyed a successful career in Leningrad and had been a
pupil of the redoubtable Georgy Tovstonogov, director of Leningrad's Bolshoy
Drama Theatre, which was considered to be 'virtually the strongest Russian
company of the post-Stalin period' (Smeliansky, 1999: 13). He shared Malkin's
ambition to give the Maly Drama Theatre an artistic project, which it had
failed in the past to combine with its social plan. Padve demanded more of
actors, raised the artistic and technical standard of productions, and focused on
contemporary plays, both Russian and foreign, including plays by Edward
Albee – a remarkable choice of repertoire for a lack-lustre touring company
with no authority whatsoever in Leningrad and modest achievements in the
Leningrad province. As a result of its general overhaul, the theatre was able to
build up audiences in the city while continuing its work in the region, although
now at a higher creative level and still at the gruelling pace of up to 200 performances each season, all of it in extremely difficult working conditions (Malkin,
St Petersburg, 30 September 1998).

It is here that Lev Dodin enters the Maly's history. Padve invited this young,
gifted director, among several others who had attracted his attention, within a
year of taking office, as part of his brief to develop the theatre. Dodin had graduated from the Leningrad Institute of Theatre, Music and Cinematography in
1966 and had acquired something of a reputation from the imaginative and
daring productions that he had mounted as an 'apprentice', one might say, of
Zinovy Korogodsky at the Leningrad Young People's Theatre (LenTYuZ). The
LenTYuZ had flourished under Korogodsky's leadership, and, by the time of
Dodin's participation in it, was well known nationally for its experimental work.
At the Maly, Dodin staged *The Robber* by Karel Čapek in 1974, *The Rose Tattoo*
by Tennessee Williams in 1977 and texts by important Soviet writers of the
1970s such as Aleksandr Volodin and Valentin Rasputin, who disclosed grim
realities usually beautified in the official media. Rasputin's *Live and Remember*
staged by Dodin in 1979, for example, treated the taboo theme of desertion by

Soviet soldiers during the war. In 1980 came *The House*, which Dodin had adapted from the novel by Fyodor Abramov, a major figure in the newly emergent 'village' literature.[3] This was a rather curious genre which, in one variation, idealised peasant life, thereby echoing Soviet propaganda on the subject, and, in another, exposed the considerable deprivations imposed by the state on the peasantry, especially during the Stalin period. Abramov belonged to the second, critical strand for which Dodin had a deep sympathy. *The House* made a huge impact, and more or less consolidated Dodin's growing fame as a renegade director.

Other productions followed elsewhere, in particular *The Meek One* after Dostoevsky at the Bolshoy Drama Theatre in 1981 (revived at the Moscow Art Theatre in 1985), and *The Golovlyovs*, which Dodin adapted from Saltykov-Shchedrin's novel, at the Moscow Art Theatre in 1984. Innokenty Smoktunovsky, a riveting stage actor best known outside Russia for his Hamlet in Sergey Kozintsev's 1964 film, played the leading role in this epic production in which Dodin attempted to transfer the collaborative working methods that he was developing at the Maly to a house that was anything but open to innovative approaches. Luminary figures like Smoktunovsky, or the MKhAT's director Oleg Yefremov, were the exceptions that confirmed the rule.[4] Saltykov-Shchedrin's book is a denunciation of empty talk, which was taken by Dodin and his audiences to be an extremely relevant theme for the times.

Dodin was obliged to work in a freelance capacity because he did not have a 'theatre-home' of his own – that institution of the Russian theatre dating from the historical meeting in 1897 between Stanislavsky and Nemirovich-Danchenko when they resolved to create the Moscow Art Theatre. The Art Theatre was founded on the idea of a collectivity that would stay together a long time, bound by common artistic goals and perceptions which would come to be shared by its audiences. It was to be a 'home', too, in the sense that it would require the sustained care and loyalty of its members. The idea persisted right through the Soviet period, and its creative principles survived despite the fact that state bureaucrats decided who would run the theatres. Yefremov worked with a group of students that was to form the Sovremennik Theatre (*sovremennik* means 'contemporary') where, despite the bureaucratic impositions placed upon him, he created a veritable 'home', a tightly-knit organisational and creative unit with a distinctive theatrical style. He was transferred in 1970 to the MKhAT, basically to revive this once-glorious establishment. Yury Lyubimov, who was a highly esteemed actor at the Vakhtangov Theatre, managed to win over officials to give him the run-down Taganka in 1964, where he built a company of world renown. Tovstonogov, after a period in Moscow and his native Tiflis in Georgia, was appointed to the Bolshoy Drama Theatre. Anatoly Efros was the only one of the four major directors of the 1960s and 1970s who did not have a sanctified 'home', although he worked with his own actors at the Malaya Bronnaya and, from there, commanded the love of the Moscow public.

Efros unwittingly demonstrated the power of the theatre-home, not least in symbolic terms, when he was moved, in 1984, from the Malaya Bronnaya to the Taganka. The transfer occurred shortly after Lyubimov had been dismissed from his position of artistic director and deprived of his citizenship (ostensibly for criticising the Soviet government to the British press, although old scores for his outspoken, quasi-dissident productions were being settled for good measure). That Efros accepted the position and, further, appeared to believe that he could thrive in somebody else's nest was met with incredulity in the theatre community, as well as with hostility from a sizeable number of the Taganka actors. Anatoly Smeliansky, when referring to Efros's ill-starred move, observes that his own 'family' at the Malaya Bronnaya was breaking up and, consequently, the move was 'prompted by a crisis in the very idea of the theatre-home and theatre-family'. He continues:

> In Soviet conditions, this vital Russian idea had turned into a situation where the performers were feudally owned not only by the state, but by their own theatrical 'family'. No one had any freedom, that is to say the natural right to leave – to be 'divorced'. In such conditions the threat of losing one's theatre was for both actor and director tantamount to a death threat. The melancholy fate of so-called 'free' directors and actors (of whom there were only a handful in the whole country!) was plain to everyone.
>
> (Smeliansky, 1999: 111)

However stultifying the situation may have become, the point appreciated by everyone was that the absence of a theatre-home, even in these conditions of servitude, was a terrible fate. This was precisely the fate of Dodin all through the 1970s, right up to one year before the Lyubimov–Efros misfortunes and Dodin's staging of *The Golovlyovs* at the MKhAT.

Into the twenty-first century

The reversal of Dodin's fortunes occurred in 1983, when Padve resigned from the Maly, and Dodin, on Malkin's invitation, accepted the post of artistic director. He was nearly 40 years old with at least 22 productions behind him. The company supported Dodin's appointment, for not only had it worked well with him but, by then, it numbered a few actors with whom Dodin had studied at the Theatre Institute. Dodin may have been 'homeless', but he was certainly not without a roof: his permanent teaching position at the Institute allowed him to develop his own school of acting and directing, and it was towards this source that he was able to look when considering the possibilities for the Maly's future. Yefremov, who had a nose for talent, offered him a niche at the Moscow Art Theatre. Dodin turned it down. Having been deprived of a theatre-home for so long, he was keenly aware of the lessons to be learned from its axioms and knew, therefore, that he would be able to realise his artistic vision only with actors with whom he shared a whole way of seeing and being, which was more likely if he formed them himself. The imperative to create an intimate relationship between his pedagogical practice and his theatre practice, where his pupils would become his actors and continue learning – a school in the broader sense of the term – was tantamount to reasserting the ideals of Stanislavsky's studio-theatre initiative that Dodin felt had become tenuous, even though directors continued to mould actors to their theatre's particular perspective.

His reasoning as to the immense benefits for the art of the theatre of a tight relationship between school/studio and professional stage was borne out in 1985 by *Brothers and Sisters*, Dodin's first production as the Maly's chief. He had already staged a version of this work in the late 1970s at the Theatre Institute with his friend and colleague Arkady Katzman and their students. *Brothers and Sisters* belonged to Abramov's trilogy *The Pryaslins* which, when followed by *The House*, formed a tetralogy dealing with the Pryaslin family. Many of those who had played in the student version of *Brothers and Sisters* now performed in its professional edition, more often than not in the same roles. The great beauty of the production lay in the process of maturation undergone both by the actors and the work, and in the power of ensemble acting achieved through this process, which was possible because of the unbroken line linking pedagogy and performance. Abramov's material had captivated the actors by its sensitivity to how the villagers of an all-but-forgotten outpost in Archangelsk, in the far north of the Soviet Union, had made enormous sacrifices for their country during the Second World War and its immediate aftermath without seeing any improvement in their lot. A tale of unconquerable faith, delusion, disillusion and lies, which was performed with a finesse that can only come from total conviction, *Brothers and Sisters* bored into the very heart of people's concerns, eliciting sensations and hopes half-forgotten by them. Its reverberations nationwide have become legendary in Russia, as has the coincidence of its premiere on 9 March, the day that Konstantin Chernenko died. Chernenko's death turned out to be the prelude to the momentous transformations sparked off subsequently by Mikhaïl Gorbachev's reforms that go under the names of 'perestroika' and 'glasnost'. It was *this* Maly, the newly reconstituted company flying the colours of *Brothers and Sisters* and, with them, the signs of a new age, that was to become the Maly known to the world. Given the historical, emotional and emblematic significance for the company of *Brothers and Sisters*, the production could well be described as its signature piece.

Now, at the beginning of the twenty-first century, the Maly comprises, besides some older actors from Padve's days and several of Dodin's contemporaries at the Institute, what might be called two main generations of Dodin-trained Institute actors: those who were trained by him and Katzman in the 1970s and the brilliant trainees of the 1980s who performed *Gaudeamus* in 1990, a number of them not formally completing their course requirements until *Claustrophobia* in 1994. This last group virtually retained its student ensemble status until the mid-1990s, even though it was fully integrated in the Maly. Finally, there is a recent addition to the generational layers of the Maly. It comprises a handful of recently graduated students from the Institute – renamed the Academy of Theatre Arts in 1992 – who were taught there by Dodin's close associates – voice, music, singing and dance teachers, all of whom continue to coach the Maly actors. Since about the mid-1990s, Dodin has been prevented from taking new classes at the Academy on a regular basis by the company's commitments abroad. His teaching goes on in the daily contact of rehearsals, which means that it is now essentially done from within the company in order to keep nurturing it and stretching its capabilities.

In the year 2000, the Maly consisted of 64 actors of whom five were on probation. This is more than double the size of the troupe that Dodin had taken in charge in 1983. However, the theatre as a whole employs roughly 220 people (Malkin, 30 September 1998), who include teachers, designers Eduard Kochergin and Alexey Poray-Koshits, technicians, stage, props and box-office managers, administrators, assistants, a company manager and Dodin's assistant director Natalya Kolotova, and a literary manager-cum-interpreter Mikhaïl Stronin. It is, indeed, a large 'family' to feed, and the bread has to come from various quarters, not least because the Maly's growth has involved expanding spatially upwards and outwards. The auditorium was enlarged and a balcony added in the 1990s, the whole now seating 460 spectators. This is a noticeable increase on the number of seats available at the Maly's beginnings.

In addition, office space had to be found and decent dressing-rooms provided for the actors. The latter were built in 1997 after years of make-do arrangements. Since the Maly is in a residential building, these new spaces had to be appropriated from the communal flats (*komunalki*) packed around the theatre precinct. Malkin recalls how dozens of people living in them had to be resettled with the help of the local authorities, while the region spent huge sums of money on the theatre's rebuilding programme – its duty, according to Malkin, given that the Maly is a statutory regional rather than city theatre. Its official status has remained unchanged since the Maly was founded, although the city owns the venue as such and the Maly pays the city a nominal rent. The regional government has always paid the theatre's salaries. Always meagre, these all but stopped at the time of the national financial crash in August 1998. The city government, while not a source of funds, has provided help in kind before, during and after perestroika, the pivotal moment for the destiny of the USSR. For instance, over the years it has provided about 50 apartments for actors to live in separately, that is, no longer in the *komunalka* style where five and more families shared one kitchen and one bathroom between them. The importance of such aid to the well-being of a theatre-home cannot be underestimated.

The financial condition of the Maly was never prosperous, which meant that it was no better off than most theatres subsidised by the Soviet state. The subsidy system did not automatically cease when the Soviet Union collapsed, but became risible in the unfamiliar circumstances of instant capitalism, when prices soared and the rouble became worthless. Theatres were forced to develop survival strategies in the make-or-break climate of the 'new Russia', and this meant looking for benefactors, much as the Moscow Art Theatre had done in Morozov, and Diaghilev and the Ballets Russes in Gunzburg. Dodin and the Maly found their patron in Vadim Somov and the petroleum refinery that he runs in Kirishi, a town 170 kilometres from St Petersburg. The Kirishi plant contains a theatre, which Somov has refurbished to the Maly's specifications, and a House of Rest (as these recuperation centres were known in the Soviet period), where the Maly actors stay when on tour or on holiday. The Maly has an annual season at Kirishi and generally gives about 50 performances in the villages and towns of the St Petersburg region. By doing so, it fulfils its regional brief, albeit at a much lower rate than the old Maly.

Somov's enterprise built a studio in the Maly's theatre in 1997 as an experimental space for its young directors, and five productions were performed there by 2000. In addition, it has co-financed various projects, including *Chevengur* with the Weimar Art Festival in 1999. This patronage, in addition to being a mechanism that returns cultural capital to Kirishi, brings, in the framework of a hesitant Russian market economy, traces of symbolic capital to the Maly in so far as 'clean' business endorsement (as distinct from the 'unclean' Mafia variety) carries the scent of prestige and legitimisation, by implying that the company is worth the financial investment put into it.[5] Moreover, while national patronage has been indispensable for something more than mere survival, so too has international touring, as will be seen shortly.

Perestroika and glasnost

The reforms initiated as a top-down process by Mikhaïl Gorbachev from 1986 to 1988, which he had anticipated when he took office in 1985, became steeped so deeply in a quagmire of untenable contradictions that they led at the end of 1991 to the disempowerment of the Communist Party of the Soviet Union (CPSU) and the dissolution of the Soviet state on 31 December of that year. Gorbachev, who had been the victim of a party and state coup in August, now had neither a party nor a state to lead. He duly resigned with a short speech on television in which he reminded his fellow citizens that they were the inheritors of a great civilisation 'and now the burden falls on each and every one that it may be resurrected to a new, modern and worthy life' (Service, 1997: 507).

'Perestroika' refers to the programme of economic restructuring that was essentially to give a mixed economy, a combination of the command-administrative methods that Gorbachev believed were fundamental to the socialist tradition and the competitive enterprise of capitalism. Yet, if he did not wish to embark on the road of unrestrained freedom of market forces, he was especially anxious to weaken the authoritarian bureaucratic system imposed by Stalin in the 1930s which, entrenched, had been largely responsible for the economic stagnation of the Brezhnev 1970s. This entailed, Gorbachev argued in *Pravda* in 1989, 'nothing less than a radical reconstruction of the whole of society' (White, 1995: 226) which, in the political sphere, meant pluralism and popular sovereignty instead of one-party rule.

The people's rule, as Gorbachev envisaged it, was to take place within the framework of socialism and under the overall guidance of the CPSU. Commentators have pointed out that the tension after 1989 between the principles of democracy and the dominance of a single party (on which Gorbachev had insisted until 1990) underlay the party's 'crisis of confidence', which 'reflected a deeper uncertainty about its function under conditions of perestroika, and indeed about the direction in which the society as a whole was meant to be moving' (White, 1995: 252). The decline of the party's authority, even in the eyes of those who had supported it, coupled with the 'state of economic emergency' into which the USSR had entered ('milk, tea, coffee, soap, meat had vanished from state retail outlets even in Moscow', Service, 1997: 468, 472) destroyed popular trust in the CPSU itself. This, together with the coup against Gorbachev, in which the party leadership was implicated, enabled Boris Yeltsin, when he came to power straight after Gorbachev's resignation, 'first to suspend and then to ban the party altogether (by September 1991, following the coup, only 2.3 per cent were still prepared to give the party their "full support")' (White, 1995: 254).

Gorbachev's most severe critics, when detailing the host of factors involved in his economic and political failures, also note that the obstacles thrown immediately into the path of perestroika by the Soviet leadership (hence their indictment of Gorbachev's 'naïveté' as regards his own men) had to do with the 'cripplingly distorting Stalinism' that continued, well after Stalin's death, 'to affect the entire ruling elite, leaving them in ignorance of the real trends in Soviet society' (Steele, 1996: 143). These critics consider that Gorbachev himself was by no means exempt from a Stalinist remoteness from reality and its mindset of conformity, caution and fear. His admirers, on the other hand, point to Gorbachev's success in democratising Russia, and praise his foreign policy vis-à-vis the west, which was instrumental in bringing down the Berlin Wall in 1989 and ending the Cold War (Brown, 1997).

Perestroika inspired mistrust and confusion within Russia. This was so because it had not provided solutions to problems, as promised, and the problems looked increasingly insurmountable as time went on. The glasnost policy generally met with greater approval because its positive effects were felt immediately. Nevertheless, glasnost went hand-in-glove with perestroika in so far as it was understood to be a necessary feature of improved economic productivity and management: people could not be expected to perform better if information was withheld from them; nor could they be expected to be accountable for their performance if they had no say in the matter. Furthermore, they could not assume the active role in public life to which Gorbachev's 'radical reconstruction of the whole of society' exhorted them if they were kept in the dark as to the infrastructure and political realities governing their lives. However, for all its direct ties with the economics and politics of perestroika, glasnost was, above all, the *cultural* motor for change since its drive for 'openness', as the term is usually translated, and for articulation of worries, doubts and criticisms ('glasnost' literally means 'giving voice'), was intended to affect people's thought, perception, evaluation and behaviour, liberating them from all manner and kind of censorship and constraint, including those that they had learned to impose upon themselves.

Glasnost, then, meant that there were to be no 'blank spots' for any aspect of

the country's history: the full extent of the mass killings of peasants during col-
lectivisation; the acknowledgement (where denial had previously been current)
that their livelihood had been systematically depleted and the true picture of
their existence falsified – matters that Dodin, in advance of glasnost, had
already brought to light via Abramov in *Brothers and Sisters*; the rehabilitation of
all victims of the Stalinist purges; and so on in a panoply of horrors that, for all
its salutary honesty, left the whole nation disillusioned and discouraged. Similarly, glasnost meant freedom of speech (in reality, a qualified freedom) for the
press, radio and television, and thus exposure of present evils as well: the
appalling rate of infant mortality; inequality in salary and status of women; violence against women in the home; crime, suicide, drug and alcohol abuse, rape,
abortion, prostitution, all of which were acknowledged to be prevalent to alarm-
ing degrees and all of which had, until then, been 'forbidden' subjects. The
mere fact that data, statistical and otherwise, was now recorded fully, as against
the spasmodic and incomplete information gathered previously, was in itself a
measure of the seriousness with which glasnost was being taken. Not seriously
enough, however, especially in its early days. Thus, the Chernobyl nuclear
explosion of 1986 was not reported in the press until more than two weeks after
the disaster, and Gorbachev took even longer to make a televised public
response (White, 1995: 98). His delay appeared to be a reluctant admission, at
the very best, of the existence of such a momentous problem.

Albeit inadequate in numerous respects, glasnost was beneficial for literature
and the theatre. Key books that had been banned were serialised in the literary
journal *Novy mir* – for instance, Boris Pasternak's *Dr Zhivago* in 1988 and Aleksandr Solzhenitsyn's *Cancer Ward* and *The First Circle* in 1990. Solzhenitsyn's
political programme 'How to rebuild Russia' was printed in two mass-
circulation newspapers in the same year (Brown, 1997: 9). Banned émigré works
also began to appear. Thus, Vladimir Nabokov's *Lolita*, a notorious émigré
piece, was published by the government publishing house in 1989 (White, 1995:
91). Solzhenitsyn, as well as being sent into exile, had been stripped of his
citizenship in 1974. It was restored in 1991, although he did not return to
Russia until 1994. Lyubimov, who had suffered a similar humiliation in 1984,
returned in 1988 and, in 1989, resumed the artistic directorship of the Taganka
Theatre (Picon-Vallin, 1997: 426). A comparable case occurred in the field of
music. Rostropovich and his family were given permission to leave by Brezhnev
in 1974, but discovered four years later from a news programme in France that
they had been stripped of their citizenship. Rostropovich refused a subsequent
offer to have it restored. His path was to cross that of Dodin in Tokyo in 1989,
where Rostropovich and the Maly were performing, and eventually gave rise to
a collaboration between them on the opera *Mazepa*.

Censorship, which had been a constant blight on the theatre, was officially
abolished in 1990. Its countless ravages included, in the case of Lyubimov, four
productions banned between 1964 and 1982. He was refused permission to
rehearse several works (notably an adaptation of *The Devils* by Dostoevsky) and
constantly reminded that he was not even to entertain the idea of staging

anything considered to be subversive by the powers that be (Picon-Vallin, 1997: 142).[6] The most significant censorship incident in Dodin's case occurred in the early 1980s when party bosses suddenly stopped his rehearsals for a production based on Yury Trifonov's *The Old Man* at the MKhAT (Stronin, Weimar, 9 July 1997). This production never materialised, but Dodin was to return to work on Trifonov with his students and show it at the Maly Drama Theatre in 1988. Lyubimov, for his part, was finally able to mount his banned productions in the perestroika and post-perestroika periods, both at home and abroad. Perhaps the most poignant example was *Alive* by Boris Mozhayev, banned by the Minister of Culture in 1968. Its theme of peasant destitution, which it shared with *Brothers and Sisters*, was unacceptable to a regime bent on embellishment. In 1989, 21 years later, Smeliansky observes, the revival of *Alive* was 'a great theatrical occasion . . . And yet, there was a feeling of tremendous sadness that the production had come too late, that it had withered, having been born in a different age and suffocated by silence' (Smeliansky, 1999: 44).

The Taganka's history illustrates the trench warfare waged between the authorities and the theatre, that allowed the former to invade theatres, while the latter were unable to reciprocate in kind. The theatre resorted to ruses and wiles in order to speak, thereby practising a type of covert glasnost long before its formalised appearance. This helps to explain why the theatre served the multiple functions of newspaper, television, forum for debate, and – possibly of foremost importance – a socialising space where people could be united by awareness, understanding, emotion and a feeling of solidarity which had become dissipated in the wider society. It is small wonder that the regime feared the theatre and sought to keep it down. And in this lies the paradox that Georges Banu identifies for Eastern European theatre in general, namely, that 'the adversary did not only do harm, it was also useful' (Picon-Vallin, 1997: 21). It would be spurious to romanticise totalitarianism by arguing that its bleak conditions allowed the theatre to flourish; equally spurious would be the assumption that the lack of leisure and pleasure under totalitarianism had opened up a niche for the theatre to fill. But the adversary *did* prove to be useful in Soviet Russia, albeit indirectly and at huge human cost, because, apart from its leisure/entertainment and glasnost purposes ahead of glasnost's time, the theatre was able to channel its energies into the artistic, as well as moral and spiritual development of its spectators. If this made it a 'church' – Smeliansky's slightly malicious term – it also ensured that it explored the art and craft of the theatre, thereby sustaining a process that had begun with Stanislavsky, Meyerhold, Vakhtangov, Taïrov, Okhlopkov and Mikhaïl Chekhov. The facts that the theatre was powerful (why else would it be censured and banned?) and was a magnet for gathering people together, were the necessary complements of its dedication to a heritage whose pioneers had invented the modern theatre. It was the flame of this theatre that had to keep burning anew. For the practitioners and spectators who had not been worn out by cynicism or exhaustion, the survival of the theatre, 'church' or 'home', was tantamount to a sacred duty.

Contributing to glasnost: **Stars in the Morning Sky**

Dodin was immersed in this complex ecology which, little by little, had contributed to the need for change officially recognised by Gorbachev. As Dodin has remarked more than once, the benefits of perestroika and glasnost were not given to the theatre as a gift: practitioners had worked hard for them for a long time and their efforts should not be diminished by the publicity given to official decrees. *Brothers and Sisters* is a case in point from the Maly's repertoire alone. However, the production that actually coincides with the glasnost period and is the closest to it in spirit is *Stars in the Morning Sky* by Aleksandr Galin, which Dodin staged in 1987 and took to Moscow in 1988. It was performed at the Taganka Theatre, the place of performance symbolising as much as anything in the production itself its immediate relevance to the decade.

The play is set on the outskirts of Moscow in 1980 just before the opening of the Olympic Games. The streets of the capital had been swept clean of the beggars, drunks, prostitutes, drug addicts and other human 'debris' for the occasion. This bit of window-dressing for the world coming to Moscow does not fool any of the characters in the play. The four prostitutes who have been shunted out of sight into a dilapidated barracks used by the mental asylum next door are Anna, who is well past her prime and a drunk; hard-bitten Klara, who earns her living well; young and beautiful Lora, who dreams of becoming a trapeze artist in a circus; 15-year-old Maria, who, glad of the opportunity to see the Olympic torch, has left her baby in town with girlfriends but, in the second half of the play, fears that her baby might be thought abandoned and sent to an orphanage. These women are guarded by Valentina, a fire-fighter who also works in the asylum, and her militia son Nikolay who falls in love with Maria, much to Valentina's consternation. Lora and Aleksandr, one of the asylum's patients who wanders into the barracks, have a quasi-mystical love affair. The play ends when the four women break through the doors locked by Valentina and rush up onto the roof to cheer the Olympic torch. The taboo themes let out of the box by glasnost are in full view, including the subject of children signed over to state orphanages by alcoholic mothers.

Galin's is a picture of surfaces. He does not probe the motives for actions. (Why, for instance, did Anna, who speaks at length about her past – she has placed two children in orphanages – believe she would find her happiness in the trade? Why did Maria leave her baby behind? Nothing in the playtext suggests that she was forced to do it.) Nor does he develop situations or the conflicts inherent in them, starting with those involving Anna and Valentina, and Valentina and Nikolay. There are obvious stereotypes such as the good prostitute (Anna), the 'holy' lunatic (Aleksandr), the diffident 'innocent' (Lora), and so on, which call upon the Bible and Dostoevsky, but sink into melodrama. The dialogue is often funny, which takes some of the edge off its coarse language; and it flirts with blasphemy, of which the brashest example is Aleksandr's explanation as to why the Virgin Mary was called a virgin, and Jesus, the Son of God. The main message appears to be that all the characters who are outcasts are victims of 'the system'. It is a tendentious play that captures the sullen, abrasive mood of the day, when a sudden kick or lashing out could be delivered virtually with impunity.

Yet Dodin turned this unprepossessing material into a star show. It is drawn in bold strokes, without any nuances, as Marina Dmitrevskaya accurately observes in the influential Moscow journal *Teatr* (1988: 48).[7] Which, as the very antithesis of the finely honed *Brothers and Sisters*, is precisely why the production generates such savage energy. The Maly actors muster all their talents to give depth of characterisation and insight, not so much into the causes of actions as into their desperate finality. That is to say, the four women see themselves as utterly worthless and superfluous. Nobody needs them and their abjection drives them to heedless irresponsibility and self-abuse. The actors create their characters' trauma through the violence and vulgarity of gesture: Anna (Tatyana Shestakova) is all angles, Lora (Irena Seleznyova) all legs, Klara (Marina Gridasova) all arms, thrown about; Maria's trauma, on the other hand (Natalya Akimova), is expressed through her childishness with the older women and her dependence on Nikolay (Sergey Kozyrev). While all characters are drawn sharply, it is, above all, the interaction between them that gives scene after scene its dramatic intensity, the whole building up to the finale when Valentina (Galina Filimonova, in a sterling performance of unremitting, embittered harshness) blocks the doors with her heavy body while her charges all but tear their way through her to get out. No sooner are they on the roof shouting their liberation than the squalid, narrow set of creaky beds, old chairs and peeling walls (by Alexey Poray-Koshits) splits apart. Clearly, the simultaneity of action suggests that the hope for something better configured in the ecstatic women on the roof is bound, like the decor, to break up and disappear. The last conversation between the characters no longer takes place against the wall which, to all intents and purposes, was a visual metaphor for the spiritual imprisonment of all, male and female, but against a space that has opened out into the darkness of the back of the stage and the wings. Soviet Russia may well have been poised to make good the promises of perestroika and glasnost, but Dodin's stage resolution of the dilemmas posed by social destruction and self-destruction is in the form of a question mark, in the dark.

Dodin deals quite brutally with the sentimentality of Galin's text and, without escaping sentimentalism altogether, generally manages to bring it into line with the hard tone pervading the whole. Some of this deviation from the letter of the word is brought about through Shestakova's gift for comedy, which she puts to good use in her inflections and intonations, lifting insubstantial dialogue to the drama of gallows humour. The production offers another alternative to the text, this time through narrative. In Galin's text, Maria jumps out of a moving car full of Klara's clients, and returns bloodied and bruised, possibly with a broken leg. In Dodin's production, Maria is gang-raped by Klara's clients. Dodin, in other words, dramatises a weak incident in the play and, by transforming it into an act of horror, both raises the stakes of the production and drives home his point that sexual violence is an integral part of the violence endemic in Soviet society.

The event, moreover, is designed to make an impact. As the women laugh, shout and weep for joy on the roof, Nikolay breaks into the barracks and lifts Maria, half naked and covered in blood, up in his arms. The composition is a *pietà*, and asks for commiseration and compassion for all the Marias of this world (Mary Magdalene woven, of course, into this figure of *caritas* and mercy). In one strong Christian image, Dodin dignifies Galin's trivial Christian references. A similar image, as if inverted, appears when Lora, in the very first scene of nudity ever to appear on the Soviet stage, cradles Aleksandr (Vladimir Osipchuk) in her lap. Here again, what is bland in Galin is transformed by theatrical means into a powerful moment. Dodin also fleshes out, as only a stage director can, the play's – and the production's – topical allusions. This is done primarily, rather too obviously, through music. The selection includes Georgy Sviridov's signature tune to the television news programme *Vremya* (*Time*), whose familiar ditty 'Time, Forward!' serves Dodin's ironies on the Brezhnev cult of optimism, which simply hid unpalatable truths; the popular song which, in English, is known as 'Midnight in Moscow'; the stirring, raucous singing voice of Vladimir Vysotsky, the icon of radicalism in the pre-glasnost era, who, in the 1970s, played an unforgettable Hamlet in the equally unforgettable production by Lyubimov. Vysotsky died in 1980 at the early age of 42. The production's use of his voice singing one of his many protest songs may also be read as its tribute to him.[8]

Russian critics showered the performers with praise. *Leningradskaya pravda* spoke of their 'brilliance' in a piece of 'honest and passionate' theatre (December 1987). The *Pravda* critic in Moscow cast his disapproving eye on the season as a whole, only to light up at the Maly 'where the actors really show the highest level of craft' (30 March 1988). Many recalled Gorky's *The Lower Depths*, one describing *Stars* as its '1980s variation' (*Literaturnaya gazeta*, 24 April 1987). The comparison provoked some soul-searching into the country's state of affairs. Dmitrevskaya dwelled on the plight of children abandoned by their mothers, arguing that the production's clemency towards such mothers as good as condoned their behaviour. *Vecherny Leningrad* argued that the production was not about prostitution but about 'our life, where we have become accustomed to thoughtlessness and treachery, indifference and spite' (3 August 1987). *Literaturnaya gazeta* noted that, although newspapers were endlessly running articles on prostitution – it had become a fashionable topic – the production had nothing to do with sensationalism. It 'was a response to the moral crisis of the late '70s and early '80s' and, in fact, was to some degree a product of this crisis. The critic defined 'crisis' as 'a threshold from which there was no going back, while everything ahead was unclear, vague'. All in all, the view held more or less unanimously was that *Stars*, in a time of re-evaluation, was not throwing morality overboard but instead was in search of a deeper common morality, something closer to a 'common humanity' (*Literaturnaya gazeta*, as above) that bound people together: the production's prostitutes were saints *and* sinners, like everybody else. The love scene between Lora and Alexey was viewed as a scene of purification (*Leningradskaya pravda*, as above), the *pietà* as a sign of hope for all those 'forgotten by God and human beings' (*Vecherny Leningrad*, as above). More than once, the world of Dostoevsky's insulted and injured was evoked, and especially Sonya Marmeladov from *Crime and Punishment*.

Again and again, critical reviews were couched in the language of morality, occasionally with religious overtones, as the production permitted. *Literaturnaya gazeta* is representative of them in saying that the most important feature of *Stars* is the question it raises as to what constitutes 'good and evil, morality and immorality, honour and dishonour'. This may not be surprising, given that the language of morality was deeply ingrained in the pre-glasnost mentality even when – and, indeed, because – it frequently served as a blind to cover social and political deficiencies. What *is* surprising is that social and political participation and critique, which Gorbachev's policies aimed to encourage, barely skimmed across the reviews' surface. In other words, the critics were not prepared to engage openly in sociopolitical discussion and debate even though Dodin's production, albeit not confrontational in the manner of Lyubimov, had given them plenty of leads in this direction. Glasnost had still to come of age, and Russians still had to overcome their mistrust of politics and politicians. According to Stephen White, glasnost was 'at best, in its early stages by the end of the Gorbachev era' (1995: 99), which suggests that it was, at best, merely a glint in people's eyes at the beginning of this era.

Theatres in an era of crisis

The erosion of established moral, ideological and social values in this era of crisis, in the sense of the term defined by *Literaturnaya gazeta*, also deeply affected the theatre as an institution. The immediate cause of disaggregation was something close to a market-economy approach to theatre management for which the state control that had bogged down many permanent companies had hardly prepared them. In 1987, in anticipation of a law to be introduced in 1989, state control was lifted and theatre organisation put in the hands of elected artistic councils whose members were not apparatchiks, but actors and theatre staff. The theatres were to be responsible for their budgets, although a fixed and, to all intents and purposes, smaller subsidy would continue to be granted by the state and municipalities. What was undoubtedly a step towards autonomy resulted in major disagreements within companies as to how they should be run and for which objectives.

First, in 1987, came the split of the Moscow Art Theatre into two entirely separate companies, Oleg Yefremov retained one 'part' of it; the other 'part' was taken over by Tatyana Doronina, the MKhAT actor who led the opposition.[9] Next came the Yermolova Theatre. More shocking still, for the profession and audiences, was the division of the Taganka.[10] The internecine struggles within the company had gone on for some time – since Lyubimov's return to Russia, according to his detractors, and because his frequent commitments abroad thereafter gave the company little opportunity to develop its repertoire. In June 1993, the City of Moscow ruled that the new stage should go to actors led by Nikolay Gubenko, while the old stage, where Lyubimov had made the Taganka's reputation, should stay with Lyubimov. Gubenko was not an 'outsider' like Efros, but a Taganka actor, and had served as Gorbachev's Minister of Culture. Lyubimov refused to share *his* theatre, but was forced later in the year to accept the ruling. Moscow was the hub of theatre life in the Soviet Union, so it was logical that the spate of separations should have occurred there on an impressive scale. Moscow, moreover, played the role of leader with considerable aggression and considered its nearest rival Leningrad – Tovstonogov and, then, Dodin apart – rather like a province that might emulate but never match the capital. Yet Peter the Great's city showed its mettle when, in 1991, the artistic council of the ultra-conservative Pushkin Theatre (now the Aleksandrinsky, as it was called when Chekhov's *Seagull* flopped there in 1896) ousted its tyrannical artistic director. Not only did venerable institutions break up or shake down, but there were deaths – Efros in 1987, Tovstonogov in 1989 and superb actors, too – all of which marked 'the end of an epoch' (Autant-Mathieu, 1994: 22).

An epoch had indeed ended where economic security was concerned. Recourse to market-economy practices after 1989 meant the end of the principle of tenure for actors: theatres could now hire by contract, and actors were liable for any deficit to theatres by their absence when, say, they took up film or television work. So much for the ideal of a 'theatre-home'! Even so, Yefremov continued to operate his 'half' of the MKhAT along the lines of this ideal. Dodin, for all the pressures on the Maly, economic and otherwise, has insisted upon preserving it. Furthermore, Anatoly Vasilyev and Pyotr Fomenko, who in the 1980s had concentrated their efforts on teaching and developing studios, re-emerged in the 1990s to foster the ideal of a close-knit 'family' group in their own idiosyncratic way: Vasilyev in monastic seclusion with his disciples, Fomenko, according to more earthy, guild-like workshop methods.[11] The prominence of these two figures suggests, in other words, that the laws of free enterprise had not entirely swept away the cultural precepts that have given the best of the Russian theatre tradition. However, the problem thrown up was not how to maintain these precepts (maintenance would amount to mere inertia), but how to innovate and develop from them while dealing intelligently with both the advantages and the disadvantages of the market economy. The worst effects of inadequate government subsidy for the theatre have been felt in Great Britain, for example, since the days of Margaret Thatcher. Time alone will show which effects are the worst in Russia. But the mechanism is in place. In 1994, as Autant-Mathieu records, the newly reconstituted Russian Ministry of Culture subsidised no more than 25 theatres, whereas the Ministry had subsidised 370 of them while the country was part of the Soviet Union as the Russian Federation. It assigned 2 per cent of the national budget to culture (with, apparently, no ceiling specifically for the theatre); 6 per cent of municipal budgets was designated for cultural activities in general, the theatre not being selected for special attention (Autant-Mathieu, 1994: 22).

The upside of the liberalisation of the theatre was its diversification. Alongside the state sector were theatres funded by businesses (2 per cent of their profits could legally be invested in culture), independent theatres run by actors' agencies, sponsored projects, including those funded by foreign sponsors, and co-productions of various kinds. Autant-Mathieu cites the example of Alla Demidova, a pillar of the Taganka and Gertrude in its *Hamlet*, whose recently formed company Theatre A staged *Quartett* by Heiner Müller. The Taganka provided the space, Theatre A paid for the translation, and Attis Theatre from Athens paid the Greek director and designer. Financial aid came from the International Confederation of the Union of Theatres and the business company Mirteatr. There was a proliferation of studio theatres, many of which travelled abroad to subsidise their work, notably Yury Pogrebnichko's Theatre on Krasnaya Presnya in Moscow and the group in St Petersburg that came to be known as Teatr Mon Plaisir. The 1990s also saw a diversity of spaces for performance such as basements (many converted into what were then known as 'free' spaces from the clandestine basements of previous years), derelict build-ings, art galleries (including the grandiose Hermitage in St Petersburg), staircases and streets. Andrey Maguchy performed an itinerant *Petersburg* based on the novel by Andrey Bely in various interiors and streets of St Petersburg – a spatial disposition appropriate for Bely's hero's perambulations across the amazing cityscape conjured up in the book. Fomenko created a sensation in 1993 by staging *Guilty Without Guilt* by Aleksandr Ostrovsky in the buffet bar of the Vakhtangov Theatre. It was a visually and rhythmically beautiful produc-tion propelled by theatricalised, highly elegant acting. Moscow was entranced. Fomenko followed up this success by mounting Fernand Crommelynck's *The Magnificent Cuckold* in 1994, 'another dazzling show', according to John Freed-man, with which 'his position as Moscow's number one director was confirmed' (Freedman, 1997: xvii).

Fomenko, who was born in 1932, took a long time reaching pre-eminence, although his work was well known in the 1970s and 1980s. He came to the fore in the 1990s, as did other men born in the 1930s whose artistic approach was quite different from his. Prominent among these were the ironic, disaffected but hard-edged Pogrebnichko, who was born in 1939; Roman Viktyuk, born in 1936, who specialised in camp productions, usually of a homoerotic kind (Genet's *Les Bonnes* in 1988, *M Butterfly* in 1990, after which followed many more that were judged generally to be of very uneven quality); Mark Zakharov, born in 1933, who was appointed artistic director of the Moscow Lenkom in 1974 where he mounted the first Soviet musicals, used rock shows for political pur-poses in the glasnost years and, in the 1990s, opened up a foreign currency exchange (the Lenkom being the first theatre to do so) as well as a night-club in the building. Smeliansky writes that after performances 'security men would quietly fill the foyer and set up special gates like metal detectors at an airport. The "new Russians" would hand in their weapons, be given a tag for them, and go off to "relax" in the Lenkom' (1999: 164).

The 1990s also heralded the arrival of a younger generation born in the early to mid-1940s: Valery Fokin, who had acquired a reputation at the Sovre-mennik and Yermolova theatres in the 1980s and is now head of the Meyerhold

Centre in Moscow; Sergey Zhenovach, who had been under the wing of Efros; Kama Ginkas, master of performances in his apartment in Leningrad where, according to Freedman, 'no one would hire him' (1997: 241). Ginkas received broad recognition in Moscow in the late 1980s and notoriety there in the mid-1990s for work that stressed non-verbal play and performance so close to spectators as seemingly to absorb them in it. Vasilyev, born in 1942, belongs chronologically to this generation, as does Dodin, two years younger. What distinguishes Vasilyev and Dodin from their peers is that both of them had well and truly arrived on the Russian scene before the 1990s. The second point to note is that, of all the directors cited, Dodin is the only one to have been nurtured by St Petersburg and, as well, to have crafted his great works in St Petersburg. Fomenko worked there in the 1960s and 1970s, but blossomed in Moscow. Ginkas, a pupil of Tovstonogov, was there for a while, but invisible. His fame also came from Moscow.

What emerges from this panorama is the fact that the most prominent directors in Russia in the 1990s, several with varying degrees of international fame, are men – women being conspicuously absent from the scene – who learned the ropes and established themselves in the profession in the Brezhnev and Gorbachev years. Some, like Dodin and Vasilyev, also created a firm audience base at this time. Others, like Ginkas, only came to fruition with and after perestroika. Unlike these prestigious elders who sought wide public exposure, the adolescents of perestroika are essentially the purveyors of small-scale theatre and alternative spaces, economics as much as rebellion playing an important part in their choice of practice and venue. The children of perestroika have yet to show what it was like to have been carried in the womb of these crucial years and be born to the theatre in the first quarter of the twenty-first century. For them, Dodin's *Stars* may well appear to be from another galaxy. Vasilyev's production of *Cerceau (Hoopla)* by Viktor Slavkin, which could not be more different from *Stars*, might also look to this new generation as if it had landed from another planet. This is how it already looked in 1985, when it was first shown. It appeared just as strange during its reprise in 1987 precisely because the image of social harmony glimpsed by its protagonists, but which they cannot achieve, seemed to belong to a long-distant past so far away that the present could only envisage it as an illusion.

Cerceau's gaze backwards is a ploy for elucidating the glaring inadequacies of contemporary people. The production's central character, Petushok, inherits a dacha from his grandmother and invites several oddly assorted people, who do not know each other, to spend the weekend there with him. The house has been boarded up. Vasilyev has the guests pull the boards of the house apart from the inside. The performance takes place in this oblong space with the audience around three sides of it. The performers-guests come in and out of view, play with large hoops that they catch on long sticks, and read Petushok's grandmother's letters which they have found in the attic. This lyrical, dream-like production, as close to Ingmar Bergman as to Jean Renoir, relies on a formal, almost incantatory mode of play that leaves audiences spellbound. The characters recapture fragments of a graceful past, but are unable to grasp the present. Their experiment to form a community fails. At the end, they reboard up the house and leave. Dodin's prostitutes will also leave after their moment of freedom, although their temporary dwelling is a brutal barracks and not a dacha that inspires visions of beauty. However, in both cases, the promise of qualitative change fails to materialise.

By disclosing failure, *Cerceau* in 1985, just like *Brothers and Sisters* in the same year, is a precursor of perestroika. It also contributed to people's critical awareness, as did *Brothers* and then *Stars*, thereby encouraging rebuilding, which is part of what happened after 1985. The type of reconstruction that had begun to develop in the theatre varied significantly, Vasilyev and Dodin representing, as is clearer in retrospect, the two poles between which this scattered variety occurred. Vasilyev, who took to denouncing 'traditional theatre', virtually abandoned the idea of a theatre in dialogue with audiences for a laboratory enclave that rarely opens its doors. When it does, the event is for guests only who are invited to see fragments of work in progress. Vasilyev, then, after conquering the mainstage, can be said to have returned to the small-scale, experimental model favoured by the 'adolescents' of perestroika. Dodin, on the other hand, continues to make theatre productions, not for elected spectators, but for a wide and heterogeneous public.

'*Only theatre*' – with '*shock therapy*'

The paradoxes of the 1980s and the 1990s are immense. The cultural fermentation to which the theatre contributed opened up multiple channels of self-expression. This has led, Smeliansky believes, to the loss of the theatre's super-status: 'it has become only theatre'; and spectators who once went there to change their lives now go to confirm that they are alive, or merely for entertainment (Smeliansky in an interview with *La Croix*, 23 January 1994). Smeliansky additionally observes that the new culture is 'a low-level mass culture' (in an interview with *L'Humanité-Dimanche*, 20 January 1994). His phrase encompasses the sensational magazines, pornography, popular music, videos, films and drugs – in short, the whole paraphernalia of consumerist culture from the west that flooded the Russian market and was idolised, imitated and reproduced within Russia. Nor did consumerism retreat after the financial crash in August 1998 when international corporations were, nevertheless, still urged by their international peers to keep their eye on potential customers in Russia. 'Never forget', said an executive from one such company, 'there are still 50 m[illion] women out there who don't shave their legs' (*The Economist*, 24 October 1998). You might say that this was 'low level'!

Boris Yeltsin was inaugurated as Russia's president in July 1992 following Gorbachev's resignation in December of the previous year. The office of president, which Yeltsin held until late December 1999, when he was succeeded by Vladimir Putin, had unprecedented legal powers – greater, by far, than anything allowed constitutionally to Gorbachev. Crime and corruption flourished in a country whose riches had been siphoned off by former communists and the Mafia, and where billions of dollars loaned by the International Monetary Fund were squandered, no one knows how or where. All social services, most alarmingly public health, deteriorated below the level of developing countries; infant mortality, malnutrition and psychological maladjustment increased significantly. The apparently limitless problems in all areas – industrial, agricultural, financial, moral, social and cultural – all of which impact heavily on the quality of life of individuals and have thrown communal life, that is, 'society', into chaos, sharply foreground the huge rifts and cracks in the country's infrastructure that had been painted over before Gorbachev's time and which were exposed but not repaired by him. The problems thus sorely displayed were left open to further abuse after Gorbachev's departure. 'Shock therapy', inspired by western monetarists, was the most important contributing factor to this scenario of human disarray. The ingredients of the therapy, which came into effect from January 1992, entailed, among other things, the liberalisation of retail and wholesale prices and wholesale privatisation of state property and enterprises, all of which, until 1998, left Russia 'in a major [economic] depression, unprecedented in the twentieth century' (Gill and Markwick, 2000: 138–40).

The 'new Russia' has experienced capitalism so primitive that its manifestations have been compared, among brazen parallels, with the lawlessness of Chicago in the 1920s and 1930s. For a brief period in the mid-1990s, consumer goods that had become freely available were more or less affordable by ordinary people, although pensioners had borne the brunt of the uncontrolled prices by which the idea of a free market had been most literally manifested. Pensioners were also worse off than most when the social security system collapsed. By the end of the 1990s, violence in all its forms – local and regional, personal and social – had escalated to immeasurable proportions. It ranged from child delinquency to vendetta-style killings, from intra-Mafia thuggery to the unexplained but seemingly political assassination of the St Petersburg politician Galina Starovoytova in 1998 (*The Times*, 6 December 1998), and from full-scale war against Chechnya, on which Yeltsin had embarked in December 1994 without popular support, to the supposedly Islamic reprisals of the Moscow bombings in September 1999 in which about 300 people were killed in a total of four or five bombings. In 1999, one-third of the country lived below the poverty line (*Le Monde: Dossiers et Documents*, April 1999). And, despite optimistic accounts as to how, paradoxically, the collapse of the rouble in 1998 had boosted domestic production which, together with higher prices for Russian oil and gas had curtailed Russia's economic landslide and allowed the economy to grow by 8 per cent in 2000 (*National Geographic*, November 2001), the reality of daily life is such that only the new entrepreneurial middle class – a tiny minority of the population – can currently enjoy the fruits of this statistically defined growth. It is nothing short of a miracle that, in these conditions, people still make and go to the theatre.

Peter's 'window to Europe', or Lev's door

The year 1985 saw, besides *Brothers and Sisters*, Peter Brook's *The Mahabharata* at the Avignon Festival, and, in the autumn, Ariane Mnouchkine's *L'Histoire terrible et inachevée de Norodom Sihanouk, Roi de Cambodge* (*The Terrible and Unfinished Story of Norodom Sihanouk, King of Cambodia*). It was the year of super-grand epics and, as such, marks a high point in the history of the European theatre. They were epic in length: *Brothers and Sisters* lasted some seven hours (till it was shortened to six) and *The Mahabharata* and *Norodom* were even longer at nine and ten hours, respectively. The trend to create marathons had started in the 1970s, probably largely due to the ritualisation of the theatre, formally and stylistically, through the idea that the event required a pilgrimage, almost as if the journey itself conferred greater sanctity still upon the sacred act of performance.

All this was tied up, of course, with the euphoric 1960s and with Grotowski's notion of the 'holy' actor, Brook's 'holy theatre', and the various counter-cultural movements in the United States, ranging from flower-power celebrations to the self-expression of performance art. The effects of soul food, together with the dynamic of the various sociopolitical movements of the 1960s, were thus loud and clear in Peter Stein's two-evening *Peer Gynt* in 1971 in Berlin, Brook's *Orghast at Persepolis* in 1971 at the Shiraz Festival, and Robert Wilson's as yet unsurpassed-for-length *KA MOUNTAIN AND GUARDenia TERRACE*, a seven-day spectacle performed in 1972 on seven mountains near Shiraz. As far as mainstages rather than arcane spaces were concerned, Wilson had already outmatched most directors interested in the long haul with his 1970 hypnotic *Deafman Glance* (ten hours' worth in Paris, shorter elsewhere), and was to produce, six years later, the path-breaking hybrid opera *Einstein on the Beach*, a mere five hours by comparison with his earlier mute work.

Length, then, was not an altogether unusual feature of contemporary epics. Its most elementary purpose was to counteract, by taking one's time to perform and to absorb the spectator in the performance, the materially driven, fast pace of market economies and, for Dodin, the no less materially driven hard slog of a command economy under communism. Not surprisingly, the term 'unhurried' recurred favourably in reviews of *Brothers and Sisters* in the Soviet Union, usually accompanied by implied criticism of the tendency of the majority of theatres to turn out conveyer-belt productions, speed being equated with quick, easy digestion. The view that rapid dispatch and commodification were interrelated was shared by Dodin, Brook, Mnouchkine, Stein and Wilson, irrespective of the differences that distinguished them from each other.

Length and its reasons aside, the epic quality of *Brothers and Sisters*, *The Mahabharata* and *Norodom* stems above all from their subject matter and how it is communicated through narrative. Russian critics invariably described *Brothers and Sisters* as 'an epopee' and invariably linked this idea, whether explicitly or indirectly, to Pushkin's aphorism that drama is a matter of how a people's fate is played out. They reverted, in other words, to the classical conception of an epic as a collective history, which is also perfectly adequate for *Norodom*, given that the production centres on the genocide of the Cambodian people by the Khmer Rouge, and is adequate enough for *The Mahabharata*, where Brook adheres to the holy book's claim that it is the 'history of the human race'. For Brook, moreover, its story about the war between two rival branches of the same family is at the very heart of this history. This is why Brook's *Mahabharata*, with its focus on the split between two halves of the human race looks now as if it must have contained a secret parable about the Cold War that was missed at the time, even though its cryptic allusions to the inevitability – 'fate', indeed – of nuclear extinction did not go unnoticed.

The connection *by substance* between these three productions throws into relief their particularities which lie, first, in their attack, namely, in the way that Dodin focuses on his own national context, while Mnouchkine and Brook move to a foreign location to explore the ramifications of 'a people's fate', and, second, in their stylisation: Dodin draws, for his brand of theatricality, on Russian culture, while Mnouchkine and Brook explore a range of Asian modes of performance, the former doing so far more than Brook, although the latter has been criticised far more than Mnouchkine for alleged 'orientalism'.[12] Since Brook and Mnouchkine were among the figureheads of western European theatre – Brook virtually promoted to the status of guru, 'above' Wilson, Stein and Giorgio Strehler – they are excellent indicators of the kind of Europe that the Maly entered when it travelled there for the first time in 1988. The company arrived well aware of the achievements of the leading western directors, not least because Peter Stein had only very recently been to Moscow with his production of *The Three Sisters*. Accounts of Strehler's and Mnouchkine's work had been followed closely, although Wilson remained an enigma, and Brook had simply become a legend after his *Hamlet* with Paul Scofield at the Vakhtangov Theatre in 1955 and *King Lear*, also performed in Moscow with Scofield in 1964. Brook's film of *Lear* was released in 1971 and had become an important touchstone for Russian theatre makers and audiences alike.

First international tours

The Maly Drama Theatre was introduced to the west in 1988 at the Glasgow Mayfest and the London International Festival of Theatre (LIFT) with *Stars in the Morning Sky*. It continued with this production to Toronto and New York. Its second tour, later in the year, was to the Festival d'Automne in Paris with *Brothers and Sisters* which, along with *Stars*, was to serve as the Maly's international showpiece for the next few years. French critics praised the cast's 'superb performances', but were just as impressed by the fact that *Brothers and Sisters* was part of the USSR's massive export of theatre 'on all fronts' (*Le Monde*, 22 September 1988). The *Monde* correspondent listed them with excitement, like trophies: 'Federal Germany, Great Britain, Canada, the United States, Japan, Greece, Italy, Yugoslavia, etc.' There was reason enough for such jubilation: the feeling that the 'Iron Curtain' had at last been torn down and the world had become more free; the old historical ties between France and Russia, maintained throughout the Cold War, could now be activated vigorously; the impression that treasures were to be discovered, as had happened during Stanislavsky's and Diaghilev's glorious *Saisons russes* whose impact was embedded in France's cultural consciousness; the thrill of knowing that Paris was at the hub of it all. For, in addition to the Maly, the Paris Autumn Festival included Vasilyev's productions of *Cerceau* and *Six Characters in Search of an Author*, both of which had been fervently acclaimed at the Avignon Festival during the summer. The Moscow Art Theatre had not set foot in France since 1964 (after its first visits in 1922 and 1923 with Stanislavsky, then again in 1937 and 1958) and was to present Yefremov's *Seagull* and *Uncle Vanya*. A dark horse, Yury Yeremin, was to show his adaptation of Chekhov's story *Ward Number 6*.

The response was significantly different, more politicised, more ideological, in the German Federal Republic one year later. The Maly's tour to Hamburg, Berlin and Munich with *Brothers and Sisters* began, quite fortuitously, at about the same time as a state visit from Gorbachev – a detail observed discreetly by the German press. Yet, if little was made of the coincidence, a great deal of mileage was to be had from underlining the political significance of perestroika and glasnost for German–Soviet relations ('romance', in the words of *Die Zeit*, 9 July 1989). The *Hamburger Abendblatt*, after stating that spectators had perestroika to thank for the production's appearance in the country, reassured them, by first asking a series of ironic rhetorical questions, that it did not deal with the 'victory of the Soviet Union' or 'the pall of tragedy over a war-torn people' (19 June 1989). In view of Germany's role in the Second World War, these and similarly tactical moves could well be taken as examples of what Sartre calls *mauvaise foi*. Beneath the ironies, however, was an assumption – shared, to varying degrees, by other newspapers – that perestroika had facilitated a process of healing between the former enemies and possibly even fraternity between them. The *Frankfurter Allgemeine Zeitung*, for example, referred to the audience's applause as 'a storm of gratitude, like an expression of solidarity with these brothers and sisters from Leningrad' (20 June 1989). No one with any kind of historical sensitivity could have ignored the reverberations of the name of this city, given the siege of Leningrad and Germany's ultimate defeat. Nikolay Lavrov, who performed in the production (and, incidentally, had family who had survived the blockade) felt that, artistic merit aside, the public's overwhelming reception was bound up with the great loss of life sustained by Germany during the war and the hardships and humiliations experienced by her people after it (Paris, 9 February 1994).

Generally, press reviews took the line of least resistance by barely mentioning the production's war motifs; and, since perestroika and glasnost were the order of the day, held that the true significance of Gorbachev's reforms lay in how openly the production was able to treat the sufferings of the Russian people at the hands of their own system. In other words, communism and not the Nazi onslaught of the war was the villain of the piece. Some mistakenly thought that the production was a consequence of perestroika, whereas, in fact, it was part of the many subterranean pressures that had made perestroika a necessity. Others referred to the opportunities opened up by perestroika for cultural exchange, the *Berliner Morgenpost* citing the presentation of Stein's *Three Sisters* in Moscow in return for which, the newspaper's critic presumed, *Brothers and Sisters* had been invited to Berlin (14 July 1989). Most reviews spoke of the powerful, unsentimental acting, effective sets, and Dodin's cinematic or saga-like scope and poetic sensibility. The *Berliner Morgenpost* saw the work as a 'monumental epic', as 'authentic epic theatre' and, further, as 'the best kind of epic theatre that Brecht had dreamed about' – minus the doctrines espoused by Brecht, however, as the reviewer felt obliged to point out. Suggestions here and there that its realism was 'old-fashioned' (a normal quibble in a theatre climate that had gone wild, for several years now, on the non-realist Wilson – his Hamburg *Hamletmaschine*, for instance, dates from 1986) were outweighed by admiration for its unforced vigour and strength.

It is worth comparing the reviews in Federal Germany and the United States. The political points regarding Stalinism and perestroika were similar in both countries, but were nowhere near as sharp in their thrust in the United States. Aesthetic issues were another matter. When *Brothers and Sisters* travelled, several months after its German tour, to San Diego, American critics were singularly unimpressed by its 'clapped-out style, namely, social realism . . . No amount of admiration for its sincerity and verisimilitude can conceal the sentimentality and melodrama filleted away in its center' (*Los Angeles Herald Examiner*, 24 October 1989 – to take the unkindest of them). And, although there was praise for the production's political, emotional and moral sincerity as well as for its 'impressive ensemble work' and 'the power of its images and the sweep of its saga' (*Chicago Tribune*, 24 October 1989), there were reservations about its content. In the words of the *Chicago Tribune*, 'In content, it veers between the poles of *Peyton Place* and *The Odyssey*'. The same reviewer went on to liken it most to the Royal Shakespeare Company's *Nicholas Nickleby*. The critic from the *Herald Examiner* damned it by describing it as a 'propaganda piece'.

These, like the preceding comments from Federal Germany and France, indicate how great a role is played by cultural perception, let alone sociopolitical stance, disposition and prejudice, in the evaluation of works of art, theatrical or otherwise. Second, if perception, sociopolitical stance, and so on, help to construct their object, they also suggest the kind of conjuncture of politics, culture, social shift and institutional mediation that is operative in a particular time-space, or chronotope, as Bakhtin calls the where-when of history (1981: 84–258), and which penetrates the way works are appreciated, interpreted and assessed. It is this nexus of energies that, fundamentally, paves the way for receptivity, allowing works to cross historical contingencies and cultural specificities and find their audiences wherever they may be.

This very brief survey of the first impressions made by the Maly on the western world – and formed *of* the Maly there, as well – cannot be closed without some reference to the response of the British press to *Stars in the Morning Sky*. British reviewers were almost as prone to noticing glasnost as their German colleagues, although perestroika seemed to fade into the background. They might well have noticed it more if '"Gorby" mania', as the Germans called it, had been fuelled as vociferously in Britain as in the Federal Republic. But welcoming a company from the Soviet Union to Britain was nowhere near as politically loaded. Britain had not been separated into ideologically opposed countries and London had not been divided by the equivalent of a Berlin wall. The Thatcher government, unlike its Federal German counterpart, did not have to come to terms with the idea that the leader of a former enemy, who had defeated Germany in the Second World War, was now being 'sold' as a friend.

British critics made less of perestroika, possibly because less was made of it, politically, in Britain; and the Thatcher government was going about a 'perestroika' of its own, dismantling the welfare system. They saw *Stars*, whose content cannot be compared with *Brothers*, as being in a similarly subversive vein and 'the fruit of *glasnost*' (*The Independent*, 5 May 1988) rather than integral to the wider phenomenon of perestroika. The *Financial Times* (11 May 1988) takes up the theme:

> This cultural symptom of *glasnost* would be interesting enough in itself. But the production goes way beyond that. It is a theatrical performance of sensational histrionic intensity, deeply moving, often funny, boldly and brilliantly orchestrated, sardonically punctuated with the brassy Socialist anthems of a suite composed in the 1970s by Georgy Sviridov and the raucous fervent ruminations of the late Vladimir Vysotsky (Lyubimov's unforgettable Hamlet with a voice like a gravel mixer and himself a beacon of pre-*glasnost* radicalism).

This review, foremost among several that widened the implications of Dodin's production and/or Galin's play, noted that 'the play tells you much about Russia, but even more about the world'. Critics were unanimous in their enthusiasm for the production's 'fine passionate performances', 'blistering energy' (*The Independent*), 'powerful punch' (*The Daily Telegraph*, 20 May 1988), 'sharp, poignant juxtapositions of beauty and squalor, romance and sordid copulation' (*The Guardian*, 11 May 1988), 'astonishing physicality' (*The New Statesman*, 3 June 1988) – in short, 'wonderful company' (*Financial Times*). With accolades like these, a return to Britain was assured.

Touring on a grander scale

This came, in fact, with *Brothers and Sisters* in 1990 (Glasgow) and 1991 (London) and *Gaudeamus* in 1991 and 1992 (which travelled also to Ireland). Glasnost and related novelties had by now worn off, leaving critics to focus on the Maly's ensemble work, which they all experienced as a revelation and to which they again referred rapturously during the Maly's fifth tour to Britain in 1994. This was part of a larger European tour lasting nearly six months. By 1994, the company had been ecstatically received throughout western Europe. Its sway included the 1991 opening of the Maly's eight-hour *Devils* from Dostoevsky's novel at Braunschweig, making it a *European* premiere and not a Russian one, as would normally have been expected, and, in 1994, two commissioned works in Paris – *Claustrophobia* for the MC93 Bobigny, and *The Cherry Orchard* for the Odéon-Théâtre de l'Europe. By 1994, *Gaudeamus* had been seen in Europe by 500,000 spectators. The British tour in that year was billed as a retrospective and comprised *Brothers and Sisters, Stars in the Morning Sky, The House, The Devils* and *The Cherry Orchard*. It ran for seven weeks in five cities (Glasgow, Newcastle, Manchester, Nottingham, London), heralding the consortium-style organisation, primarily for reasons of cost, which would cover the Maly's future visits to the country. *Gaudeamus* and *Claustrophobia* were not part of the programme, although they had inaugurated the Maly's European tour at the beginning of the year in Paris and had gone from there to Marseille and Geneva. Italy was not to see them until the end of the year when the Maly undertook a three-month tour, a mere mini-tour by comparison with the earlier tour. However, it was by no means smaller in ambition since it now incorporated the United States. The Maly's virtually non-stop travel throughout 1994 gives some indication of the prestige it had by now acquired worldwide.

Impressive though the Maly's journeys may be, it would be wrong to assume that they are noteworthy predominantly for the long spans of time and distance that they cover. What must take precedence over these factors is the sheer scale of the endeavour in human terms. Well over 80 company members were involved in the European tour, *Brothers and Sisters* alone taking some 40 actors, most of whom appear on stage at any one time. Since the company is very closely knit and operates on team effort, designers, technicians, stage and other assistants, and voice, movement and music teachers were all part of the tour, all striving to provide the best conditions possible for performances of the highest quality. The presence of teachers was axiomatic, for their task, as in St Petersburg, was to coach the actors to perfect their work and conduct warm-up sessions before performances, on the principle that training was never finished. In addition, there was the problem of juggling programming so that, say, the student ensemble could return to St Petersburg to play *Gaudeamus* before it left again on tour, and the productions of other directors affiliated in one way or another with the Maly could keep the theatre open at home while the company was abroad. Time-extensive tours are usually time-intensive as well, and those of 1994 were no exception. Performances followed hard on one another's heels and, because the productions are as artistically demanding as they are long (shorter ones, like *The Cherry Orchard* run for two and a half hours without an intermission), required particularly concentrated attention and stamina. None of this could have got under way without entrepreneurial acumen and planning from the Maly, let alone from its international partners, and the immense financial expenditure and managerial and administrative co-ordination on the part of the countries, cities and theatres hosting the company.

It was again in France that the 1994 tour took on the aura of an epoch-making cultural event. Once again, as had happened six years earlier, the Maly was integrated into a larger Russian programme, only this time the company brought six productions instead of one. (*Brothers and Sisters* returned, to greater glory, with this visit.) Moreover, the company was not one of many stellar attractions, but the main star in the firmament. This time, too, the contextual associations were explicitly spelt out. It was explained that this *Saison russe* was named in memory of the dynamic *Saisons russes* of the 1910s and 1920s (*Libération*, special edition, January 1994) and was a tribute to the great Russian traditions of theatre, dance and music that had nurtured the arts in France throughout the twentieth century. Much was made, especially by *Libération* and *Le Monde*, reputedly the newspapers of the French intellectuals, but also by the popular press in magazines such as *Télérama*, of how the past efforts of 'theatre people' in France to stay linked up with Russia had paid off; the *Saison russe* would otherwise not have come about, especially because ties were fragile in what, until the advent of perestroika, had primarily been a one-way process, France initiating and sustaining contact with the USSR. *Libération* cited Roger Planchon, who visited Moscow in 1963 with his celebrated theatre from Lyon-Villeurbanne, making this one of the rare foreign influxes of the not so thawed-out 'thaw' of the Khruschev years:

> I always thought we had to go there, that it was as important for them as for us. At the time, no English, American or German troupe went to the USSR, barely any Italian ones. France was, above all, their opening to the west, as I understood very quickly.
>
> (Planchon, quoted in *Libération*, special edition, January 1994)

The broader picture, drawn with more detail than the 1988 coverage, gave the *Saison russe* special appeal. But the season's main thrust, as perceived virtually unanimously, was not Russia's debt to France, but France's debt to Russia. Borja Sitja, who was in charge of the programming of the *Saison russe* at the Odéon-Théâtre de l'Europe, then directed by Lluis Pasqual after Giorgio Strehler's tenure, summed up the general view succinctly. The question put to him was whether the Odéon-Théâtre de l'Europe had a particular mission as regards Russia. Sitja replied:

> This season is simply a promenade to our sources. For, the Russian tradition has nourished us all for 100 years: modern acting and staging were invented by Russians, Stanislavsky, Meyerhold, etc., which must never be forgotten. I believe that Russia is the only place – along with England, perhaps – that ought to be constantly in the mind of a director or of a theatre. There is nothing conjunctural about this operation: it is a necessity pure and simple.
>
> (*Journal de Genève et gazette de Lausanne*, 19 February 1994)

Further on, Sitja adds the following to his notion of necessity: 'When you frequent the Russian theatre, you discover new ideas. Or old ones that you had forgotten.' Thus, apart from the Maly's programme, which was in the lead, the ideas were to come from the Moscow prodigy Ivan Popovsky's production of *The Fairground Booth* by Aleksandr Blok, the very same play that had received scandal status when Meyerhold performed it in 1906; from the extended workshops of Pyotr Fomenko, Popovsky's 'master', with acting students of the Conservatoire national d'art dramatique; from the work of MKhAT stars Anastasia Vertinskaya and Aleksandr Kalyagin who, with French actors, were to stage the third acts of Chekhov's major plays in one performance. Then there were Pasqual's productions: *Summerfolk* by Gorky, *Roberto Zucco* by Bernard-Marie Koltès, performed in Russian by the Maly, and *Phoenix*, a little-known play by the well-known poet Marina Tsvetayeva. To cap it all, there were public lectures by contemporary Russian dramatists and readings of Russian plays considered to be among the most radical available. The whole was subsidised beyond expectations by various organisations of the French government, notably the Association française d'action artistique in the Ministry of Foreign Affairs, which goes to show how much can be achieved for the arts when a government not only has a veritable cultural policy, but also is willing to put its money where its mouth is, and its policy on the line.

The magnitude, in imagination as well, of France's Russian season, and the fact that the Maly had been showcased in such an event, highlighted the company's importance, transmitting it well beyond France's borders. At the epicentre of the forces deployed for its success was its phenomenal artistry, which will continue to be its primary resource in the twenty-first century. Arguably, the 1994 tour put the finishing touches to the Maly's international reputation and ensured that it was known to be among the very best of our time: in the words of Peter Brook, 'the finest ensemble theatre in Europe' (*Time Out*, 13–20 April 1994). Touring continued after 1994 beyond Europe to Brazil in 1995, Israel in 1995 and 1998, and Australia and New Zealand in 1996. Within Europe, tours included the Scandinavian countries, Spain, Greece, Romania and Hungary and virtually annual visits to France, although Italy and Britain also did well. Take Britain as an example: the Maly's seventh visit in 1998 with *The Devils* at the Barbican Centre in London was followed in 1999, also at the Barbican, by Chekhov's *A Play With No Name* (better known as *A Play Without a Title* and known, best of all, as *Platonov*). The Chekhov play had been premiered in 1998 at the Weimar Art Festival. In 1999, Weimar was the Cultural Capital of Europe and featured another new Maly work *Chevengur*. Both of these instances of international recognition were singled out by the fact that, as had happened before with *The Devils*, a production germinating and generated in Russia was premiered outside Russia.

How the Maly was castigated by certain Russian critics for its relations with the west will be discussed in a later chapter of this book. The point to be made at present is that the Maly's outstanding quality has appropriately earned it all the touring that it can handle. For, without selling itself cheap, while being, nevertheless, on the market, the Maly's capacity to live and work with high seriousness has been facilitated by the touring network. At home, as we have seen, it is assisted by the Kirishi factory. Roman Malkin accurately observes that touring, with its fee usually at US$50 a day per person, literally feeds the actors, but also sustains them and their families in St Petersburg (St Petersburg, 30 September 1999). Actors' salaries before the August 1998 crash were around the equivalent of US$100 a month. The cost of living was, however, much higher than the rouble's buying power. In the months after the crash, when the rouble lost up to two-thirds of its value and the cost of living tripled overnight, salaries almost stopped. Some redress since then has not radically altered a dire situation. Malkin makes no bones about it: the chance to earn foreign currency is of enormous help to individuals. He adds, however, that it only minimally helps the Maly Drama Theatre itself towards running costs. Clearly, then, the major benefit to be had for the company as a whole is sponsorship of the work itself – the guarantee, as had happened in Paris, Braunschweig and Weimar, that it would see the light of day.

Given the vicissitudes of Russia since the dissolution of the Soviet Union in 1991, and given the disappointed promises and hopes that the conditions of daily life would improve, it is small wonder that Dodin had this to say in 1997, when *Brothers and Sisters* returned to the Odéon-Théâtre de l'Europe, once again to standing ovations, for its third run in Paris since its debut in 1988:

> We had the impression in 1988 that we were showing a little of our past. In 1994, we felt that we were staging our future – and we have this feeling again today. For twelve years now, we have been living with the idea that each day might be fatal. We are told, each day, that we must hang on, wait a little, that everything would sort itself out. And each day we read the most alarming news in the newspapers.
>
> (*Le Monde*, 4 February 1997)

It is possible to extrapolate from Dodin's acute observation and note that, if you are playing your future, what you play is bound to be meaningful and bound to be alive. History, in other words, will not have outdated it. This is a clue to why *Brothers and Sisters*, after so many years in the repertoire, could continue to be performed meaningfully by its performers and so become meaningful for its spectators.

Collaborative projects – and The Winter's Tale *directed by* Declan Donnellan

Touring had more than one spin-off. It enabled collaborative projects, the first of which was *Roberto Zucco*, in the 1994 Paris season, as already mentioned, and in 1996 *Reflets (Reflections)* staged by Georges Lavaudant.[13] Written by Lavaudant with writers of some repute, Jean-Christophe Bailly, Michel Deutsch and Jean-François Duroure, *Reflets* is probably best described as a suite of images meant to suggest reflections upon states of mind and soul. *Roberto Zucco* was another story altogether. The last play by Bernard-Marie Koltès before his death from AIDS in 1989, it was given its premiere in 1990 by Peter Stein in Berlin. Koltès had, by then, an international standing largely acquired through Patrice Chéreau's productions of his work in the 1980s, and most of all through *Combat de nègre et de chiens* (*Black Battle with Dogs*) whose extraordinary scenic effects and mythical grandeur recalled the *Ring* cycle directed by Chéreau to immense acclaim in Bayreuth during the previous decade. Some of that Wagnerian aura had enveloped Koltès.

Pasqual had already directed *Roberto Zucco* in 1993 in Barcelona, in Catalan. The Russian production entailed several months of rehearsals in St Petersburg, as did *Reflets* after it. The 'deal' – a Koltès word if ever there was one – was that these productions would be first performed in France before returning to Russia. *Roberto Zucco*, like all plays by Koltès, belonged to a Genet-like world of formal structure combined with physical and psychological violence. Where Chéreau had given that universe mythological proportions, Pasqual sought its horrors where Koltès had found them in the streets of modern society. He did so, however, by studiously avoiding slice-of-life pictures, which were inconsistent with Koltès's aesthetics, so as to plumb the emotional depths of the Maly actors and have them bring out the pulsations of Koltès's text.

The play concerns gratuitous violence which, Koltès implies, is a social norm that is both private and public, and beyond repair. Zucco kills his father before the play begins, strangles his mother in the second scene, rapes a teenage girl, who has already been subjected to continual violence from the members of her own family, and murders a policeman and then a child. An episode where Zucco takes two hostages, a woman and her son, occurs in a park in front of bystanders who appear to have lost all feelings of humanity and are fascinated by the crime as *crime*. This incident is the public face of the endemic violence observed dispassionately by Koltès and which Pasqual wished to communicate without the intrusion of any moral judgements whatsoever. The girl, the only person with whom Zucco is able to establish a relationship, betrays him to the police. He dies spectacularly by appearing to plunge down from a scaffold built into the flies and open to view throughout the performance. A blinding light symbolises his fall which, in the text, occurs during a hurricane. Two video screens track the whole performance, their very presence accentuating the distance from violence taken by Pasqual and conveyed to the audience. Visually, the production was a stark, expressionistic study in etched-out silhouettes and sombre tones and shadows. There was no sign in the Maly actors' vibrant performances that they had found the play's 'black, glacial and morbid universe very shocking' (Pasqual quoted in *Télérama*, 16 March 1994). They did find it shocking, but were not going to show it. Besides which, the challenge lay in performing a play that, by its coldness, was fundamentally alien to them.

The play closer in temperament to the Maly was *The Winter's Tale*, the first by Shakespeare ever to be staged at the Maly Drama Theatre. In 1997, the British Council brought Cheek by Jowl director Declan Donnellan and his designer associate Nick Ormerod for two months to St Petersburg to work on the play with the company. Donnellan and Dodin had met in 1986 in Helsinki, where Donnellan was directing *Macbeth* and Dodin Ostrovsky's *Bankrupt*, both in Finnish. When he and Ormerod saw *Brothers and Sisters* in that same year, they were, in Donnellan's words, 'completely blown away' by the 'overall quality of the acting' and 'the extraordinary rapport between the audience and the actors' (London, 30 December 1998). The admiration became mutual, and their friendship was cemented as the paths of Cheek by Jowl and the Maly crossed at various international festivals and the Maly saw such productions as *Angels in America* staged by Donnellan in Düsseldorf. Cheek by Jowl had performed *Measure for Measure* and its celebrated *As You Like It* with an all-male cast in St Petersburg, which had given Donnellan a significant following in the city. By the time he and Ormerod came to work with the company, their contact over 11 years – the French collaborations had not undergone a similar maturation – had prepared their welcome into the 'family', into the theatre-home that Donnellan himself believes is an ideal model. Donnellan: 'I knew them so well that Nick and I cast the whole thing in one morning, whereas the casting period normally takes us months and months' (London, 30 December 1998).

The *Winter's Tale* did not disappoint the public or the press. None was impervious to the 'minimalism that hides painstaking work' (*Kommersant*, 12 November 1997), the economy with which Donnellan had caught intense passions, and the way he had encouraged the actors to bring out the qualities of vowels and consonants, thereby 'stylizing tragic theatre' (*Chas pik*, 12 November 1997). In addition, 'Donnellan makes Shakespeare understandable, clear, logical' (*Kultura*, 12 February 1998). None had missed the delicious comedy of the rustic scenes, nor the sly parody of their great roles in *Brothers and Sisters* and *The Devils* made by the actors who played the Old Shepherd (Nikolay Lavrov), the Young Shepherd (Sergey Bekhterev) and Autolycus (Sergey Vlasov). Nor could anyone miss the atmosphere of suspicion and fear: 'Here are tyranny, borders, refugees, dissidents, negotiations, prisons' (*Chas pik*, as above). Donnellan's brilliant stroke of having Hermione's trial look like a Stalinist show trial (Natalya Akimova as Hermione) inspired immediate recognition, as did Pyotr Semak's dictatorial Leontes. The production played in Moscow, where in April 1999 it received the Best Production Award at the Golden Mask, the equivalent of the Olivier Awards in Britain. This was the first time that a production by a foreign director had won the award. It was received when the NATO bombardment of Serbia had provoked violent street protests, and 'anti-western sentiment in the country [Russia] was running at a vertiginous 15-year high' (*Financial Times*, 25 April 1999). Donnellan was deeply moved by the gesture and the fact that 'despite everything that was going on in Serbia and with the situation in Russia, the theatre community could rise above it all' (*Financial Times*, as above).

The production was no less apppreciated in Britain during its six-city tour in May 1999. Like their Russian colleagues, British critics highlighted Hermione's show-trial scene, and connected it to the production's multiple references – of action, costume, gesture – to totalitarianism. A comparison between the reviews shows that, while the semiotics of totalitarianism had the deepest of resonances for the Russians, the British, judging by their consistent attention to them,

responded most deeply to the themes of forgiveness, reconciliation and redemption foregrounded by Donnellan with ambiguity and a terrible sense of loss. In
the last scene Donnellan has Hermione and Leontes, both of whom are worn
by pain and time, bend with grief before their daughter, while the ghost of their
son Mamillius places his hand on his father's head in an act of forgiveness. This
closing moment is shot through with an unbearable feeling of waste – of joys
that can never be retrieved, of broken lives that can never really be mended. So
intensely powerful was the scene that audiences choked with emotion, knowing,
moreover, that the road to salvation, if feasible, was taken at an inestimable
cost. 'The greatness of Shakespeare', Donnellan argues, 'is that, at any given
moment, anything could happen, that it could go in any direction, that things
are completely open' (London, 30 December 1998). He continues:

> You have to leave yourself open to ambiguity, ambivalence and, very, very
> importantly, to conflicting action. And the conflicting action is this. Anzhe-
> lika [Nevolina, who plays Perdita] asked me whether Perdita wants to know
> Florizel or not, and I said 'Yes, she does, and yet she doesn't, and you have
> to play both of those' . . . It has to be open. At any given moment she
> might be wanting this or wanting that, and the two things come into con-
> flict . . . *The Winter's Tale* starts with the stakes impossibly high . . . and you
> have to keep the stakes there and at that level of energy so that people are
> torn in two directions, in equal conflicts in their souls.

The Shakespeare of torn directions, which start with an unresolved conflict in
Leontes that drives his jealousy and finally leads to an amazing but dreadful
grace, is the Shakespeare discovered by the Maly through Donnellan.

Prizes in Parnassus

The Maly has not been short of prizes, although the Golden Mask won with
Donnellan is, to date, unique. *Stars in the Morning Sky* received the Olivier Award
in 1988, *The Devils* the Moscow independent prize Triumf, for direction, in 1992
and *Gaudeamus* the UBU Italian theatre critics' prize in 1994, also for direction.
Dodin also received such honours as the State Laureate of the Russian Federal
Republic for *Brothers and Sisters* in 1986 and, among several in Russia after the
dissolution of the USSR, a prize for theatre pedagogy in 1996. In 1998, *A Play
With No Name* won the Moscow Golden Mask, twice over, for best direction and
best production. In 2000 *Chevengur* received the Golden Mask for best direction.
More national glory came in April 2001 when Dodin received the President's
Prize, an award established by Putin, for his contribution to the arts. From an
institutional point of view, rather than that of financial reward or pure prestige,
perhaps the most important recognition yet has come from the Union of European Theatres which, in September 1998, gave the Maly Drama Theatre the
title of 'Théâtre de l'Europe'.[14] The Odéon was the first to receive this title and
Strehler's Piccolo Teatro di Milano was the second, each theatre taking its

individual perspective on how to foster and develop the theatre in Europe. While the Maly can only dream of the government subsidies received by its predecessors for the vocation bestowed with the title, the status conferred upon the Maly makes it a Russian European Theatre like no other.

International parity was reconfirmed in April 2000 when Dodin received the Premio Europa per il Teatro (Europe Theatre Prize) at Taormina in Sicily, an occasion which also saw the world premiere of his production of *Molly Sweeney* by Brian Friel. Dodin was the eighth winner of this prize after Mnouchkine, Brook, Strehler, Heiner Müller, Robert Wilson, Luca Ronconi and Pina Bausch. A Parnassus of this kind can look, to the cynical eye, like a boys' club, but, irrespective of the worldly values attached to the presentation of laurels, the quality of the work of this group will go down in the history of the theatre as nothing less than stellar (Bausch's *Tanztheater* here generically included as theatre). Its brilliance does not in the least diminish the many fine practitioners who shine without titular glories, and on whose creative activity the entire constellation of the theatre depends. Where Dodin's Parnassian status is concerned, it is inseparable from the phenomenal abilities and dedication of his troupe. Sicily featured in more ways than one in the company's fortunes. *Chevengur* was performed in Gibellina in July 1999, and *The Seagull* was given its western European premiere in Palermo in October 2001 at the annual festival held in a European city by the Union of European Theatres.

Finally, a postscript of importance regarding the Maly's impact and influence abroad. Alan Lyddiard, artistic director of the Northern Stage programme at the Newcastle Playhouse, was inspired by the Maly to establish a permanent company and an ensemble theatre in Newcastle, in the sense in which the Maly is both these entities. The project, the Northern Stage Ensemble, was funded for a two-year trial period by a major award from the National Lottery Arts for Everyone scheme. At the beginning of June 1999, Lyddiard invited Dodin to conduct a three-day workshop with his newly formed company, which was to close with the arrival of the Maly at the Newcastle Playhouse with *The Winter's Tale* directed by Donnellan.

The workshop was at Allenheads in County Durham in an exquisite landscape. The focus was *Uncle Vanya*. Neil Murray, Northern Stage's designer, prepared the old school-house where the workshop was to take place so that it suggested a home in the country, a warm, inviting environment in which a Vanya and a Sonya could welcome Elena and her retired professor husband. Candle-holders with burning candles were fitted to the whole of the back wall of the main room. Candles burned on a long table covered with an Indian cloth and leaves and twigs from the garden. A fire roared in the small fireplace. Urns filled with long branches stood on pedestals, one near a pile of newspapers neatly stacked and tied up with red ribbon. Here the assembled company worked in the day, and dined in the evening. We worked essentially on the text and with the text, as actors and scholars usually imagine Stanislavsky and Chekhov might have done with the Moscow Art Theatre. Dodin spoke, read and thought aloud in Russian. The actors followed the words on the page in

English, but they especially followed Dodin's gestures and the movements of his face. They felt, strongly, that these non-verbal means of communication led directly to their designated goals, as in any performance. They improvised several scenes in the late afternoon, when the room was suffused with its inhabitants' trust. Languages were interpreted, but over and above language was a common will to go somewhere, and hearts to go there, too. Out of this, theatre is born.

2 The work process

Improvising, devising, rehearsing

Training an ensemble

No company in the world today has ensemble dynamics comparable to those of the Maly Drama Theatre. Where others claim ensemble status because of the fact that they are repertory companies, none is as tightly knit, as exclusively focused on working intensively, continually and permanently together as the Maly. Nor does any have such a single-minded commitment to company objectives. The Maly is unique even in Russia where cohesive units based on the idea of the 'theatre-home' have been the established norm and where existing repertory companies and even workshop studio/laboratories like those of Fomenko and Vasilyev no longer constitute ensembles in the strongest sense of the term, that is, as a permanent group breathing as one. Given Russia's precariousness and speed of change, the Maly's tenure may be at risk in the future. However, as the twenty-first century opens, it is its own best advocate of survival.

The Maly ensemble was founded on the school–company continuum referred to in the preceding chapter and, consequently, on how the various generations of actors produced by the continuum nurtured one another. In Dodin's words: 'I need a new generation so that someone can always nudge someone else along' (Weimar, 9 July 1997). All of the Maly actors, barring the oldest and the few youngest recruits of the late 1990s, have spent four years studying acting with Dodin, or five in the case of those who progress to his directors' course. Studying does not stop when they join the company: they build on what they have learned as students through the working processes adopted by the company as a whole. Intimate work on a daily basis, which enjoys duration as well as the mutations brought about by time, allows the Maly to fashion a 'common language', this phrase being one Dodin uses frequently to identify what is specific to the company. What this means is that its practice is symbiotically bound up with its principles. Performers and non-performers, most of whom have collaborated with Dodin for decades, are tuned in to each other, can spontaneously go into action with one another, and can understand and discuss their work effortlessly because of the philosophical, moral, cultural and social values and assumptions underlying their work as a collective entity. The voice, music and dance specialists who taught Dodin's students continue to teach, coach and exercise them as professionals; and the administrative staff do not merely push paper, but come into rehearsals to see how work is progressing.

The fact that the Maly is a community does not mean that it is an ideal world free of tension and strife. People do experience conflict, hurt or anger, as Dodin well recognises. Furthermore, apart from the stresses that might be expected of any work situation, the logistics of maintaining strong links between the school and the company so that the experiments of the one can enrich the other, have proved, at times, to be 'like a cobra that was very difficult to hold' (Dodin, Weimar, 9 July 1997). This difficulty took a different turn in the mid-1990s when it became quite clear that extensive touring abroad was preventing Dodin from working consistently with new students at the Academy of Theatre Arts. It was, therefore, more important than ever not to lose the ongoing recip-rocal relationship that had been vital both to the training programme at the Academy and the Maly. Dodin was obliged to shift more responsibility to his associates at the Academy who continue to transmit the school of acting and directing that he has developed there for three decades. Thus, although the Maly's most recent recruits have not had an intimate connection with Dodin prior to joining the company, they have nevertheless entered it with some sense of its principles and ethos and on the assumption that they share them. Such is the binding power of the Maly's 'common language' that all its members have the 'sense of going in the same direction', as Dodin puts it, and 'follow a "higher" right' that transcends individual interests and makes their *practice* the primary purpose of their being together. Dodin says: 'I am convinced that, in principle, theatre lives only according to this "higher" right' (Weimar, 9 July 1997).

'Aliveness' in the nervous system

Close observation of the Maly's working patterns indicates that, like any lan-guage, its language of practice evolves through use by its users. This openness allows it to avoid the codification that Dodin believes has afflicted Stanislavsky's alleged 'system' both inside and outside Russia. To his mind, the problem inside Russia dates from Stalin's time when 'all had to account for themselves by saying that they worked according to Stanislavsky's system' because 'Stani-slavsky had been forcibly planted everywhere, like potatoes or corn, except that no one had any clear sense of what was growing there, if, indeed, anything *was* growing there' (Paris, 8 April 1994). According to Dodin:

> The problem outside Russia, which was also repeated inside the country, arose from the way Stanislavsky's preliminary investigations and experi-ences were transmitted by those who had left him early, say [Richard] Boleslavsky in America. These investigations emphasised rational analysis . . . [and] confirmed, especially in the west, the rather naïve notion that the system was a collection of determined, fixed exercises and principles.

Yet what matters most in Stanislavsky, Dodin argues, are not his pedagogical devices, but his perpetual dissatisfaction with himself, his endless research and discoveries, and his coming to grips, increasingly as he grew older, with an idea of theatre that gave priority to sensations, feelings and emotions rather than to reason and cognitive understanding. This is the Stanislavsky whose artistic notebooks and diaries Dodin considers to be more potent by far than his canonical texts. The latter are

> textbooks which suffer, as textbooks do, from the fact that they stop in time, whereas the others go day by day; everything that belongs to yesterday is repudiated in the name of the new and yet goes into the new.
>
> (Paris, 8 April 1994)

Dodin's commentary holds clues to his view of the theatre. His constant emphasis, as he works with his actors, on the 'living life' of moments and the actors' 'aliveness' to them is related to what in the later work of Stanislavsky, as interpreted by Dodin and reformulated by me, may be termed research into possibilities at the quick of feeling. Dodin was sensitised to this visceral approach to acting by his teacher at the (then) Institute, Boris Zon, who had studied with Stanislavsky for several years and was able to communicate with extraordinary facility the lessons he had learned, not about methods and systems, but about the endless capacity for life of something alive. When this idea, inherited from Stanislavsky, is reviewed in the context of Dodin's practice, it can be paraphrased as follows: something that has come alive in the actor takes root, which ensures its regeneration and growth in successive performances where it is fresh every time.

Dodin's commitment to the actor's 'aliveness' is fundamental to his whole approach and also undergirds his notion of 'authenticity', which he claims he also gleaned from Stanislavsky. However, Dodin's conception of it has nothing to do with the orthodox views according to which Stanislavsky's 'authenticity' is bound up with verisimilitude – naturalism for the reproduction of natural and social environments ('exact', 'faithful' reproduction), and psychological realism for the 'truthful' construction of character.[1] The issue, for Dodin, is not one of aesthetic categories such as naturalism or realism, as is absolutely clear when he refers to how much *Claustrophobia* relies on the actors' authenticity (Weimar, 9 July 1997); *Claustrophobia*, a collage of highly theatrical, non-character-based fragments, is antithetical to all naturalist and realist conventions. 'Authenticity' comes from the *quick* of performance, which is not contingent on the formal-stylistic features (aesthetics) of the performance any more than on its subject matter or content. In other words, something is 'authentic' if it is felt in the moment and done precisely as it is felt. 'Authentic' theatre, for Dodin, is a theatre of the 'living life' of performing, that is, of *play* itself (*igra* in Russian).

Dodin's fluid conceptions have a hint of New Age go-with-the-flow about them and, as such, may appear to give short shrift to the systemic part of acting known as training. The point is that Dodin does not define training in terms of exercises geared towards immediate, tangible results, but as a 'training of the heart and the nervous system' (Paris, 8 April 1994). This generates an approach that, although not a method in the sense of a set of procedures, is nevertheless *methodical* and, as will be shown in the course of this book, quite draconian in its expectations of its participants. Training the sensory receptivity and responsiveness ('nervous system') *of* each actor and *between* actors allows them to find an appropriate physical expression for whatever internal action transpires ('heart'). The actor's body, in other words, is in a position to articulate the impulses that drive it at *any given instant* of a performance. My italics intend to draw attention to Dodin's concern with the mutability of performance, whatever its style or genre, where every mutation must x be given full value so that it matters neither before nor after it happens, but at the very moment of its being done. There is a clear relationship between Dodin's focus on the immediate moment and Stanislavsky's on the 'transient now'.[2]

Dodin's emphasis on corporeality and, consequently, on a physicality that is integral to the ebb and flow of performance, is to be seen as his development of Stanislavsky's research on physical action and its connection to the actor's emotional and imaginative resources – those 'inner' resources that an actor must fathom in order to play. At the same time, his emphasis on *play*, that is, on heightened *outward* manifestations, conjures up the name of Meyerhold whose passion for inventiveness in play had been imparted to Dodin by Matvey Dubrovin, his teacher at the LenTYuZ in the 1950s (Weimar, 9 July 1997). Dodin recalls how openly Dubrovin discussed Meyerhold, with whom he had worked during the 1930s, in class. Subsequent chapters will indicate the Meyerholdian touch in a number of Dodin's productions whose play is highly articulated, self-aware, reflexive, ironic, brazen and charged with the actors' fantasy, which they keep going at a high pitch. In other words, the play at issue exploits what Meyerhold termed *teatralnost* (theatricality), all of it enhancing the process of performance or what could be described as the show of theatre-in-the-making as it is being made.

By combining theatricality with the principle of 'living life', Dodin has arguably worked towards the convergence latent in Meyerhold's and Stanislavsky's respective research that both men recognised at the end of their lives, but which neither was able to bring about alone. It is important to remember that Meyerhold had been imprisoned, tortured and shot by Stalin's secret police, these facts only coming to light after his 'rehabilitation' in 1955, when Dodin was 11 years old. Consequently, his influence on Russian teaching institutions and the theatre profession was, at most, clandestine and indirect – albeit charismatic – and could not flourish openly until several decades later, precisely when Dodin had become a mature director.

Nevertheless, despite the appeal of Meyerhold's elusive image, the most important figure in Dodin's approach to acting is Stanislavsky. Stanislavsky is behind all the explorations of physical action which led Dodin to the psychosomatic forces of action, an area of research now associated with Grotowski who, as is well known, spent his last years pursuing Stanislavsky's unfinished research.[3] The connection between Dodin and Grotowski may not be apparent at first glance, especially because Grotowski's legend is dominated by his earlier experiments with myth, ritual and paratheatre and so with the spiritual dimensions of play. However, regardless of appearances (and Dodin's unawareness of his affinity with Grotowski), this deep connection emerges from their insight into Stanislavsky's search for the principles of cohesion in, by and through the actor, namely, for what is possibly best defined today as the psycho-physical-spiritual fusion understood to be the necessary condition for performance.

That Stanislavsky is the mediating link between Dodin and Grotowski becomes striking when Dodin reflects upon the psychosomatic impulse of psychophysical projection by actors. He observes how sensory imagination makes its impact on the body and how the body instantaneously physically reacts to it. There is a difference, he remarks, when it comes to training an actor, between the actor's imagining that he/she has hurt a finger and playing how much it hurts ('Oh, oh, it hurts', Dodin's mock cry accompanied by a shake of his finger) and imagining the hurt so acutely that a fine streak of blood appears on this very finger (St Petersburg, 29 September 1999). What can be inferred from Dodin's comparison is the distinction he makes between codification, which is intrinsic to Stanislavsky's 'system', and 'aliveness', which is not a matter of knowing, conceiving or reconstructing, but emanates from 'the nervous system' expressing itself through the body. A question then follows. If psychosomatism constitutes the actor's 'aliveness', or at least is constitutive of it to varying degrees, where is the dividing line between the imaginary and the real? The answer might lie in Dodin's belief ('increasingly a conviction, over the years') that the theatre is the space of everything that is imaginary and, although other than life, is a continuation of it; and the imaginary is itself real, like the blood on the actor's finger (St Petersburg, 29 September 1999). The rider to this is Dodin's observation that the theatre plays what 'in life, would have happened in another rhythm, on another nerve, and in another plastic expression' (Novosibirsk, 15 December 1997).

Although 'aliveness' cannot be taught according to rules, it can be fostered by awakening the actors' emotions and imagination. Training in the classroom involves doing this in a number of different ways. Irina Tychinina and Maria Nikiforova of the class that devised *Gaudeamus* recall how stimulated they had been, in their first year of study with Dodin, by work with imaginary objects. (Clearly, despite his qualms about *the system*, Dodin found this quintessentially Stanislavskian exercise useful.) Various methods, some of which included real objects, were used to excite the senses – taste and smell not excluded – and by these means open the students up to free association. Tychinina remembers how she created chain upon chain of associations from a smell, building countless actions, events and stories from them. The process of awakening facilitated her receptivity to poetry, which members of the class read aloud to find its meanings. But these readings also trained the students' sense of musicality. In Tychinina's case, reading poetry aloud developed her plasticity, since the poetry guided her gestures and movements whereas she had had a tendency to 'just move' in a random fashion (St Petersburg, 22 September 1998).

Nikiforova's imagination, on the other hand, was 'fired up' most of all by voice teacher Valery Galendeyev's classes on Shakespeare (St Petersburg, 19 September 1998). Each student was asked to choose a Shakespeare play and read every part and stage direction in it aloud. Galendeyev's purpose was not to study texts analytically, but develop alertness and awareness. The student reading a play was obliged to change roles suddenly, change the relations between characters, change rhythm, tone timbre and register and, just as suddenly, shift to different points of view, all of which taught him/her how to deal with a volatile whole. The text could not be fixed at the outset precisely because what might have looked like a whole altered with the arrival of new characters and new occurrences. This changed the balance between the characters and the balance between the characters and the person reading them. As is clear from Nikiforova's account, work of this kind trains actors to work beyond roles they covet and take on fully what others are saying and doing. This is essential for *ensemble* playing. Furthermore, its attention to pace sensitises them to movement. Igor Chernevich, also of the *Gaudeamus* group, recalls his pleasure from physical work with Dodin when they undertook arduous imaginary journeys in class together, climbing mountains and crossing rivers to reach seemingly impossible goals. When asked what he thought training was, Chernevich replied without hesitation that it was, above all, the exercise of the imagination and its search for a way to express physically what the imagination had discovered (St Petersburg, 22 September 1998).

Preparation, warm-up, immersion

Training can take a more indirect course than that of the above examples, as happens with the task of preparing Dodin's table in the studio before a class begins. The preparation is a daily ritual carried out according to a rota system. It inculcates discipline but, above all, its purpose is to develop the spirit of fantasy and of what might be called extrapolation, since the arrangement on the table must express in some way, by image, symbolically, or through the atmosphere it creates, the work to be done that day. By giving individuals free rein, it obliges them to use their imagination about the group's collective activities on a particular day and, consequently, asks them to be answerable to the group as a whole. From the sense of responsibility towards others, which this task stimulates, come the personal ethics and work ethics that Dodin takes to be indispensable for the Maly and the theatre in general.

A more complex version of this kind of training occurs in the *zachin*, which Dodin appropriated from Korogodsky and the Youth Theatre movement. The word means 'beginning', and a *zachin*, in Dodin's pedagogy, is a prelude to a class, organised by a group of students. Like the table arrangement, a *zachin* is meant to be related to the intentions and themes of the session, or to crystallise them. The activity develops a flair for devising and is, in fact, a form of devising itself. The students who are responsible for a given *zachin* compose songs, ditties, poems, short narratives or pieces of prose, which activate their creativity and, at the same time, their willingness and ability to perform. The activity also nurtures their capacity for the collaborative input necessary for devising and for commitment to the team. Sometimes a *zachin* inspires work in subsequent lessons. At other times, pieces devised for a *zachin* resurface during sessions specifically set aside for devising, where they are explored and reworked. Some of these metamorphosed pieces may eventually find their way into a production, as happened in the case of both *Gaudeamus* and *Claustrophobia*.

The practice of *zachin* is carried over into professional life, thereby sustaining the continuum between early training and continual training at the Maly. It happens backstage in the form of music, songs, poems and readings before the opening night of a production, whether of one just launched or of one already in the repertoire. There are several reasons for its occurrence. It is a ritual that celebrates and reinforces the Maly's ensemble ethos, which Dodin believes is crucial for the theatre as such. Its binding power is particularly important when the company is abroad, adjusting to unfamiliar surroundings and performance spaces. It is a way of blessing the cast as well as the performance about to begin – an additional ritualistic aspect of the *zachin*. It prepares the actors inwardly for the performance, since its motifs or moods are related to it in some way. The actors tune up 'the heart and the nervous system', as orchestral players tune up their instruments before they play. The *zachin*, in this particular respect, is comparable to the Maly's regular pre-show warm-ups whose aim is to activate the actors' nervous system so that they are alert, vibrant and spontaneous on the stage, and hear and feel each other and the audience. This, too, is an essential aspect of Dodin's notion of 'aliveness'.

The Maly's warm-ups are integral to the company's training and are generally in three parts comprising voice, classical ballet and music, to which the actors have been introduced during their student days. It is clear from the school/company's programme, and from Dodin's conversation, how deeply convinced he is that ballet and music are the best models for actors: dancers and musicians, he observes, exercise their instruments daily, and actors must treat their bodies like instruments to keep them in form so as to be capable of delivering anything required of them. One does not have to look too far to see why, in his view, ballet and music are such great resources for the art of acting. Ballet, for instance, although ruthless in its demands on the human body, is designed to give it strength, stamina, poise, equilibrium, co-ordination, precision and grace, among other qualities, including mental stamina, which are necessary as much for stage work as for daily life. And while ballet plays a fundamental role in the actors' mental and physical development, its benefits are extended by gymnastics, acrobatics and circus skills, usually learned on a one-to-one basis with their teachers.

How far actors develop an idiom, say acrobatics rather than ballet, depends on their needs for a particular production. *A Play With No Name*, for instance, requires acrobatic and circus skills from a number of its players, some of whom perform such dangerous feats as leaping from a balcony into water or juggling fireworks. Special attention was given to these actors according to their own perception of their needs. *Gaudeamus*, on the other hand, is far less concerned with fine-tuning individual requirements in that it operates on group ability, thus on the balletic skill of the whole cast. By the same token, the perfecting of skills is not seen to be purely functional, that is, solely for the ends of performance. The Maly actors also improve skills they would like to master for personal satisfaction.

The Maly's pre-show warm-ups are arguably closer to the warm-ups of a dance company than a theatre one (thereby justifying Dodin's dance model for actors) in so far as, besides covering routine exercises such as *pliés, battements tendus*, arabesques and bends, their exercises target the specificities of a production. This holds as much for their voice and music components as for their ballet work. A good example of how warm-ups are adjusted to precise objectives is the voice series conducted by Galendeyev before *A Play With No Name*, which I observed in Weimar in 1997. He paced the actors through exercises on tenacious breathing so as to prepare them for speaking with water in their respiratory canals. The production requires many of them to go in and out of water right through their performance and drops of water stay in their nose, throat and ears, affecting their vocal delivery. Sometimes they simply cannot hear themselves talk. Galendeyev also had them articulate sets of syllables to different kinds of movement involving their whole body – the purpose being the effortless control of breathing. He worked on consonants – fricatives, for example – to help their voices resonate in the watery environment. Exhalation exercises, with sounds but not words, were done in time to release exercises of the body so as to expel tension from it. This was to help the actors cope with the heat coming from the light projectors placed very close to them on the stage. In addition, Galendeyev's exercises for the release of tension had a therapeutic goal in that they allowed the actors to deal better with the hot weather in Weimar.

The light projectors have a dramatic purpose since they evoke the summer heat to which Chekhov's characters refer. They are there, as well, for visual impact since their proximity to the water allows them to make startling contrasts of light and shade. Thus they are used to combine semantic meaning and attractive composition, and logical sense and theatricality.

Galendeyev's warm-ups prepared the actors both technically (performing in water) and artistically (keying in the production's summer motif and its characters' sensuality). They were not done, in other words, just to get the body going, literally warm it up, as usually happens in companies, but to get it going in a particular way for the performances at hand. Yet although Galendeyev's pre-show warm-ups responded to immediate conditions, including Weimar's weather and the actors' vulnerabilities, which varied from day to day, they had long preparatory work behind them. He had anticipated the difficulties peculiar to working with water during the production's three-year period of gestation and had trained the actors through that time to be ready for them. Furthermore, dialogue in *A Play* is usually accompanied by the abrasive sound of trumpets, clarinets and trombones and not by the quieter tones of a string quartet or a piano in the background, so Galendeyev researched the use of 'those resonators that would allow the voice to break through the brass music' (Weimar, 7 July 1997). In summary, Galendeyev's warm-ups, like all at the Maly, operated on a triple principle embedded in the company's work as a whole: responsiveness to given circumstances, exploitation of acquired techniques (diction, vocal line, clarity, rhythm, tempo, speed, among others in Galendeyev's rudiments of play) and a stretching of what had already been acquired on the assumption that training is, in Dodin's words, 'an uninterrupted process, without end' (Paris, 8 April 1994).

The idea that training is both a process and uninterrupted is probably best described as organic, and pre-empts a distinction between two notions of technique, one understood as an integrated component of cumulative learning and the other as mechanics. Sergey Bekhterev illustrates well how the Maly privileges the first. When I asked him how he would define technique, he referred to the company's production of *The Devils*, explaining that he has to wait a long time in this production before he appears and always watches it closely from the wings or the lighting box (St Petersburg, 30 September 1998). Technique, for Bekhterev, is this very act of watching a performance closely, and is essential, he believes, because no actor can walk straight out of a dressing-room and automatically cue in to the action on the stage. And observation is fully useful when it is serial, allowing an accumulation of gleaned insights, all of which sustain each other. Consequently, Bekhterev observes the changes in the performance from one day to the next, catches mistakes, assesses the performance's strengths as it evolves, and gauges how he will fit into its momentum. His single most important concern is to interact with his partners *now*, and not according to his memory of something that they had achieved in previous performances. Incidentally, Bekhterev's remarks demonstrate, since he does not set out to do it, what Dodin's axiom of acting in the 'living life' of moments might mean.

Training as an ongoing process 'without end', involves, as well, a principle of immersion. Tatyana Shestakova, Dodin's wife, recalls how they returned one summer to Verkola, Abramov's village in the Archangelsk region, to recharge their bodies and spirit (St Petersburg, 29 September 1998). Shestakova also wanted to replenish the roles of Anfisa (*Brothers and Sisters*) and Lizka (*The House*), which she felt she had played for too long away from their source of inspiration. She remembers how they travelled on a small, decrepit train that progressed so slowly as to allow them to touch brilliantly coloured flowers as big as footballs and run their fingers through long grass greener than anyone could imagine. The opulent landscape through which they travelled threw into sharp contrast the empty supermarket in the village, described by Shestakova as a huge edifice sticking strangely out of the vegetation like a flying saucer. This desolate supermarket was a constant reminder to the villagers that the food shortages discussed by Abramov in his novels had not disappeared with the Second World War and the post-war years of reconstruction, but had continued into the 1960s and 1970s and seemed, by their persistence, to be endemic to the Soviet system. Dodin and

Abramov loved fishing, and spent their days by the river, talking more than catching fish. Shestakova spent her time with the women, sharing their work and hospitality, and renewing her contact with what of them and of herself had helped her to invent her characters. The picture of gender division emerging from Shestakova's reminiscences indicates that the social relations of Verkola had not changed since the post-war years, which Dodin conveys in his productions.

Dodin had first come to Verkola with his students in the late 1970s, when they were working on *Brothers and Sisters* as part of their course. They settled down for a month in a disused monastery on the river, on the opposite side from the village, and gradually became involved in village activities. Abramov resisted any contact with them since he was suspicious of their interest in staging his novel and had misgivings about their ability to articulate its concerns, given their youth, city background and relative ignorance of history. Nikolay Lavrov, who plays Anfisa's husband in the production, recalls how curiosity eventually got the better of Abramov, and he crossed the river to see what they were doing (Paris, 10 February 1997). A passionate meeting ensued, establishing the strong ties that facilitated a second journey to Verkola in 1985. This was the time when the whole company was preparing its professional version of *Brothers*, so some 60 people rather than 16 students now came to the village to rehearse. The enormous distance from Leningrad was daunting, and the logistics of the venture were complicated, entailing arrangements for families left behind and for the difficult living conditions that lay ahead in Verkola, among them the empty supermarket shelves that Shestakova had noted previously. Training by immersion was hardly a straightforward business.

The purpose, of course, was for the actors to undertake what was tantamount to ethnographic and ecological research, not as an academic exercise, but as an act of absorption in body memory. Their research, in other words, was to become embodied for re-embodying in performance with ease, like a second nature rather than a show of skill. There were numerous demands on their sensitivity to nuance. Lavrov observes how they had to avoid 'actorly' renditions of peasant accents which, on the Russian stage, were typified by uniformly long vowel sounds, regardless of region. They had to grasp the peculiarities of the Archangelsk dialect where, among other things, speech is differentiated by gender: women speak with a sing-song intonation, while men flatten it and harden consonants. It was vital, as well, to capture details of gait, posture, gesture and mimicry and of how men and women related spatially to each other, proxemics being integral to the social relations between the sexes. While gathering impressions, they gained some insight into Verkola's history and noticed, for instance, the indifference of field workers to the quantities of grain left behind to rot by antiquated combines. This kind of negligence was, in Lavrov's view, a consequence of state control and its disincentives to individual initiative. Seeing it in the present helped him to sharpen his perception of the past and also to penetrate the issues regarding the struggle of peasants for diminishing returns against state demands on production – issues explored not only by *Brothers*, but also by *The House* in which Lavrov performs as well.

A similar type of research by immersion was taken up by the *Gaudeamus* class on the Don, the setting for Yury Trifonov's novel *The Old Man* from which Dodin and his students were devising a production at the time. In the early 1990s, in anticipation of *The Cherry Orchard*, the Maly enjoyed several brief periods in the country, both in Russia and abroad. The company's sojourn abroad involved two weeks at Whitmuir Hall near Melrose in the Scottish Borders where it workshopped the play with international participants under the auspices of the International Workshop Festival. In 2000, the company stayed by a lake at Kirishi, sponsored by Somov's refinery, as part of its preparation for *The Seagull*. Little, if any, ethnography was involved in these immersions in quasi-Chekhovian surroundings. Their principal purpose was to stimulate the actors, in suggestive, convivial contexts, to feel their way around Chekhov's plays.

The actor as researcher

Immersion in social and natural environments is, however, a relatively small part of the Maly's programme of research, given that the idea extends well beyond its most obvious environmental application. Dodin: 'What is immersion for an actor? It is, before all else, a matter of taking in, going through and feeling [*prozhit*] everything offered by an author' (Weimar, 9 February 1999). By this, Dodin alludes to a process whose complexities may be likened to multiple intermeshed layers that become even more thickly entwined with the passage of time. Although this complex phenomenon is not ordered hierarchically, either in Dodin's mind or in the actors' way of proceeding, my presentation of its various strands must follow some sort of sequence to be intelligible.

First of all, it should be remembered that Dodin's 'author', although referring to dramatists as well as novelists, certainly must encompass novelists since the 'theatre of prose' is fundamental to the Maly's work. The question is: how does the company create productions out of novels? The simple answer is that it plays novels right through, *in their entirety* – dialogue, narrative, description, expository passages, and everything else between the covers of the book. While Dodin's use of novels is not unusual in the Russian theatre, *how* he appropriates them is quite different from the usual practice of adaptation, when a playtext is scripted from a novel and handed over to be played. What is unique about the Maly is that a script only gradually emerges from the performance of a book. Furthermore, countless possible versions or 'virtual' scripts are played before anything like a final script appears. This process is unmatched even by radical directors like Lyubimov, who, apart from a few experimental steps in Dodin's direction, essentially adapted novels within literary parameters – that is, by establishing texts – rather than striking out to create new, performance-led texts, as Dodin had done. Dodin's 'theatre of prose', then, is constructed out of performing on your feet, performing as you go, which is a process that can be described as research-during-play-*into*-play, and is viewed very much as such, if not formulated exactly in these terms, by Dodin and his actors.

The process takes hours of work in any given day and covers any number of years, depending on the book chosen. Performing *The Devils* right through, for example, took three years, and occurred while the Maly showed productions already in the repertoire. This was also the case with Chekhov's *A Play*, whose length and style Dodin saw as novelistic rather than dramatic. The same happened with *Chevengur* (1999), the company's last 'theatre of prose' to date. Long time-span, then, is the single most important prerequisite of the company's research-during-play, the latter facilitated by its ensemble idiom or 'common language', which is used intuitively rather than strategically, as dancers use their idiom when they spontaneously try out steps with each other, or jazz musicians when they improvise. However, the process, although centred on spontaneity, is by no means anti-intellectual in the sense of being suspicious of all conceptual thinking and discussion. It is simply that table talk neither pre-empts play nor dominates it. Discussion among the actors occurs between their various tries. Dodin, for his part, tends to reserve talking for after a run-through. While he might suggest alternatives for this or that aspect, he generally takes a circuitous route around and behind what the actors have played, inviting them in this elliptical manner to investigate further. This is why his talk may appear to be tangential to the subject, and philosophical rather than pragmatic. As Dodin sees it, his commentaries should not focus on getting immediate results – how someone could do something differently – but aim to motivate thought, since thinking, in his view, is part of training and more important for the development of the actor than any 'technique' for attaining short-term ends (St Petersburg, 29 September 1998). Motivating an actor to think makes an actor 'a researcher instead of a mere interpreter, or just a wearer of masks' (Weimar, 9 July 1997).

Dodin deploys another method for stimulating thought, and this is reading aloud. Reading aloud Shakespeare when they were students would have prepared company members for reading whole novels aloud to each other, Dodin also participating in this pleasure. Reading of this kind usually takes several years, and what is especially interesting for an outside observer is that the process of reading varies. Once again, there appear to be no fixed rules as to whether a book should be read aloud before its pages are played, in conjunction with play, or in parallel with it. *The Devils*, for example, evolved with reading in parallel. Reading for *Chevengur*, on the other hand, chopped and changed, although it interrupted play more often than not, operating like a cross-check for what was being played out.

The company has no doubts as to the numerous benefits to be accrued from their reading aloud. It sharpens the actors' capacity for limitless attention both to their partners and themselves on stage. It encourages their immediate response to a specific situation and hence stimulates research-during-play around that response. It helps them, with Dodin, to make discoveries together, which, while reinforcing their ensemble identity, fosters their sense of co-ownership of the virtual production. Finally, although not exhaustively, reading aloud inspires them to build up their imaginative, emotional and intellectual resources by further reading at home. From Dodin's point of view, 'the actors read a lot, which allows them to quickly catch references that are not merely cerebral and in their head' (St Petersburg, 29 September 1998), but come from their 'immersion in the human heart' (Weimar, 9 July 1997). To claim that the latter immersion is of paramount importance to the Maly is not an over-statement; and literature has pride of place because it is taken to be a conduit to the 'human heart' which, Dodin believes, actors must study to be able to *act*.

Reading, albeit textual, is also contextual. Hence it involves immersion in an author's cultural, social and historical context – in fact, an engagement with what Dodin calls 'everything offered by the author'. For example, the actors rehearsing *The Devils* (and this included two to four actors working on each role) compiled a list of some 240 books that they, together with Dodin and other company members, thought were relevant to Dostoevsky. They read, first of all, everything that Dostoevsky as well as his fictional protagonists might have read: Goethe and Schiller and other early nineteenth-century German philosophers and poets whom Dostoevsky had admired; Russian liberal philosophers of the 1840s like Herzen, anarchists like Bakunin, and nihilist political philosophers, notably Nechayev and Chernyshevsky, all of whom Dostoevsky had disliked. Then they read the Russian religious philosophers contemporary with Dosto-evsky, as well as those like Berdyayev and Bulgakov who had been influenced by him. They also read Nietzsche, whose desire for the destruction of the authority of God, Church and state in the name of individual freedom – Nietzsche's version, through the 'transvaluation of values', of anarchism – Dos-toevsky had vehemently refuted. *The Devils* explores from a negative point of view, contrary to Nietzsche's positive outlook, a very similar network of issues.[4] Last of all, the Maly read critical studies and books about Dostoevsky. Dodin claims, as do the actors of *The Devils*, that this massive contextualisation showed them how to link time to history and culture, to make time concrete, and to 'one's relationship to oneself and others' (Weimar, 9 July 1997). What is more, according to Dodin, the actors had discovered so much by going through the process of reading-research that 'this very discovery changed them, as if all by itself'.

An ongoing process

The value Dodin places on change is closely linked to the principles of accumu-lation and maturation guiding his work. The actors store up knowledge, sensations and so on, and how they draw on their stock and add to it feeds into a production, its maturation depending entirely on their growth and change. Maly productions have a long life-span not because of repertory inertia, but because maturation is integral to the company's commitment to what I have termed research-during-play-into-play. This drive to keep discovering makes a production a matter of process every time it is performed rather than a com-modity put out on display. In 2000, *Brothers and Sisters* turned 15, and, as Nikolay Lavrov notes with satisfaction, many of its performers had gradually caught up with the age of their characters, which altered their relationship to the production and, consequently, affected it as a whole, in some cases quite deeply (Weimar, 11 February 1999).

The Devils in 2000 was ten years old. Dodin observes how this production took three years of intensive preparation, another three after it was first performed before the actors felt relatively ready for it, and more years again before it began to settle. (The comparison with wine here is irresistible!) Pyotr Semak, who undertook the role of Stavrogin only towards the end of the preparatory period, remembers that the first three years of the production's public life were a torment (St Petersburg, 26 April 2001). Gradually, after sleepless nights, anguish and constant search for his character, he began to feel some kind of freedom with his role. But the substance he feels it now holds is only a recent development. The production, he notes, has shifted considerably with time, infused by the growing understanding of its performers. This evolution is known in the Russian theatre as the 'life of a production'; and while longevity is a feature of repertory companies, what distinguishes the Maly is its absolute commitment to the principles of rediscovery and renewal at the 'quick', as I have called it earlier, so that longevity does not become a matter of mere reflex and repetition.

The moment of freedom in his role experienced by Semak was familiar to the actors, all of whom had suffered tremendous doubt in themselves during *The Devils'* evolution. Dodin, moreover, did not cushion them from it, believing that self-doubt, rather than confidence, is the catalyst for creativity and the flux and change required by it. He puts the network of issues concerning maturation, creativity and freedom in this way:

> A big production is like a big book that is created over a long time, as you might build a church with stone over a long period of time, and which then lives for a long time. It does not live with a dead life, but changes with time, with the physical, physiological, biological experiences of those who created the show and who continue to play it. If it is alive, it is not staged, but continues to develop. Of course, the production has been drawn, so actors do not have the freedom to reorganize it and say 'I'll go out here, now' or 'I'll come in from there'. They cannot improvise on the drawing that we have found together, but they have maximum breathing space for internal improvisation in it, and this inner freedom is the space of creative investigation and change.
>
> (Weimar, 9 July 1997)

As I interpret Dodin, 'internal improvisation' refers to the actors' capacity to make fresh discoveries, which is contingent on their openness to themselves and their partners. Only when they are uninhibited are they fully in contact with what Dodin frequently calls, during rehearsals, their 'spiritual life', his phrase alluding to that mind–body–spirit fusion at the heart of his research.

His focus on this fusion explains why he thinks of energy, a term used by directors and actors the world over, as 'inner energy' rather than as outward physical expression. Dodin: 'Energy is the feeling and thought that move, disturb and excite us, and do not give us peace; energy does not mean doing something more loudly or nervously, but asking sharper, more astute questions about what we are doing' (St Petersburg, 29 September 1998). This pulsation of heart and mind coming together ('feeling *and* thought' – my italics – as quoted above) generates the actor's actions, and sets off a chain reaction from actor to actor to spectator, and back again. Dodin terms what I have called a chain reaction a process of 'infection'. His idea of the spectator as someone who is energised by the play of actors and who returns this energy back to the stage is far removed from the empathetic, passive spectator who, ever since Brecht and Brecht's polemic against Stanislavsky (in the guise of an argument against Aristotelian poetics), has been presumed to be the norm of dramatic theatre – Brecht's epic theatre posited, of course, as the latter's exact opposite.[5]

It should be clear that Dodin's idea of the actor's research, as specified by my account, has far more to do with development than with bullet-point, check-list method. Yet the development of the actor per se is not, to his mind, the vital issue. The Maly actors certainly acquire skills and techniques for acting. However, what interests Dodin over and above the acquisition of craft is the spiritual, intellectual and cultural development of the human being who *inhabits* the actor. The quality of the human being, in whom the quality of the actor is embodied, is precisely the target of the extensive reading for *The Devils*. Another example of this holistic approach – the actor developed out of the developing human being – is the *Gaudeamus* students who learned to play brass, percussion and wind instruments. Most of them had never played musical instruments before, and although this skill, at least at the most basic level, was required for the production, it was developed into a musicality that extended them as people.

As noted in the preceding chapter, their music teachers usually travelled with the *Gaudeamus* students on their international tours, monitoring their progress as they went. So effective was this ongoing learning that, by the time Dodin staged *A Play With No Name*, the same performers were able to play entire pieces, instead of isolated bars of music – furthermore, at an extraordinarily high standard quite at odds with their late start. Galendeyev observes that Oleg Dmitriyev, for example (Sergey in *A Play*), who had never held a clarinet in his whole life, prepared 24 pieces for this production, including works by Mahler and Vivaldi (Weimar, 7 July 1997). Not all 24 were used, but Dmitriyev had built up a genuine repertoire and the knowledge of music that goes with such an endeavour. All the actors, without exception, felt pride in their technical accomplishment, which is the result of training in the mundane sense of the word. However, as Sergey Kuryshev observes, before all else, they valued the opportunity given them by their apprenticeship to gain a musical culture and enrich their internal world (Weimar, 7 July 1997; Kuryshev learned to play the trumpet which, in *A Play*, he must blow while swimming in the water). To their mind, their professional development was dependent on their personal development.

Devising and improvising

It is evident from the foregoing observations that Dodin's is a Renaissance, humanistic perspective in a social climate pervading Russia as much as the rest of Europe that favours specialisation, competition, scoring and results, and what Dodin describes as a 'conveyor-belt mentality' (Newcastle, 2 June 1999). His faith in well-rounded human beings underpins his predilection for actors who are not 'mere interpreters', but researchers who become 'active co-authors' of a production in 'its journey of birth' (Weimar, 9 July 1997). For Dodin, a production is a 'living organism', which is why he speaks of performances as 'giving birth anew'. In this framework of thought, the theatre can be nothing other than a place of spiritual regeneration and renewal – *re*birth, in some sense of the word – for all who engage with it. Spectators are necessarily included, as is clear from how frequently, in rehearsals, Dodin urges his actors to look at their play with the eyes of spectators. By asking them to exchange places, he reminds them that spectators are participants in the theatre-making process.

How does co-authorship at the Maly come about? Essentially, everything revolves around devising, which starts with *études*, Stanislavsky's method for stimulating the creativity of actors. An *étude* may take many forms, but always involves an actor's personal sense of something, say, an incident or a situation, as she or he perceives it at a given moment, thereby making the *étude* provisional and exploratory. An actor performing an *étude* may work by association, pursue a memory, or go further still and tap into the unconscious. An *étude* does not have to be based on personal experience. It may focus on something that an actor anticipates, or fears could happen, or desires. It may be inspired by a poet, playwright or novelist. It may be put in an author's historical context, or be updated to the present. *Etudes* at the Maly are never solo pieces, but always with partners, in keeping with the company's collaborative practice. They are never prearranged. At the very most, the actors may briefly discuss a theme for an *étude* just before doing it, while its actual physicalisation carries the theme through, usually for up to 15 minutes. Partners do not give instructions to each other. Play evolves organically, largely aided by the intimacy between them that originated in their student days and has been cultivated systematically in their professional life.

The Maly actors work through hundreds of *études* as they prepare a production. They usually start by inventing their own dialogue which may be tangentially related to the play or novel to be performed, or may mix pieces of this source text with their improvisations, all of it of course physically expressed, corporealised and embodied, on the go. These *études*, which clearly are devising processes, may last for a relatively long period before the actors devise directly from a source script. But even then, they first only give an approximate version of it, or paraphrase it before they actually speak it as written. In each case, the process takes its own course, allowing the actors a freedom not possible when practice becomes routine.

Two examples will illustrate this open attitude. Devising for *Lord of the Flies* started with performing a range of themes extrapolated from the novel: domination, conformism, scapegoating, youthful curiosity, the fun of enterprise, and so on. A good deal of this preliminary work was acrobatic, and eventually evolved into the production's ritual dances, circular runs, and all kinds of daring feats, like leaping onto the walls of the stage, suggesting a rock face, or dangling from them. Work directly with Golding's novel came well afterwards. Devising for *The Devils*, by contrast, started straight off with Dostoevsky's text, the actors simply playing the book through. They teased out this or that motif to see how much they could invent around it. They picked out, for instance, all the threads of the political debate between the 1860s generation and that of the 1840s, sons against fathers, radicals against liberals. Slowly, they linked the characters, events, scenes, dialogue and narrative relevant to this debate. They also selected other leitmotifs, building up actions around them and testing whether cross-connections were possible between them.

Writing with the body

Whatever course the process takes, the physicalisation of novels is none other than a process of writing drafts *with, through and in the actors' bodies*. This way of working must surely make the Maly a foremost example, in the early twenty-first century, of a theatre written on the body, as a choreography is crafted on the body of dancers. In the case of *The Devils*, it generated countless hours of play over the three years spent devising. The embodied mass of drafts was whittled down through a series of showings to about 20 hours; then, for the first runs of the production, to about ten hours divided into three parts and then eventually reduced to the eight or so, as the production now stands. Dialogues were memorised and rememorised, and noted down by Sergey Bekhterev and Tatyana Shestakova, Dodin's assistants for *The Devils*, in a myriad of scripts. Both of them also participated in devising and subsequently performed in the production. Apart from its choreographic quality, the Maly's scripting method is incredibly like oral culture, where songs, poems and tales are remembered and transmitted orally long before they are written down. The process of this work is its own result. That is to say, it is not driven by a predetermined goal – a scene, for instance, that has to fit into 'the' production. It is fluid, with a try-and-see approach. In addition, nothing in it is merely marked out, or held back to preserve energy. The actors give themselves fully, as if they were already acting on the stage in front of an audience. Dodin maintains that only by giving their all, every time, can actors surpass something they have already achieved and discover something new; and only in this way can they be liberated from all inhibitions and constraints.

Devising can also be a matter of free play, away from its source of inspiration. This was the case with *Gaudeamus*, devised from Kaledin's novel *The Construction Battalion*, but which bears little structural and narrative resemblance to it. Dodin gave his final-year students the task of inventing reams of script written on the body, in the Maly fashion. Only afterwards were they asked to commit some of it to paper. The disjunction between Kaledin's and the production's texts explains the latter's subtitle of *Nineteen Improvisations on a Theme of 'The Construction Battalion'*. Unfortunately, this subtitle is translated in most languages as *After Kaledin*, thereby losing the nuance implied by the term 'improvisations', namely, that the production was devised through and through. Dodin had read the book aloud to his students. They were shocked by its sordid contents and relentless negativity as regards the Soviet army, whose violence Kaledin took to be a microcosm of society at large. They were doubly shocked when Dodin asked them to turn this grim world into fun, using song and music (Maria Nikiforova, St Petersburg, 19 September 1998). Gradually they realised that such horrors as blind submission to authority, which in their totalitarian regime they had all known since childhood, could be viewed in an absurd light. This realisation freed them to devise comic pieces. One such piece lampooned the Soviet army's booklet of rules of combat, which some of the young men in the group had been obliged to learn by heart during their military service.

Invention followed upon invention. At Dodin's suggestion, they performed a series of military exercises to rock music, which gave rise to numerous hilarious sketches. One of them, whose refrain 'One-way ticket' was put into Russian nonsense rhymes, was subsequently kept for the production. Another of Dodin's suggestions was for them to imagine the soldiers' dreams, and then imagine these dreams as a ballet. A surrealistic ballet minuet came out of the *études* on this idea and was also kept for the production. The themes of excessive eating and drinking were explored comically. An *étude* was built on the commands 'Don't overeat!' and 'Don't get drunk!' which, in the final script, gave the colloquial 'Don't stuff your face!' and 'Don't get pissed!' It became the basis of an extraordinarily funny section in the production involving an officer and a dead-drunk soldier. These orders were to become an in-house joke during the *Gaudeamus* tours and survived thereafter as a wicked allusion to Dodin's injunctions, every time before the Maly set out on a tour, that they were not to eat or drink themselves to death, since they had to turn up the next day for rehearsals!

There can be no doubt that devising at the Maly is infinitely complex and time-consuming. But what is Dodin's role in it? It should be said at the outset that the Maly's collaborative work is not the same as co-directorial work, which means that Dodin retains his role of director throughout the entire process. The actors show him their devising, usually at regular intervals. The single most important verb in his feedback to them is *poprobovat* which means 'to try out', and they usually redo their work, improvising afresh, before a showing session is finished. At some point, when they and Dodin feel they have accumulated enough physicalised drafts to warrant an overview, Dodin begins to layer them, taking this or that layer away from the existing range, or adding a newly minted layer of devising. In the case of *Gaudeamus*, the students presented him with some 40 hours of devising, which took three days of play, before Dodin put his hand in to shape the material. Whatever type of devising is involved, Dodin culls, cuts, condenses and connects, much like a literary editor, except that he does this with living people. This editorial procedure in the flesh is another defining characteristic of his concept of the 'theatre of prose'.

However, the notion of editing deployed by me is not altogether adequate since Dodin brings his own imagination, innovations and creative wishes and decisions to the process. Sometimes he interferes quite radically in what the actors have devised. He asks them to 'try out' other possibilities, which means that scenes that may have begun to take root are pulled up and either thrown away or transplanted and transformed beyond recognition. His prime responsibility as a director is to hold the mass of material together so as to shape from it a compelling stage work. The long process from the first drafts to the one presented to the public is integral to what Dodin understands by a production's 'journey of birth'. Many scenes created by the actors go by the board, as do those shaped by Dodin. Nevertheless, all the excess material that disappears leaves its mark on how, having integrated it in their body, consciously as well as unconsciously, the actors actually perform. Dodin frequently refers to his practice of amassing much more material than he ultimately uses as the principle of the iceberg, here citing Ernest Hemingway's famous dictum that a piece of writing only shows the tip of everything that has gone into its making. The same principle could well apply to how the actors amass acting so that, on stage, the visible tip is sustained by everything invisible beneath it. The immense impression left by the Maly actors everywhere in the world, as witnessed by critical reviews, is bound to be tied up with this power of the unseen palpable in the seen.

Dodin sometimes turns sharply against his own decisions, as may be illustrated by *A Play With No Name*. The actors had been working hard on the love relationships in the play, when he suggested that they look at other themes, in case the latter illuminated the former. Months were devoted to improvisations on the theme of money, which is central to Chekhov's plot in so far as two of its moneylenders, Abram Vengerovich and his son Isak, finance its protagonist Anna Voynitseva. Additional months were spent on the scenes featuring Vengerovich and his son; similarly, on scenes where other characters talk about them in dialogue verging on anti-Semitism. The actors explored several possibilities: satirically undercut this anti-Semitism, play it in a lighter tone so as to diffuse it, or play it straight. Their aim was to make discrete units of action from which Dodin, rather like a panoptic eye, could select the most promising.

Dodin watched a wide range of drafts, prompting the actors to rethink them, until eventually he settled for two variations of the production, one sustaining the theme of money, and the other without it. These two variations were rehearsed alternately right up to the eve of the Weimar premiere. Then, suddenly, Dodin decided that the money theme was superfluous, and the first variation was scrapped. The company had started devising *A Play* during the financial crisis in Russia in the early 1990s. At the time, the theme had been urgent, but Dodin now felt (1997) that everyone had lived helplessly with the problem for so long that it had become stale. He felt, additionally, that this theme muddled the issue rising to the surface from the whole devising process, which was the tragedy of wasted lives. Even at the last minute, Dodin had no qualms about deleting material on which great quantities of time and effort had been spent, for such is the liberty of a theatre that takes research seriously and does not capitulate to commercial pressure. By 1997, such pressure had become part of Russian 'new' capitalism and, perforce, of the Russian theatre.

Becoming

Dodin's role is also catalytic in what amounts to a phenomenological conception of the theatre as a place where human experience is materialised and which in itself is an experience through and through. Thus, when the Maly was performing *A Play* at Weimar, he organised a visit to the Buchenwald concentration camp nearby. The company had begun to prepare *Chevengur*, and Dodin's assumption was that the actors would draw on this experience when it came to devising. Generally, Dodin believes that an actor cannot act something that he or she does not know in some way – consciously, unconsciously or on a repressed or subliminal level. And his prompts to the actors to push beyond their limits are a way of helping them to break through to their unconscious. Here Dodin draws on a psychoanalytical perspective on acting, as Stanislavsky had done when he attempted to understand what fuelled creativity in the actor.[6] Grotowski was to do much the same, the difference between him and Dodin lying in how Grotowski ultimately abandoned the idea of the actor for that of the doer, the idea of the theatre for that of action, and the role of the director for that of a shaman.[7]

Dodin, in addition, heavily emphasises the importance to the actor of the 'self' which, in my observation of his way of working, he conceives of as anything but a fixed entity. This 'self' involves *multiple* selves in perpetual flux in time and space. Hence Dodin's argument that actors do not experience today what they experienced yesterday, and that the performance now cannot be repeated tomorrow, or in two or five years' time. Dodin's viewpoint may be illuminated by the distinction in existentialist philosophy between being and becoming, that is, between *is* and *potential*. When set against this context of thought, his devising process looks very much like research into potentiality, into what might become. The various philosophical strains underpinning Dodin's practice overall bring him close to Maurice Merleau-Ponty and Jean-Paul Sartre in whose philosophy phenomenology, existentialism and psychoanalysis intertwine. Nuances distinguish them. Sartre accentuates the existentialist question of becoming and subordinates psychoanalytical precepts to it. Merleau-Ponty concentrates on the concreteness of experience and how it shapes perception, unconscious perception included. Dodin is a man of the theatre for whom everything, however formulated philosophically, must be made flesh. Yet his philosophical links beyond Russia are via his own cultural context, particularly Dostoevsky in whom, as intellectual history has recognised, phenomenological, existentialist and psychoanalytical thinking were salient long before they found their name.[8]

Rehearsals

Rehearsals provide the space for becoming, and in this respect the devising sessions are already rehearsals. However, the more fully established rehearsals, when a production has taken shape, are no less important for exploring potential. Dodin does not like the word *repetitiya* ('rehearsal') which, he believes, implies the idea that something has already been fixed and is then merely repeated (Novosibirsk, 15 December 1997), and prefers by far the word *proba*, a 'try', from the verb *poprobovat* cited earlier. The English 'rehearsal' used in this book refers to Dodin's fluid conception of *proba*. The conception itself indicates why, for him, rehearsals are an open zone and what he calls a 'zone of freedom' in which anything is possible. What might become depends on the openness of the actors to themselves, their partners and the situation. A similar idea termed *disponibilité* is central to Sartre's philosophy, confirming the existentialist dimension of Dodin's practice. Nikolay Lavrov observes how apparent the difference is, in rehearsals, between the Maly and other companies in Russia:

> We are not driven by personal ambitions and ego, as I have found in other companies, or when shooting a film. Things are said honestly and openly so that when something is not good we say so, and say 'Let's do it again. Let's try again' . . . There are no hurt feelings just because somebody made a critical comment, or because Dodin said, after he had watched three hours of rehearsals, that he thought it was boring. We might feel discouraged, but we trust him, even though he makes mistakes – and he *does* make mistakes – or even though we might not be absolutely convinced, body and soul [about his judgement] . . . One of the worst things about the theatre is that directors are afraid to make criticisms of actors. I've heard an actor yelling at a director more than once: 'What! *You* want to help *me*! Go to hell!' This does not happen in our theatre, and the trust we have is the result of years of working together . . . of rehearsing without fear.
>
> (Paris, 10 February 1997)

Some of the trust evoked by Lavrov must surely come from learning how to encounter your 'selves' and the 'selves' of your partners during the years of working together. Dodin: 'We are not ashamed to remember everything that concerns us . . . nor admit that sometimes we simply do not know how to do something' (Novosibirsk, 15 December 1997). Lavrov recalls that they can go through 'kilometres and kilometres of rehearsals and get nowhere', yet not think the running was wasted. Dodin, for his part, maintains that the company generally feels that nothing they do is superfluous, no matter how fruitless it may have seemed at the time. In the light of the preceding section on devising, it could be said, in fact, that the surplus effort put in provides them with reserves of know-how and confidence, which they build up through tenacity and perseverance at every stage of their 'journey'.

The actors are expected to be present at all rehearsals, whether or not they may be required to try anything out. Dodin believes that a discovery during a rehearsal can transform a scene entirely, and if people miss it they merely revert to how they played the scene the day before, thereby destroying its 'aliveness'. He believes, furthermore, that even the smallest discovery in one scene has a domino effect on other scenes that no amount of retelling to people who were absent can replace. Nor can retelling recapture the impact made by a shared discovery, which has long-term repercussions on how the productions-in-the-making take their course.

Role change

There is another reason for the imperative to attend in that actors are free to try any role they wish when the spirit moves them, or when Dodin invites them to try. He has this in common with several contemporary directors in Europe, notably Mnouchkine, whose experiments with actor–role combinations and per-mutations have been exceptionally consistent. However, Dodin, more than Mnouchkine, allows time to work for him much longer. The Maly combinations change slowly, allowing numbers of actors to rehearse the same role, or several roles, for a considerable period, even years. Yet, suddenly, Dodin may ask an actor who has been watching rehearsals for months on end to try a role, where-upon the whole range of actor–role combinations can swiftly change. Such was the case with Kuryshev for the role of Platonov in *A Play With No Name*, which he had not dared to try. Months of observing his colleagues and benefiting from their research had prepared him to step into the role quickly. Dodin also unex-pectedly invited Nikiforova to try the role of Sasha, Platonov's wife. She had been rehearsing the role of the rather feckless Maria Grekova and had not imagined herself as a wife, mother, and home- and family-maker: none of this was comparable to her own life. Nevertheless, it was precisely her *lack* of experi-ence in these areas that ignited her desire to experience them, and enabled her, through her imagination of what it might be like to be such a woman, to perform the part. Having observed all the rehearsals, she had a reasonably clear sense of how she might give the role of Sasha her own individual stamp.

Sometimes an actor may volunteer to play a part that does not appear to be suitable in the slightest. This happened during rehearsals for *The Seagull* in 2001, only weeks before the production was to go to Moscow for the third Theatre Olympics. (The Olympics were created on the initiative of a group of inter-national practitioners, among them Georges Lavaudant and Robert Wilson, the first being held in Delphi in 1995, and the second in Shizuoka, Japan, in 1999.) Aleksandr Zavyalov, who had been rehearsing Medvedenko, unexpectedly offered to play Konstantin in a scene that had been giving the whole cast some difficulty. Konstantin is usually played by a *jeune premier* – not Zavyalov's case who, besides being older than Chekhov's character, is rather stocky and florid. Despite his rustic appearance, Zavyalov brought such tenderness and vulnera-bility to the part that all stock notions about it showed their emptiness. Dodin was provoked to comment on the deleterious effect of stereotypes: there was no reason at all for Konstantin to look like a dashing hero (St Petersburg, 24 April 2001); and indeed there was not, as the actor had demonstrated.

Some actors play all the parts until they find the one most suited to them. Some who begin to alternate in a role play it less and less and then fade out of view. This happened to Pyotr Semak, who, after a year of waiting, thought Dodin had forgotten he was to rehearse Stavrogin. Then, after a summer's break, Dodin asked him to play the role (St Petersburg, 26 April 2001). What Dodin relies upon, as actors change parts, is the moment of recognition when they see the right cast emerging from the process. Rehearsal participants express their opinions and options, although Dodin most definitely takes the director's prerogative of having the last word on casting. It is not uncommon for the Maly to have two actors for selected roles when the production is performed.

It would be utopian to assume, irrespective of Lavrov's good faith, that the feelings of the Maly actors are not hurt. It must surely be extremely difficult not to know whether a role will be yours and then, after such uncertainty, endure disappointment. Yet, like Lavrov, Semak endorses Dodin's claim that the Maly ascribes to a '"higher" right', for the goal at stake is to get the work right. The procedures for matching players to roles are loose in the extreme. Nevertheless, there appears to be general agreement among company members that a role, once cast, may 'rightfully' belong to someone. Such was the case of the principal role in *The Broken Jug* (1992), which was performed by Nikolay Pavlov, 'as no one else could', according to both Lavrov and Galendeyev (Weimar, 7 July 1997). When Pavlov died prematurely of a heart attack in 1996, the production fell out of the repertoire for want of anyone who could replace him. Occasionally, actors are no longer collectively 'right' for a production. This was the case of *Lord of the Flies*, whose original performers felt they had aged too much to play Golding's schoolboys of 12, although, to this day, Dodin is not convinced that age is a problem. Other problems, he believes, are more to the point, like the disappearance (or possibly theft) of the fuselage, which is part of the production's scenography. *Lord of the Flies*, while considered still to be in the repertoire, has been rarely performed in recent years; but Dodin's confidence that it could be reactivated at a moment's notice is well founded. Such is the intensity of the Maly's long, infinitely exploratory rehearsals that the actors retain their creation inside them for years, permitting this most transitory and ephemeral of arts something like 'fixity' in the relentless flow of time.

Co-authorship

What further distinguishes the Maly's rehearsals is the participation in them of scenographers, costume designers, technicians, stage and props managers, teachers, administrators and various assistants – in short, the whole company taken in its broadest dimensions. The frequency and length of their participation vary, as does their contribution to co-authorship. Let us take *A Play With No Name* again. The teachers Mikhaïl Aleksandrov, Yelena Lapina and Evgeny Davydov, the company's brass teacher, were especially important for the musical co-authorship of this production, for which 12 hours of music had been gathered by everybody. They found scores, transcribed pieces from recordings, transposed music to different keys or vocal registers, arranged it for instruments other than those for which it was written, and so on. They gave Dodin advice as to how to narrow the sheer quantity of music down to three and a half hours, the time it takes to play it virtually non-stop in the version that became the production; and their contribution was invaluable since *mise en scène* and music are so tightly intertwined in the work as to be inseparable. This music covers several centuries and genres – jazz, blues, classical pieces, Russian Romances, opera arias, waltzes, Charlestons, tangos, all of which reflect the different kinds of input made by different members of the company at some stage of the work's development.

The non-performers who participate facilitate the orchestration of all the artistic elements necessary for the show. They anticipate where they may be needed, propose alternatives, and identify the vocal, instrumental or physical difficulties of an individual or a group, providing coaching as required. The designers Eduard Kochergin and Alexey Poray-Koshits are in close consultation with Dodin all the time so that design and direction are related symbiotically. Moscow-based David Borovsky, who had collaborated for several decades with Lyubimov, had a similarly tight-knit relationship with Dodin when he designed *Lord of the Flies* and *Molly Sweeney*. Borovsky, as we shall see towards the end of this book, works abroad with Dodin on opera in the same symbiotic way as occurs in their work for the theatre.

Design ideas are born from these effortless collaborations. Dodin and Poray-Koshits were in London in 1991, when the Maly was on tour in this city, and the company had begun preliminary work on *A Play*. Both men were by the Thames, discussing the play, when Dodin exclaimed how wonderful it would be to have it on water. Water is suggested, if only by its absence, by Borovsky's design for *Molly Sweeney*, which evokes an empty swimming pool. Water appears as a channel in *Chevengur* and reappears as a lake in *The Seagull*. Both productions are designed by Poray-Koshits. Apart from the fact that water is closely connected to these plays (*A Play* is set on a river, *The Seagull* on a lake, and blind Molly excels at swimming), water is Dodin's favourite element. Its presence in most of his productions in some form (apart from being a feature of the scenography, the actors also wash in it) belongs to his personal iconography and, as such, is encoded into his share of that co-authorship of productions in which he so deeply believes.

The expenditure of energy in rehearsals is immense. Dodin believes it is worthwhile especially because extreme creative effort, when the mind-body is pushed beyond its limits, releases tension, relaxes the mind-body and lifts it onto another plane of spiritual awareness. This is the point when an actor can make a breakthrough and achieve what cannot be achieved in any other mind-body state (Paris, 8 April 1994). What, at times, must appear from the outside as a punishing regime is perceived by the Maly actors as a prelude to those moments of exhilaration when bodies become light and transparent and free. Actors,

Dodin frequently says in rehearsals, must always be interested in what they are doing. If they are interested, their spectators will be interested, since actors cannot be so totally different from everybody else (Novosibirsk, 15 December 1997). He also says that nothing is as compelling as transparency, because only then are spectators lifted out of their skins. What he means is that focused interest compels attention, but transparency makes people fly.

Part II

The major productions

Part II

The major predictions

3   Dodin's 'theatre of prose'

Three main reasons emerge from Dodin's account of why he dramatises prose fiction. Prose is 'often richer than drama with the exception of Shakespeare and Chekhov who can hold their own' (Novosibirsk, 15 December 1997). Prose has broad dimensions that playwrights tend to fear when writing their own plays. Prose is liberating for directors because they are not obliged to follow the theatrical rules that plays generally impose upon them. Consequently, instead of falling back on established ideas about the theatre and what it is supposed to be, directors are forced to look for it specifically in terms of the book in front of them: 'You have to find the theatre *in* the book.' All the productions discussed in this chapter were motivated by Dodin's desire for a theatre able to transcend the boundaries set by a practice largely dependent on pre-existing plays.

Furthermore, as is clear when Dodin's 'theatre of prose' is assembled and studied as a corpus, prose allows him to restore a cultural memory that had been damaged, lost or threatened with loss by censorship and semi-clandestinity – the case of Dostoevsky's *Devils* and Andrey Platonov's *Chevengur* – or by the solitary exercise of reading in a country that had stifled public debate. The theatre, the most immediate and collective of artistic practices, is the keenest means by which culture, and thus also the history that it carries, can be re-membered (as happens to a body, since it is pieced back together to be embodied by the theatre) and remembered (since it is restored to memory) at the quick. All participants partake in it and incorporate it simultaneously. This, indeed, is the power of the theatre, as Dodin knows full well.

Brothers and Sisters, although mounted after *The House*, needs to be discussed first since the epic scope and historical resonance of these productions are all the more impressive when the stories they tell theatrically are given in chrono-logical order. Also, since my readers are not likely to know Abramov's novels, narrative sequence will make it easier to understand who the characters are and what part they play in each production. The fact that different actors play the same characters indicates that, irrespective of Abramov's order in which *Brothers* precedes *The House*, Dodin intended his productions to be autonomous and have their own artistic integrity. It is important to remember, as well, that they are not dramatic adaptations of novels as such, but works of the theatre in their own right. The devising process for *Brothers*, in particular, was so creative and free that, in Dodin's words, 'When we re-read the novel we forget that this or that scene was not in it at all; we forget that we have put a scene together from different dialogue, or have displaced a scene altogether' (Novosibirsk, 15 December 1997). Abramov, who became a friend of the Maly and saw both productions more than once, never thought for a minute that the company had taken untoward liberties with his texts. On the contrary, he took its inventiveness as an honour, which is precisely the spirit in which these productions were created.

My study of these productions, as of all in this book, is based on multiple viewings, sometimes across several years. This is probably the only way of stabilising in words something that is necessarily unstable since it is performed differently every time. A composite analysis derived from a number of performances is all the more important when a production undergoes subtle changes, let alone obvious ones, during its 'life' in a repertoire. The Russian notion of the 'life of a production' is particularly relevant for Dodin's theatre where organic development and maturation are understood to be paramount. My analytical account of *Brothers* will be especially detailed because it is seminal to the Maly's work as a whole, even when various productions take directions quite different from it.

Brothers and Sisters

Narrative structure

Part One of *Brothers*, which is titled *Meetings and Partings*, is in two acts and opens with a documentary film screened on an upright platform of logs at centre stage suggesting the wall of a peasant hut or *izba*. Designed by Kochergin, this platform swings, lifts and falls throughout the production. On it are images of victorious soldiers who return from the war greeted by crowds of smiling faces, flowers, kisses and cheers. The music is a buoyant Soviet march, a recurrent motif that signals a change of focus, time or event in Part One and comes over the top of deeply painful moments like a voice-over, sonic juxtaposition putting emotions into a gently ironic but compassionate perspective. A speech beginning 'Brothers and sisters' penetrates the music and is a quotation from Stalin's famous 1941 address to the Soviet people exhorting them to defeat the Nazi invader.

The wall swings up to reveal a crowd of villagers who surge forward as if to welcome their own heroes. More villagers enter through the audience, among them two running children. There is noise, chatter, laughter, movement and dance. The scene, however, is a sleight of hand because what spectators think they are seeing – the return of Pekashino's heroes – turns out to be a welcome for two younger men, Misha and Yegorsha, who have spent the winter at a logging camp cutting timber for the state. Ambiguity of this kind, when two or more events merge, momentarily confusing perception, is typical of the way the production works in layers of simultaneous action rather than along a single straight line. These are the marks left behind of Dodin's layering method during rehearsals, when the moments of creativity and the processes of creativity are rendered visible through the way layers are combined or cut, and the production is slowly shaped by the process.

It is spring 1945. The quick flashback to Stalin's speech in 1941, together with the film celebrating victory, firmly anchor the time, place and cultural space of the story about to unfold. Most of its protagonists are in the crowd of some 40 people on stage. All of them are important, and even the smallest roles are shown to be essential to the texture of the whole. However, a number of these protagonists are the narrative's main references. They are the Pryaslin family – Misha, his mother Anna and sister Lizka; Anfisa, Chairwoman of the Pekashino *kolkhoz* 'New Life'; Ganichev, the representative from the district committee; Yegorsha, who will marry Lizka, and Varvara, a young war widow. Two more characters who are indispensable to the plot, Grigory and Pershin, appear in the second act. Misha is barely out of his adolescence, but is the head of a family of five children, his father having been killed during the war. He will soon lose his friend Yegorsha, who, tired of Pekashino penury and sweat, will seek work in town. Misha and Varvara fall in love and have a sexual relationship. She is older than Misha and is accused by the villagers of having seduced him. Varvara is disgraced and ordered to leave the collective farm by Anfisa. Misha is ordered to return to the logging camp. Anfisa's husband Grigory, who had been presumed missing, returns unexpectedly. Anfisa tells him that she cannot forget how he had beaten her and is waiting for Ivan Lukashin with whom she fell in love when he was convalescing in Pekashino after a war injury. Grigory and Varvara leave for the town together – this part of the plot being reported by one of the villagers when Misha is logging in the forest. Ganichev deplores the poor economic results of the *kolkhoz* and, blaming Anfisa for them, proposes that Pershin, a former army officer, replace her. The *kolkhoz* workers cast their votes against Anfisa, ignoring how much she has done to keep Pekashino from starvation during the war. Misha is adamantly against her because he cannot forgive her for breaking up his relationship with Varvara.

Part Two, *Roads and Crossroads*, is also in two acts and begins with images of extraordinary harvests from *The Kuban Cossacks*, the 1949 propaganda film distributed across the country to bolster faith in collective farming. By this time, the production has made it quite clear that political rhetoric and peasant reality are at odds and that the immense efforts, good will and endurance of the inhabitants of 'New Life' have brought none of the economic and social improvements promised them. Some five years have passed. Anfisa and Lukashin are now married, and he is the *kolkhoz*'s new leader.

Numerous details complicate the story. All have to do with the economic ruin of Pekashino: the way the men are sent to lumber camps in the forest and are thus forced to neglect the farm; how officials seeking to fulfil production plans propose farming methods that destroy the land; how the machinery is old and broken; how the roof of a recently constructed stable is left unfinished because the men building it are fed up with not being paid; how the harvests are taken away by the state for distribution elsewhere; how the women continue to work hard, sowing and reaping and doing multiple other tasks. The role of women during the war effort as well as afterwards is consistently highlighted in the production, as is their capacity for fierce truth-saying when the men bow to pressure from the various apparatchiks controlling the *kolkhoz*. Then there is a campaign for collecting money for state loans from the villagers, who resist handing over their paltry savings; accusations of malingering, including by Misha, against the returned soldier who had been imprisoned in a concentration camp and who eventually takes himself to the hospital in town where he dies of cancer; talk of communism and 'enemies of the people'; hunger, fatigue and discussions on where the fault lies for the *kolkhoz*'s ruin, in the devastation caused by the war or in the politics pursued by the state.

All of this is structured by a collage of scenes of varying length and punch, public issues constantly overlaid by personal events and the presence of politics pervasive, although never in an agit-prop form. Even the most overt political episodes in dialogue echoing Communist Party ideology are not 'set-up' for scoring points. Instead, whatever political and critical point can be extracted from this or that episode *emerges* out of it and, especially, from how it is interwoven in the network of scenes whose full significance appears only gradually. Similarly, although the personal and the political are closely connected, the personal is not reduced to the political as the single causal principle behind all behaviour and action. What is personal also has to do with morality and with the complex, often half-glimpsed or simply hidden motives that pump through what Dodin calls the 'human heart'.

This 'human heart', which is as capable of love and courage as of betrayal and fear, shows its many colours right across the production, leading the work to a conclusion where the 'heart' and moral fibre, or lack of both, converge with the broader political situation. Yegorsha, who comes back to the village with news of better economic conditions in town, flirts with Lizka, and they marry towards the end of the second act. Lukashin is appalled by the deep-seated resentment that drives the men to abandon the stable roof so as to unload a river steamship for goods as payment. He decides to give each one of them a 15-kilo bag of grain in order to persuade them to stay, even though this is illegal. Yegorsha stops the bags from being distributed and, out of sycophancy, reports the incident to the district authorities. Lukashin is arrested and imprisoned. Misha asks the villagers to sign a letter in his defence. They all refuse out of fear except for Lizka, whom Yegorsha forbids to sign. She does so nevertheless and, in the nearest thing to a 'message' in the whole production, argues that it is better not to live at all than to live without a conscience. Yegorsha leaves her. Meanwhile, Anfisa learns from Varvara in the town that she still loves Misha. Anfisa exclaims that she has ruined Varvara's life and asks for her forgiveness. She also asks two rhetorical questions, 'Why do we trample on each other?' and 'Why don't we let each other live?' which resonate with still greater strength as the production draws to its close. Misha, like Lizka, ends *Brothers and Sisters* on a high moral note, but his life is in pieces. It is clear why, by its scrutiny of life in a political system claiming to improve it, including relations of solidarity among people, *Brothers* was a harbinger of glasnost and still a daring expression of it in the Gorbachev period.

The production ends with a reference to the 1958 film *The Cranes are Flying*, which also treats the theme of hope for the future after the traumas of war. The Pekashino characters group together at the entrance of their village – denoted by two huge swinging gates made out of poles. They listen to the call of cranes flying above, a symbol of an indomitable life force that is beaten down by disillusion, but not destroyed by it. The sound of cranes in *Brothers* cites and thus recalls the end of *The House*. Quotations from one production in another and cross-references between them occur frequently in Dodin's body of work, creating what Bakhtin calls a 'dialogical relationship' between them.[1]

The principle of perpetual motion

This bare-bones account of the production's story and content cannot begin to convey the inventiveness, variety and vitality of their theatrical incarnation. The production's aesthetics are based on the principle of perpetual motion, on currents of action which pull together tableaux, sections, episodes, fragments and codas into a composition of symphonic range and depth and extraordinarily infectious joyfulness. The whole gives the illusion that time and motion have no beginning or end and, for the spectators who are willing to go with it, takes them into another spatio-temporal dimension altogether. The effect is one of simplicity and effortlessness, which is in fact a matter of *trompe l'oeil*, in that the theatrical styling of everything that looks natural, straightforward and unforced demands from the actors complete control over their vocal, gestural and kinesic skills and absolute attention to each other and the rhythms of the ensemble.

Take, for example, the closing scene of the first act of Part One which runs for some 30 minutes and is set in motion by the return of one soldier to the village, the only one out of 60 who had gone to war. The scene begins, before the preceding fragment ends, to the music of an accordion played by Yegorsha (Sergey Vlasov). He comes on to the stage from the audience accompanied by shouting children, and also by women carrying flowers, as is traditional in Russia for welcoming guests. One woman dances, swirling a red handkerchief, while others cover their shoulders with shawls for the ceremonial occasion. The silence of expectation that follows is not 'dead' silence but continues the action as the soldier comes through the audience to be met with applause when he reaches the stage. A party in his honour is created in full view as the actors mill around and set up tables, covering them with white cloth, flowers and bottles of vodka and food. Misha (Pyotr Semak) circles with a red flag. Yegorsha resumes playing his accordion and beating his feet on the ground, as occurs in Russian folk dances. Others chat, sing, or mark out dance steps here and there. Toasts are made to victory. In subsequent scenes, which are constructed as echoes of each other, toasts are made to the women for working the *kolkhoz* during the war and feeding the nation; others to the motherland and, in Part Two, to Stalin himself, by which time the deprivations endured by the village under Stalin have become well and truly apparent to the audience. Furthermore, although both the Maly actors and the spectators have a longer view of history than the characters and know full well how badly history has turned out, the actors propose these toasts without any snide overtones or didactic intent. In this, as in other areas open to damaging irony, the production places the dignity of its characters above the egos of its makers

The scene is also built on contrasts of atmosphere, mood and emotional charge. The upsurge of noise and movement suddenly subsides as everybody concentrates solely on the bliss of eating a piece of meat, the first in years. There is silence for a minute as everyone eats. This flows into laughter, then into anguish as women remember that their men have not come back, then into solemnity as Anfisa (Tatyana Shestakova) offers a toast to Misha for his tireless work for the *kolkhoz*. Humour follows as all the women follow her lead and pour their vodka into his tin mug in his honour, custom demanding that he drink it all in one draught. A slight pause, and then they pick up the movement by singing folk songs in chorus. Varvara breaks in with *chastushki*, witty folk ditties chanted to music, which create a relay of spontaneous replies going from one performer to the next. Varvara (Natalya Fomenko) is a stunning, tall blond with braids around her head like a crown. Fomenko was suitably described by an American critic, when *Brothers* was performed in its fifteenth year in New York, as a 'Slavic answer to Sophia Loren' who 'gives the work an essential sexuality that pervades the entire production like a brisk perfume' (*New York Times*, 14 July 2000). Fomenko's Loren-like beauty and sexuality are equally potent in Dodin's otherwise rather prosaic *Desire Under the Elms* (1992) whose country and western dance scenes appear forced by comparison with *Brothers*.[2] Her 'perfume' envelops a scene where Misha, inebriated by the vodka given him, first holds Varvara in his arms.

Seamless convergence

All these different activities are carried out at their own tempo, the actors always taking their time, never hurrying an action, which are among Dodin's most frequent directions during rehearsals. Above all, they are carried through without interruption as some overlap, while others, like the eating fragment, are offset momentarily. The flow of time, pace and movement of the kind observed here also allows larger transitions to occur seamlessly, thereby weaving together disparate sections across the production's six hours of performance. Often a particular motif resurges as the seamless transitions occur, operating like a recall of a previous event. This happens, for instance, with the Misha–Varvara motif, which returns at the very end of Part One after several sections have focused on other concerns. It is precipitated by Misha's altercation with Lizka (Natalya Akimova) over his vote against Anfisa. Misha, dejected, looks at his father's portrait on the wall. In the same instant his father in uniform walks through a door on the side of the stage. Varvara comes in from the shadows at centre back. She walks towards Misha, who lifts her up to the sounds of the victory march that had opened the production some three hours before. Misha's mother and siblings appear from nowhere, as does a table covered in white. Misha's father breaks the bread he has brought in his hands as women throw salt on Misha and Varvara: bread and salt – signs, in Russian culture, of hospitality as well as of a marriage. More women run in to the sounds of the popular Russian waltz 'On the Hills of Manchuria' that is played intermittently throughout the production, and soldiers pour in through the audience and embrace the women on the stage. Wheat and flakes of light fall like confetti on the crowd.

Two events converge in this conclusion to Part One: one is the return of the soldiers which, in Pekashino's case, is celebrated at the end of the first act of Part One, and the other is a wedding celebration which, to all intents and purposes, is happening simultaneously. Celebration is, in fact, the point of departure from the very first moment of *Brothers* for the diverse scenes that flow on from there, like one long stream with its different tributaries, until they eventually culminate in this feast. The great poignancy is that this magnificent celebration is in Misha's imagination, his fantasy externalised so compellingly that spectators are swept up by it and transported with him into the time of daydreams. The dead return alive in this transcendent time, as does Varvara, who has gone forever. While a great deal happens in this scene, no one speaks, which accentuates its phantasmic quality. The spectral image of happiness is all seen through Misha's eyes, Dodin brilliantly handling a character's point of view and communicating it as such to the audience. The bread cameo in it has parallels elsewhere, albeit in altogether different keys: in Part One, when Misha returns from the forest with a loaf of bread, a product his youngest sibling had never seen before; in Part Two during the collection of savings, when a woman upbraids Ganichev and defiantly gives him a piece of their daily 'bread' made out of moss.

The Misha–Varvara motif resurfaces towards the end of Part Two, once again in the world of dreams. The occasion is Lizka and Yegorsha's marriage. Fomenko reappears as Varvara's phantom, once again from centre back, smiling with joy. In some performances she dances, while in others she simply walks across the stage towards Semak-Misha and walks past him – subtle shifts of play that occur in a number of other scenes as well, giving scope to that 'inner improvisation' coming from the feelings of actors in the moment that Dodin maintains is essential for performance. The themes of love and celebration, which were intoxicating in Part One, re-emerge in the Lizka–Yegorsha wedding scene. This time, however, they are embedded in the sheer beauty of peasant ritual, which the Maly actors had observed and absorbed during their various stays in Verkola. The scene has a magical quality quite unlike any other in the production, and this is largely due to its formality: the way the women prepare the bride, the bride's lament on the loss of her girlhood, the dance between bride and groom opposite each other, holding a taut shawl folded in a V (Figure 1, overleaf), and a round dance as dignified as a courtly dance, partners changing to the rhythm of the music and the song sung by the dancing women.

Figure 1 *Brothers and Sisters* at the Maly Drama Theatre, 1988. S. Vlasov and N. Akimova dancing; T. Shestakova and A. Zavyalov seated.

Photograph by V. Vasilyev, courtesy of the Archive of the Maly Drama Theatre, St Petersburg.

Two more examples of ensemble interaction will show, as well, how the Maly's performance style relies on metaphoric, poetic levels of expression. One example involves the women sowing, early in Part One. The other concerns both women and men working in the forest and occurs closer to the end of the same part. From a compositional point of view, the two scenes are echoes, in different registers, of each other. Light is used in both to create a setting. It is also a doubling device in that it completes and repeats actors' actions. In the women's scene, for instance, scattered light duplicates the image of showers of seeds sent across a field. The performers, in the meantime, sing in harmony, swing their arms wide in unison and stomp their feet forward as they sow, their piece, for all its cohesion, managing to avoid a chorus-line effect. In the forest scene, sheets of yellow light suggest the sun coming through trees. They alternately obscure the performers, as if they were blending into the shadows of trees, or throw their silhouettes into relief. The lighting also conjures up images of falling logs. The relative silence of the forest evoked here contrasts with the noise of the women lying around on the floor in a large cluster and telling dirty jokes between sowing. The cluster of bodies is an effective metaphor in itself for the sense of ensemble established (Figure 2, overleaf).

The easy changes from place to place are made possible by the log platform that serves as a film-screen at the beginning of Parts One and Two and which can be swung to any height and set at virtually any angle. Its metaphoric capacity is boundless. It represents a field or forest, and is used accordingly at floor level. It hangs as a roof for a bath-house, or tilts to become a grain-chute or a truck on which bags of grain are loaded. It stands up to become the inner wall of a room or the outer wall of a hut. It sits to give the angle of a street or a courtyard. It is lifted to designate various spaces, among them a hay-loft where Varvara and Misha make love. It hides secrets such as the trapdoor that spectators are to imagine in the loft floor when Anfisa hounds the lovers. This particular sketch is, on occasion, extremely funny in that the timing of Anfisa's harangues is impeccable as she looks and talks into thin air rather than in the lovers' direction. In other performances it is vehement rather than amusing, and Anfisa-Shestakova will not allow the lovers to escape her gaze. Whichever way it is played, the impact of this vignette comes only afterwards from the contrast between this highly theatricalised event and its profound human consequences.

Humour is a constant feature of *Brothers and Sisters*, despite its dark undertow. It runs right through extended sequences, as happens in Part Two, for example, when Yegorsha visits the village, the sound of a roaring motorbike announcing his arrivals and departures. Golden curly-locks Yegorsha-Vlasov is all angel and testosterone to Lizka-Akimova's mixture of burgeoning love, common sense and indignant innocence at his sexual advances. One such foray, which begins with his sporting a bandaged thumb for sympathy, unashamedly plays for laughs. He is a likeable, hedonistic braggart to Misha's responsible man, and a gag-cracking, clever town boy to the village simpleton Yura (Igor Sklyar). Sklyar performs Yura's reactions with such precision and candour (the amazement in

Figure 2 *Brothers and Sisters* at the Maly Drama Theatre, 1988.

Photograph by V. Vasilyev, courtesy of the Archive of the Maly Drama Theatre, St Petersburg.

Sklyar's neck and shoulders, for instance, when Yegorsha strikes a match from within his breast pocket) that his character is a source of good-natured humour whenever he appears. Humour has a satirical thrust at particular points, as happens when an authoritarian voice can be heard barking orders and abuse down a telephone, Yura becoming their accidental recipient rather than Ganichev, for whom they were intended, but who is on his rounds of the *kolkhoz*. Humour also ripples across such disturbing sequences as the one between Anfisa and Grigory who brings her gifts from the city – a pink nightgown that he clumsily drapes over her peasant dress and black patent leather high-heels that he puts on her feet. Since Anfisa cannot walk in them, the heels slide along the side of her feet on the ground as she moves, telling him how she remembers his physical violence against her. The layering of vignettes in this sequence bears out Dodin's claim during one of the Maly's Italian tours, long after the making of *Brothers*, that 'No book, painting or performance worth its salt can be limited to being beautiful, but must radiate something, must let people feel the creative process behind it' (*La Repubblica*, 11 December 1999).

The House: but not a home

The House is in two acts and takes the story of *Brothers and Sisters* into the beginning of the 1970s. Misha (Nikolay Lavrov) is now married to Raisa, who figured in *Brothers*, and they have three daughters. The couple have killed a sheep for the arrival of Misha's twin brothers, Pyotr and Grigory, whom he had sent to Moscow to study. Pyotr is an engineer. Grigory is an epileptic. They learn from Misha that he has quarrelled with Lizka (Tatyana Shestakova) because she had illegitimate twins, now small children, after the death of her son by Yegorsha (Igor Ivanov). Misha has built a new house. Lizka lives in the house she inherited from Yegorsha's grandfather. After a number of scenes concerning Pyotr, Grigory and Lizka, which include Misha's fury against his brothers for staying with Lizka, the focus of attention falls on Yegorsha's return to the village after an absence of 20 years.

Delightful scenes showing Yegorsha's encounter with the women of the village and then with Lizka who, to their disapproval, greets him warmly and invites him home, are followed by a scene in which Yegorsha, cocky as ever, though the worse for wear through drink, attempts to seduce Lizka whose laughter from happiness Yegorsha mistakes for derision. Anfisa (Galina Filimonova) tells Lizka that Yegorsha has sold her house. Lizka is forced to move out. Meanwhile, a series of scenes involving *kolkhoz* disputes and Misha's consternation at how the villagers have lost all interest in work and the welfare of the village leads to a long sequence featuring the old commissar Kalina, who is fatally ill, and his wife Yevdokya (Vera Bykova). Yevdokya tells the story of their life. The sequence is hard-hitting, and is essentially a synopsis of the history of the Soviet Union. Kalina had participated in the most important events of this history as he, with Yevdokya, travelled the length and breadth of the country building socialism, only to end up in a Gulag. Kalina had protested against Stalin's suppression in 1937 of the old communist vanguard of the 1917 Revolution.

The second act is fundamentally a close-up of domestic details concerning the Pryaslin family, Misha's daughters and Anfisa's son being foils for their parents' generation. This is situated, however, in the wider context of *kolkhoz* politics and the politics of the nation, the domestic and the public constantly rubbing against each other, though not so tightly intertwined as was to occur in *Brothers*. Kalina, on his death-bed, asks his wife to sing his favourite revolutionary song, which Bykova, soon joined by Lavrov in an undertone, performs with a mixture of verve and stoical sorrow, Dodin preventing this scene from degenerating into mawkishness or despair. Kalina's funeral follows, and no sooner does this scene end than Anfisa rushes in to tell Lizka that her house is being demolished for firewood. Pyotr and Lizka attempt to haul the carved wooden gable of the house sold by Yegorsha onto the home of their childhood. The old rope holding it breaks and the gable falls on Lizka. (The accident is not shown in the production, any more than the gable, which is metaphorically indicated by one of the wooden beams that operate like swings in Kochergin's design.) She dies in hospital. News of her death is brought to Misha, and the production ends with an elliptical, implied funeral instead of a performed one as had occurred in the case of Kalina. The cranes fly past as Misha recalls his father's question to him when he went to war: 'Have you understood me?' Of course, what Misha understood, 30 years later, was that people had to protect and preserve their house and home.

One can see in the production a number of the qualities, in smaller doses, that would become such great strengths in *Brothers*: ensemble power, emotional and physical vitality, poetic configuration, precision, tragedy blended with humour, the use of contrast and juxtaposition, and the symbiosis between direction and scenography. Where *Brothers* is fluvial, *The House* operates in terms of clusters of juxtapositions that identify and distinguish sequences from each other, the latter by no means as multi-layered as in *Brothers*. Also, similar devices have dissimilar purposes, notably the jump-cuts that in *Brothers* are wish fantasies and in *The House* are flashbacks. The wish fantasies have a stronger psychological thrust than the flashbacks, which highlight narrative and mood.

And the politics of *The House* are more direct than in *Brothers*, as is evident both in Yevdokya's mordant account of Kalina's life and the scene of Kalina's funeral. In the latter scene, a female party ideologue berates the villagers for giving Kalina a hero's burial. When they defy her command, which is tantamount to defying both the party and the state, she insists on observing formalities by calling for Kalina's medals and decorations to be displayed. In a supremely stinging moment, she discovers that Kalina had none. Nor was this possible, the production makes plain, for a commissar who had fought in the Revolution but was sent during Stalin's purges to a Gulag. The funeral scene ends as the villagers, who hold Kalina's coffin and their red flags high, turn in a circle to the music of a brass band that has been playing on stage throughout it. As *The Independent* noted with reference to this scene during the Maly's 1994 tour of Britain: 'And for a moment, as the villagers, bearing their red flags bury the old commissar, you realise the enormity of their betrayal by the state. You also realise just how courageous this company must have been in staging this production' in 1980 (5 May 1994). Indeed, its courage, in hindsight, is quite staggering, especially as Dodin had not been a 'permitted' dissident as Lyubimov had been right through the 1970s.

Misha's father's question is all the more trenchant because Misha remembers it against the background of Lizka's and Kalina's deaths. Misha had symbolically deprived Lizka of a home by quarrelling with her. Kalina, according to Yevdokya, had been too busy building socialism to care about having a home at all: 'The whole country was his home!', she comments scathingly. The question's significance did not escape the Soviet public, although its answer was not articulated openly in the press until glasnost and perestroika. Thus in 1986, six years after the production was first performed – and its release took place only after rehearsals had been monitored by various officials – *Sovyetskaya kultura* (*Soviet Culture*) wrote that Dodin's actors had played the fate of millions of Pekashino characters across the Soviet Union. These millions had built 'our Home', even though 'for many years they were unable to satisfy their children's hunger or build their own house' (29 July 1986). The production had shown, as well, 'how difficult it had been to change the smallest thing in our Home, even though we had aspired to this goal'. In this, as in other respects, *Sovyetskaya kultura* concludes, *The House* had gone to the source of the problems that had beset Soviet society and were undermining it still in the 1980s.

Lord of the Flies

From the novel to the script

The destruction of house and home would become a major preoccupation of Dodin's work in the 1990s. In the meantime, he focused on the dark terrors of the 'human heart', as presented by William Golding's *Lord of the Flies*. He found the 'theatre in the book' in its straightforward and abundant dialogue, its simple sequence of events and its underlying idea that the descent into savagery of the English schoolboys, who had been stranded after a plane crash on a desert island, was all too human and could have happened to anyone, anywhere, in any putatively civilised society. Published in 1954, Golding's tale of struggle for domination and control, submission to authority from collective fear, mass hysteria, mob violence and murder – all of it among children – had huge implications for a world that had only relatively recently witnessed the unprecedented horrors unleashed by Nazism, Stalinism and the Second World War. It was for his insight into the modern world and his warnings to it that Golding received the Nobel Prize in 1983.

The fact that the book had appeared at the height of the Cold War also gave it a topical ring. The 'beast' on the island feared by the schoolboys could be interpreted as the communist bogey fabricated by McCarthyism, or the 'enemy of the people' fabricated by Stalinism. Yet, whichever way it was interpreted, the book explained that the 'beast' of evil did not emanate from alien forces, but was an integral part of all human beings. Dodin's production elicited precisely this kind of response from the Russian critics when it was first performed (*Izvestiya*, 17 April 1986; *Vecherny Leningrad*, 8 December 1986). However, they reacted differently in that they related the idea of inherent evil directly to local concerns, alluding, albeit in rather veiled terms, to the repression, fear, betrayal and general moral degeneration that had prevailed in their society. Dodin, on the other hand, alluded only *indirectly* to Soviet society, and then only by association: *Lord of the Flies* was not, after all, a re-run of *Brothers* or *The House*. The clue to the distinction he drew between these productions lay in the passage by Golding that Dodin had inserted as a separate leaf in the programme. Golding asserts in this citation (from his speech at a conference of European writers in Leningrad in 1963) that 'humanity is afflicted by an illness. I do not mean humanity with a capital letter, but those people with whom I rub shoulders daily'. Dodin saw his production in similarly universal – but not abstract – terms.

The script, which this time was arranged by Dodin, closely follows Golding's plot while condensing it for dramatic impact. It is in two acts, the first corresponding to the first five chapters of Golding's novel and the second to the rest, giving two and a half hours of performance. Concision is here the objective, by contrast with the epic magnitude of *Brothers*. The script begins with Ralph and Piggy's discovery of a megaphone – a conch in Golding – which becomes a symbol of legitimate and something like democratic authority. Simon, Sam, Eric, Roger and others emerge from the forest at Ralph's call, as do Jack and the choirboys who soon become Jack's army of hunters. (Golding's 'little 'uns' are omitted from the script, with the exception of Percival.) A fire lit by the hunters burns out of control. The incident exacerbates the antagonism between Ralph and Jack, who contests Ralph's leadership of the group. Ralph and Piggy see a ship on the horizon but discover, when they clamber to the top of the mountain, that the hunters, overexcited by the prospect of killing pigs, had let the fire die down. Thus, there was no smoke signal for the ship to detect. Jack insists that they need meat, Ralph that they need huts for shelter and fire for rescue. Dodin builds up the unresolved tension between them meticulously, taking it to a plateau in all the boys' talk of snakes, ghosts and the beast who supposedly lives on the island, which closes the first act.

An interval leaves spectators in suspense, which is intensified when Sam and Eric claim in the opening scene of the second act that they have seen the beast. From here on Dodin speeds up the action, cutting away anything he considered superfluous in Golding to the very core of the plot. Jack and Ralph seek the beast, but abandon their search out of fear. Jack challenges Ralph's right to lead, fails, storms off and returns with a pig's head to appease the beast. Jack wins the boys over, thereby destroying Ralph's position. Simon talks with the pig's head and discovers two beasts, the real one, which is within, and the imaginary one that had billowed in the wind which, in Golding, is a dead pilot in a parachute and in Dodin, a pilot's spare suit – in other words, without a cadaver in it. Simon is killed by the maddened pack of boys. They raid the shelter of Ralph, Piggy, Sam and Eric, who have not joined Jack's 'tribe' (Golding's term), to steal Piggy's glasses, which they need to make fire to eat pig, all thought of fire for rescue forgotten by them. The foursome go to Jack to retrieve the glasses. Roger kills Piggy. Sam and Eric are coerced into joining the tribe. Ralph is about to be hunted down like a pig – the island, by now, raging with fire – when there is a black-out and a pause. A man's voice offstage asks whether they were at war and whether anyone was dead. Children's voices, not the adults playing the children, reply, also offstage.

The rest is Dodin's coda. The lights come up on the voice's last lines showing a child standing in front of Ralph and facing the audience. Ralph (Pyotr Semak) turns away and wails, and then puts his arms gently around the child's shoulders, both looking to the audience. The image can only imply that the child is within the man. In Golding's novel, an officer coming to the rescue rhetorically asks whether they are 'a pack of British boys'. In Dodin's production, the anonymous voice asks, also rhetorically, whether they are 'civilised boys'. Dodin surmises correctly that the notion of 'civilised' is implicit in Golding's 'British', and avoids the specific 'British' in order to strengthen the universal embrace of his production.

Dialogue in Dodin's script serves action. He picks out lines spoken by characters concerning particular actions from across as many as ten to twenty or more of Golding's pages, making them into compact speech. (So, for example, the instances when Jack talks about meat and hunting, which recur in many chapters are telescoped by Dodin, or when Piggy supports Ralph's exhortations to keep the fire going, another repeated main action.) Usually Dodin follows Golding's order of dialogue. Occasionally he inverts the order, or gives additional lines to a character by taking them from another so as to distribute speech more evenly. (Roger's dialogue, for example, which tends to be meagre in Golding, is filled out to give the character a greater dramatic presence.) Sometimes he turns actions that are narrated in Golding into part of the dialogue. Most often large chunks of Golding's talk between characters disappear behind Dodin's stringent selection of what is essential in what they say. All in all, the script is like a skeletal version of Golding rather than a mosaic with extraneous pieces brought in, as occurs in *Brothers*. But it is precisely its pared-away quality that gives us insight, as an X-ray may be said to do for the body, into one of Dodin's most important creative principles, which is that of transforming novels into theatre.

Dodin's theatricality

Very recognizable though it is, the script nevertheless incorporates a number of insertions that, although foreign to Golding, are crucial for the theatricality pursued by Dodin. They involve Simon's speech in the second act, when he confronts the 'beast' in the form of the pilot's suit and reads instructions on its label for use in case of an emergency – lines that do not exist anywhere in Golding's book. These lines, coming at the moment of epiphany that there is no beast, throw into relief Simon's dialogue with the pig's head, which Sergey Bekhterev performs bivocally, that is, as Simon's interior monologue and as the head's address to him. Thus, the 'I' of 'I am the beast' refers both to Simon and the beast at one and the same time. In this way, the production accentuates the issue of the beast in humanity inscribed in the novel.

The remaining insertions are musical – hymns, nursery rhymes and other songs that underscore given actions. 'Abide with me' is sung by Jack's choir beneath the stage before they file up from there onto it. This, together with their red choirboy dress, tells the audience their identity before Jack explains who they are. The hymn is sung again after Jack's incitation to kill a pig, the note given by him to the choir operating like a command to his hunters. In this way, images of godliness and profanity and of civilisation and brutality are brought into one frame. 'Good King Wenceslas' is sung shortly afterwards to demonstrate that they are a troupe – and troop. The nursery rhyme 'Here we go round the mulberry bush' is sung as the boys explore the island, that is, climb the back wall of the Maly theatre, which David Borovsky exposes as part of his design. (The rhyme is not sung with its usual words but concerns a train stopping at London and Glasgow which, in the circumstances, has a decidedly bizarre ring.) Simon sings one of its stanzas in the second act when, hanging from the wall, he discovers the pilot's suit. A lullaby telling of God's love for children closes the first act. Simon-Bekhterev starts it off, gradually joined by the choir/hunters who step out of their characters to sing it, standing still, as if it were a chorale in a religious service.

This lullaby/hymn returns at the beginning of the second act, which starts after the interval, to establish continuity with the first. Otherwise song in the second act occurs at only two other moments, excluding Simon's rhyme, so as to highlight Jack's power (Igor Sklyar). The songs follow on, one after the other: the well-known English round on a cuckoo, which the choir/hunters sing as they dance around the pig's head that they have hoisted up on a rope for the beast; and a hymn sung in descant by way of Jack's riposte to Ralph who, in the face of an impending storm, has pointed out that Jack's pack did not have any shelter. Song, as all these examples show, is never decorative but, by heightening action, also heightens meaning and does so by its incongruity in the given context. Its ancillary effect is to give a slightly English touch that suggests just enough foreignness, something not Russian, to keep any kind of over-identification by Russian spectators at bay. This slight distancing, even though the songs are sung in Russian, helps to carry the notion of an identifiable, all-inclusive 'humanity' that was envisaged by Golding when he talked about his book, on the one hand, and by Dodin when he transposed it to the stage, on the other.

One sequence deserves special attention as regards the production's pronounced theatricality. It begins with Jack's return with the pig's head which Roger (Vladimir Zakharyev), who climbs up the rope at centre stage, attaches to the middle of the rope. The sequence progresses with the cuckoo round, a stomping-jumping circular dance, and the hymn in descant. Then all hell breaks loose. Thunder rips the theatre apart. Cosmic electronic sounds pulsate in counterpoint to what sound like tolling bells. A recording of a woman's gravel voice belts out a song off stage above the din (scores by Alfred Schnittke and Dimitry Pokrovsky) while the actors stamp on the floor boards, and jump and leap and chant the war cry taken from Golding: 'Kill the pig. Cut her throat. Spill her blood.' Everything occurs at once in this phenomenal cacophony of rhythms and registers in whose opening bars the actors swing back and forth, high up on the three ropes hanging from the flies, while others swing the same ropes at floor level as if they were ringing bells, aural and visual imagery in concert. As the cacophony rises to a crescendo, some actors jump on the swinging ropes while others jump off them and run, yelling and whooping at the top of their voices. They run up and down or jump across the bits and pieces of Borovsky's set – the broken fuselage of a plane, a bit of a cockpit, something that looks like a tall box, and a frame beside it suggesting the door of an aeroplane. Or else the actors vanish, only to dash out of the secret troughs hidden in the design. Their running turns suddenly into more circling as they chant and stamp around the fuselage and then change their dance by beating it hard like a drum. They then stamp and jump forward on both feet, moving in an S shape that winds its way to the back wall and along it out into the wings. They are lit against the wall from behind so that only their silhouettes are visible, light having shifted from the front of the stage to the back and from one type of *chiaroscuro* to another. The actors need, in this scene, every bit of physical fitness and balletic, acrobatic and circus skill that their training has given them.

This frenetic music-dance scene came out of the devising process and is pure theatre in the sense that it was born out of performance and not from words on a page. Dodin has not even put any stage directions for it in the script, as if to keep its performance origins intact. He makes it coincide with the climax of the story, that is, when Jack defeats Ralph and breaks away with his own group. The rest of the action, which has such high moments as Simon's epiphany, can go nowhere else but from this climax to its quasi-apocalyptic resolution. Dodin also uses his great musicality astutely by picking up the registers and timbres of this stupefying dance scene for the prelude to Simon's murder. Thunder, electronic rumbling, the blast of pre-recorded song and the actors' chanting and stomping dance, which they perform, this time, like storm-troopers, converge as they close in on Simon for the kill, his murder taking on the appearance of a ritual killing. When Piggy meets his death, which happens soon afterwards, echoes of the electronic sounds of this scene can be heard, like a musical recapitulation, so as to link the two murders in one overarching frenzy of blood.

In terms of characterisation, Piggy (Grigory Dityakovsky) is a major departure from Golding's creation. He is not a victim-scapegoat at 'the centre of social derision' (Golding, 1999: 168), which is also how Peter Brook presents him in his 1963 film version. Rather, he is not altogether different from Ralph and is also Ralph's ally and partner. Dodin's perspective, contra Brook's, means that the production, instead of centring on the suffering of an outsider and the bullying of insiders, has the scope to explore the vulnerability of solidarity in the face of destruction. In Golding, Piggy is killed by a boulder rolled over him by Roger. In Dodin, Roger clubs him to death with the megaphone that Piggy found. Hailed by Brook as 'one of the great theatre events of his life', the production was allegedly never allowed by Golding to come to Britain (*Daily Express*, 20 June 1998). Nor has it ever travelled anywhere in western Europe and beyond, to the great loss of theatregoers there.

The Devils

The hard-edged corporeality of *Lord of the Flies* – Meyerholdian in its emphatic physicalisation and thus also its theatricality – gave way, five years later, to the dark stillness of *The Devils* in which virtually everything is internalised, the whole becoming a study of movements of the mind and soul that, for want of a constructive, productive issue, turn inwards on themselves. Unlike *Lord of the Flies*, *The Devils* foregrounds its characters not so much for their psychological make-up – theirs is an enigmatic, unfathomable presence – as for how they are immersed in their thoughts, their cogitations providing the focus for the entire work. It is, before all else, a verbal piece, all nine hours of it in three parts, and the effect is hypnotic. Its minimalist aesthetic crafted out of language, which distinguishes *The Devils* from the rest of Dodin's *oeuvre* (only *Molly Sweeney* would begin to resemble it), contributes to its mesmeric influence. The smallest inflection, the slightest gesture, the subtlest change of facial expression – every tiny shift is meant to channel attention not to the speaker, but to what is being said.

The fact that the production homes in on the philosophical and moral substance of its dialogue was noted with some awe by all the critics who saw it when it was first performed in Braunschweig. The *Hamburger Abendblatt* (13 November 1991), for example, additionally observes how its almost static quality largely accounts for its force, and a critical consensus on the astounding impact of this combination of word, relative immobility and power through restrained acting would emerge wherever *The Devils* was performed thereafter: in Russia, Scotland (1994), France (1997), England (1998) and Italy (2000). Several exceptions to the rule maintained that there could be no drama without action (for example, the *Peterburgsky teatralny zhurnal* – *Petersburg Theatre Journal* – July 1992), but the point, precisely, is that the drama is in the production's non-action or, put differently, in its economy of action. The drama is so deeply entrenched in this economy that to complain about it would be tantamount to asking for another type of performance altogether – *Brothers and Sisters*, perhaps, of which *The Devils* is the exact antithesis. The Petersburg critics acknowledged its value with their prize for best production in 1993. As it stands, it would not be too much to claim that *The Devils* is a gigantic landmark in the history of world theatre.

The production was performed in Britain at London's Barbican Centre to the most rhapsodic reviews of them all. It was shown under the alternative title for Dostoevsky's book *The Possessed*, which is misleading since it suggests the passivity of possession, of being possessed, whereas both Dostoevsky and Dodin stress that devilry is active and produced consciously, voluntarily and wilfully by social agents. The awed admiration filling British press reviews is well conveyed, for example, by Alastair Macauley in *The Financial Times*:

> The greatest acting in the world? It often seems that way when watching the Maly Drama Theatre of St Petersburg in Lev Dodin's three-part adaptation of Dostoevsky's *The Possessed*. London contains a disproportionate quantity of the world's best actors, but these Petersburgers are a lesson to us all. Economical and compelling, theirs is acting both as noble craft and as a humble art, devoted to a cause larger than themselves.
>
> (30 June 1998)

Or compare this accolade with that of the *Observer Review*:

> Today is the last day of a grand theatrical experience . . . But Dodin . . . has pulled off something extraordinary. He transmits the contradictory, ducking and diving quality of the novel, but he also gives the evening an intelligible and lucid line . . . They [the actors] are a marvel.
>
> (5 July 1998)

Or take a fine actor, Simon Callow, writing in the *Evening Standard*: 'Dostoevsky's *The Possessed* . . . will tower above anything else you will see on stage this year, or perhaps this decade. On no account miss it.' Callow also writes:

> The most exciting theatrical event of the summer will be the arrival in town of the legendary Maly Theatre of St Petersburg – the greatest company in the world. The depth and power of their work is overwhelming. The stagings are inventive and the interpretations thrilling, but it is the acting, above all, that makes their work sublime . . . There's only one drawback – after seeing the Maly Theatre, almost all other companies will seem lifeless by comparison.
>
> (*Evening Standard*, 25 June 1998)

With accolades like these, mere praise pales into insignificance.

'The end of a historical period'

Rehearsals for *The Devils* (Figure 3) began in 1989 after Dodin had staged *Stars in the Morning Sky* with the company and *The Old Man* with his students. (He had also rehearsed parts of Chekhov's *Three Sisters*, but found it unsuccessful.) From the start he urged his actors not to be afraid of long and slow speeches, pointing out as time went on that Stavrogin, Verkhovensky and Kirillov, who are the main protagonists, speak in continual monologues and are, as a result, in conversation only with themselves. What binds them together is their sectarianism, each one of them doggedly pursuing his particular form of it to the last. Gradually, as rehearsals progressed, Dodin pushed back the political aspects of these characters' ruminations, leaving exposed the ethical and metaphysical conundrums that Dostoevsky had placed at their core. This entailed toning down Dostoevsky's satire of revolutionary politics, which he had envisaged as a mixture of liberalism, radicalism, terrorism, nihilism, atheism, and even certain variations of slavophilism, all of it castigated by him in the name of Russian Orthodoxy.

The book, completed in 1871, was in the limelight at the end of the 1980s not only because it had been branded 'reactionary' during the 1920s and was banned until the late 1950s, but also because the political machinations exposed in it corresponded, in the public eye, to the now-discredited strategies of the communists. The putsch against Gorbachev by communists in August 1991 only reinvigorated scepticism as to the worth of any kind of extreme partisan discourse in a country that had been steeped in ideology and was now on the verge of collapse; and responsibility for Russia's run into chaos – headlong since the Bolsheviks took power in 1917, according to her most determined anti-communists – was laid at the door of those ideologues who had placed dogma before bread. It was still too early to say where Boris Yeltsin's ostensible drive for democracy would take the nation, although hard-bitten pessimists predicted that this political venture was also doomed to failure. Now, on the eve of Russia's new future, with which the opening of *The Devils* abroad had coincided fortuitously, Dodin was more anxious than ever to avoid anything that looked like an opportunistic reading of Dostoevsky; despite the fact that he had chosen the book several years previously because its 'explosive irony' as regards visions of revolution provided a fitting 'conclusion to the end of a historical period' (*Corriere della Sera*, 28 October 2000), that is, the end of totalitarian Russia as announced by perestroika. Now, more than before, Dodin looked for support in the argument that, over and above politics, Dostoevsky had studied how human beings destroyed themselves and others and had sought enduring, universal values behind current affairs. In Dostoevsky, the love of God is foremost among these values since it is the basis of love and respect for humankind.

Sergey Kuryshev, who plays Kirillov, notes that Russians had been so bombarded by political speeches since1987 that, by the time the company was ready to show its *Devils* to them at the end of 1991, they had had enough of anything blatantly 'political' (Weimar, 6 July 1997). It is significant that Kuryshev should cite 1987 as a turning point, since this date announced Gorbachev's democratising measures vis-à-vis the political structures of the Soviet Union, which precipitated dissent and debate within the Communist Party. In this climate of political wrangling and emboldened by the beginnings of something like free speech, newspaper and television journalists communicated what could only appear to be 'messy' disagreement to their audiences. The 'political', then, as

Figure 3 Lev Dodin (standing in profile) rehearses *The Devils* at the Maly Drama Theatre, 1991.

Photograph by V. Vasilyev, courtesy of the Archive of the Maly Drama Theatre, St Petersburg.

Kuryshev implies, was more or less equated in the observing public's mind with verbiage, most of it taken to be dishonest and self-seeking.[3]

Sergey Bekhterev, who plays Pyotr Verkhovensky, notes, on the other hand, that although Russians tended to think of politics in crude terms (as pronouncements, decrees, falsehoods) as a result of their historical experience, a more nuanced concept had appeared in the production-in-the-making which had been cut away during rehearsals. The first part of this 'lost' production had revolved around the liberal generation (notably the relations between Stepan Verkhovensky, Pyotr's father, and Varvara Petrovna, Stavrogin's mother), the second around the younger generation, and the third around the theme of the city (St Petersburg, 30 September 1998).

Dodin, for his part, felt increasingly as time went on that this version had more to do with Dostoevsky's past than with the history of the twentieth century and its 'horrifying experiments – the communist experiment and the fascist experiment' (Weimar, 7 July 1997). Consequently, in order to foreground the relevance of Dostoevsky for the present, but without resorting to the clichés of the earnest, proclamatory politics that were currently in vogue, he removed the interplay of perspectives of the 'lost' production and left for the production that survived a deliberately crude version of politics taken to such a high degree of absurdity that, paradoxically, it became a work of refinement. In hindsight, especially when the August 1991 coup is kept in mind, his decision to eradicate what might be termed 'pamphleteering' content appears to have been vindicated. It is important to note, as well, that Dodin's cautious approach to what was topical in politics is illuminated by the increasing complexities of the political arena from 1987 onwards and its encroachment on the everyday life of citizens. It could be argued, in other words, that the political volatility of the times made every new event topical, almost on a daily basis, and it is precisely the evanescence of events that Dodin wished to avoid in *The Devils* in order to prevent the production from feeling outdated at birth.[4]

The crude version of politics presented by Dodin is concentrated in Part Two in the scene involving the secret society to which Pyotr Verkhovensky belongs. The scene looks like an old daguerreotype, all of its figures tightly grouped around a table and samovar swathed in cigarette smoke, the characters further away from the centre merging into the shadows behind them (Figure 4). Its opening dialogue is uttered with the utmost seriousness but is, in effect, empty babble. Several voices ask whether this gathering constitutes a meeting, while others insist that a vote must be taken to determine what it is. If spectators are momentarily bemused by the contradiction between manner and subject matter, they soon realise that the devilry to which Dodin takes a magnifying glass is nothing less than a terrifying insanity – terrifying precisely because it looks and, on the surface, sounds sane.

This exposure is carried further when Shigalyov (Vladimir Tumanov), the assembled company's prophet, propounds his social system for the future in the dictum that everything must begin in absolute freedom and end in absolute tyranny. Thus, Shigalyov's vision of dictatorship, which his colleagues take to be

Figure 4 *The Devils* at the Maly Drama Theatre, 1991.

Seated l. to r.:
M. Samochko, S. Vlasov,
P. Semak, S. Bekhterev,
I. Ivanov, M. Gridasova,
A. Koval, S. Kuryshev,
N. Lavrov.

Standing l. to r.:
I. Chernevich, N. Pavlov,
M. Nikiforova,
V. Seleznyov,
T. Rasskazova.

Photograph by
V. Vasilyev, courtesy of the
Archive of the Maly Drama
Theatre, St Petersburg.

perfectly reasonable, is set up to appear reasonable because of his sober tone and learned air, but is deflated in the very instance of its utterance by the sheer inanity of his words. It is matched by Verkhovensky's talk of equality, which he equates, in all earnestness, with slavery. Verkhovensky's absurd pastiche of socialism (little, in Dostoevsky, separates pastiche from its supposed model) is given by Bekhterev at face value as a mark of his character's cold-blooded delirium. The scene proceeds surreptitiously in this way, undermining what it presents and thereby revealing how apparently rational disquisition can mask total lunacy.

The end point of this play of dualities is Verkhovensky's peroration, in a subsequent scene, on 'the people's need' for a despotic ruler during which he attempts to persuade Stavrogin to become the society's – and Russia's – chief. Bekhterev here portrays Verkhovensky as an extremely ingenuous intriguer, while Semak's matter-of-fact response to the proposal as 'mad' indicates that Stavrogin rejects it not from any kind of conviction, but from the *ennui* bred by moral sickness. This crucial revelation about Stavrogin had been anticipated from the beginning of Part One where rumours of his immorality, which allegedly had not stopped short of murder, are discussed by Stavrogin's mother, Verkhovensky and Captain Lebyadkin whose lame and feeble-minded sister, Marya, Stavrogin had secretly married as part of a wager that he was capable of anything. To believe in nothing and yet act on nothingness is part of Dostoevsky's understanding of 'nihilism', which the production conveys gradually, slowly immersing spectators in it before they can find a name for it. (It is important to note that the production's cumulative effect on spectators on a subliminal level is fundamental to the impact commented upon by its reviewers worldwide.) Stavrogin, however, also has the power to hurt by doing nothing, that is, by *not* intervening in acts of evil. Thus, through indifference, he sanctions Verkhovensky's arrangement to have Marya and her brother murdered. Verkhovensky organises the murder, ostensibly to please Stavrogin and 'free' him for Liza, another of Stavrogin's amorous adventures. In reality, as Bekhterev's devious touches of salacity show, Verkhovensky satisfies his own lust for killing, which is stronger, even, than his eagerness to please Stavrogin down to the last detail of offering to behave like a pimp.

Pure terrorism

Every encounter between Verkhovensky and Stavrogin is a meeting between two faces of devilry, the one executing what the other inspires it to do. Stavrogin is, first and foremost, a catalyst. He is the mastermind behind Shatov's obsession with the idea of the 'man-god', the omnipotent human being created by the death of God whom Dodin and the Maly actors had rediscovered in Nietzsche. He is also behind Kirillov's 'I am God' which, the latter believes, frees his will entirely and justifies his contemplated suicide. Both Shatov (Sergey Vlasov) and Kirillov (Sergey Kuryshev) are Stavrogin's 'creatures', and the production explores the tension between Shatov's uncertainty as to the existence of

God and Kirillov's ultimate conclusion as to God's non-existence. In either case, however, Semak's Stavrogin demonstrates *his* steely, dispassionate will to harm which, in the terms taken by Semak from Dostoevsky, is the inevitable outcome of Stavrogin's godlessness. A similar capacity for wrong resides in Verkhovensky, another of Stavrogin's creatures, and overrides whatever political pretensions he may have. It is clear, by the time Verkhovensky has Shatov murdered by the secret society for his alleged betrayal, that 'political' action by Verkhovensky is a mere façade for unmitigated, gratuitous violence. This is pure terrorism. Dodin, who follows Dostoevsky particularly closely on this point, confirms the latter's argument that politics in the name of extreme causes is nothing more than a pretext for the perpetration of violence as such.

Parts One and Two are extraordinarily contained and restrained. Only in Part Three does Dodin unleash the positions, political, moral and metaphysical, put into place in the preceding two parts. Now the third main face of devilry, the power to manipulate others – since this, too, is integral to pure terrorism – takes the upper hand as Bekhterev-Verkhovensky springs into action. Shatov is killed. Verkhovensky immediately pursues his next prey, Kirillov, whom he forces to write a note taking the blame for Shatov's death and goads into suicide. The long scene between Verkhovensky and Kirillov is in two phases, the first calculated by Dodin to give greater resonance to the second. The first shows Bekhterev-Verkhovensky gobbling up a whole chicken in a cruel demonstration of greed, self-assertion, control and domination. This act of metaphoric cannibalism is all the more indecent because of Kirillov's implied poverty, on the one hand, and the very real poverty in Russia, particularly as experienced by audiences in the early 1990s, on the other. Years later, Dodin was to recall how 1991 'was a cold and hungry year with nothing in the shops' and 'people exchanged the little food they brought from home during the interval' (*Corriere della Sera*, 28 October 2000). Dodin used the chicken-devouring sketch, then, to drive home a point quite cruelly; and, apart from its flagrant relevance to the current situation, Bekhterev-Verkhovensky's act has symbolic weight in so far as the dialogue preceding it is a debate as to whether human beings devour an Idea or whether the Idea devours them. The Idea at issue concerns, of course, any all-consuming, fanatical *idée fixe* of which Shatov, Kirillov and Verkhovensky are carriers, as is Stavrogin who, in addition, is its matrix.

The second phase of the Verkhovensky–Kirillov scene is composed of a plethora of micro-scenes in which Verkhovensky plays cat-and-mouse with Kirillov. Kuryshev has Kirillov in a febrile state to start with and whips his character into a state of exaltation, now pulling out a revolver and coming close to his partner as if to kill him, now refusing to write the note about Shatov, now renouncing his resolve to kill himself and then, prompted by Verkhovensky, resolving to do it. The shuttle between the two characters generates black humour. Take the micro-scene where Verkhovensky-Bekhterev, his legs crossed, chats away intimately as if anything but death was at stake. Suddenly Kirillov-Kuryshev, in a spurt of excitement over his own words, brandishes the revolver at his interlocutor's head. The fact that his character's supreme confidence was imperceptibly shaken is indicated by Bekhterev, in an inspired gesture, when he quietly mops his brow with a handkerchief. Or take the sequence of micro-scenes when Verkhovensky dictates Kirillov's suicide note. Bekhterev here assumes a number of roles ranging from pedantic schoolmaster, who enunciates the syllables of the words Kirillov must write, to ecstatic zealot, who punctuates the air with his flaying arms, to plain thug whose eyes menace his victim. From start to finish of the long Verkhovensky–Kirillov scene, Bekhterev's is an infinitely subtle study not only of terrorist behaviour, but of the psychopathology of terrorism. The audience waits with bated breath, not daring to hear the pistol shot when Kirillov, almost out of sight, pulls the trigger.

The only scene that surpasses this denouement for sheer spine-chilling force is Stavrogin's confession in a letter to Father Tikhon, which Semak speaks as a monologue in Part Two. Stavrogin here gives an account of his rape of a 14-year-old girl and how, albeit watchful, he ignores her silent anguish after the rape, knowing that this would contribute to driving her to despair. In fact, she hangs herself shortly afterwards. Semak's quiet, dispassionate performance is riveting, uncanny in its stillness as he sits, talking, while barely perceptible movements chart his journey into Stavrogin's inner abyss. He performs in a similar fashion right through Part Three, giving his audience glimmers of those 'circles of self-destruction' in which, Dodin believes, all the protagonists of *The Devils* turn (Weimar, 7 July 1997). The production ends when Dasha, Shatov's sister and Varvara Petrovna's ward, reads Stavrogin's letter in which he states that life holds no meaning for him. News is brought in that Stavrogin has hanged himself.

Demonic darkness

The women of this male-dominated, even misogynistic world are also caught up in the vortex of madness and self-destruction, although Stavrogin rather than a lofty Idea is the object of their fixation. They are Marya (Tatyana Shestakova) who sinks deeper into derangement because of him; Liza (Anzhelika Nevolina), a diaphanous beauty, whose desire for him manifests itself through the hysteria of repressed emotion; Dasha (Irina Tychinina) who is self-effacing and secretive, but confident that she will succeed in holding on to him; Matya (Natalya Fomenko), Shatov's estranged wife, who was discarded by Stavrogin but is consumed, nevertheless, by sexual passion mixed with rage and shame. Matya appears for the first and only time in Part Three to give birth to her child by Stavrogin. This scene is alive with intersecting tensions and is all the more human for its display of vulnerability, which stands in sharp contrast to the austerity of the production as a whole. Its intersections involve Matya's verbal abuse of Shatov, which is a transference, in the psychoanalytical sense of the word, of her feelings towards Stavrogin; Matya's ferocity against the world at large, which mingles with the pain of childbirth; Shatov's dither when he runs to Kirillov for tea and boiling water, the latter also required for the birth; Shatov's humility in the face of Matya's verbal blows; Shatov's overwhelming joy that she had returned to give birth to 'his' son (although he knows full well that 'his' son is Stavrogin's); the vigorous, no-nonsense approach of the midwife (Tatyana Rasskasova) as she fills the space with her presence, sizes up the situation, upbraids Shatov, prepares for the birth and delivers the child while sitting on the rail of the bed to do so, her legs spread wide and her back to the audience – a masterpiece of discretion in what could have been a 'stagey' and banal rendition of birth. This time, if only for a comparatively short time, the tact and tenderness of the 'human heart' shine through and eclipse its demonic darkness.

The sets by Kochergin determine all the parameters of Dodin's direction. A guillotine that often serves as a door lifts up and snaps down at centre stage. Planks and pulleys swivel, lift and heave, giving narrow see-saws on which the actors walk and run. Verkhovensky and Stavrogin use them for dialogue, as if across a gaping chasm. The whole construction plunges downwards to the space below the stage, a nether world where movement frequently begins and ends. The dead bodies of Marya and her brother flash up into sight on parallel see-saws and disappear into the gloom. Shatov, straight after the birth of 'his' child, is suddenly propelled upwards on one of them, and is instantly pushed into the underground by the group of men who kill him. A starkly etched duel between Stavrogin and Mavriky, Liza's fiancé, is 'frozen' high in the air on the outer edge of the planks before the planks dip and these characters, their pistols incongruously facing the wings, dive out of sight (Figure 5, overleaf).

Movement also spreads to a narrow space that is level with the audience and holds a small round table and two chairs for the duration of the performance. It goes, as well, into two small areas on either side of the construction/stage, which are closed in at the back by black curtains. Verkhovensky eats his chicken in one of the side areas, and inveigles Kirillov on the other side. Kirillov writes his suicide letter at audience level. Dasha occupies a side area, Liza usually the sides of the stage. All the dimensions of the space are used and suggest the bridges, canals, slums, nooks, crannies and airless, tight rooms of Dostoevsky's St Petersburg rather than the provincial town in which the author set his novel. But it is an empty, haunted space in which the characters fade in and out of view, like ghosts.

This forbidding, brooding place provides no exit. Stavrogin speaks his monologue to the side of the front edge of the stage lit only by dim light. As he speaks of the raped girl's suicide, a young girl climbs a ladder, visible for the first time on the back wall of the stage. The ladder reappears to mark his suicide, now lit in red, as if in blood. This is the only colour to speak of in a composition predominantly in black and white. Costumes are unobtrusive, a period style suggested by the sleeves of the women's dresses and the tailcoats and high-collar shirts of the men. Nothing intrudes on this hallucinatory world, not even the sporadic carousel music, or a voice humming, or the sound of a beat that you dimly begin to understand is the beat of a heart. This heart beats as the young girl climbs the ladder, and beats louder still when the empty ladder comes into view at the end of the performance to remind you that the human heart can be nothing more than a heartless throb.

Figure 5 *The Devils* at the Maly Drama Theatre, 1991.

Photograph by V. Vasilyev, courtesy of the Archive of the Maly Drama Theatre, St Petersburg.

Coda on *Molly Sweeney*

Heartlessness might well be a main theme of Dodin's *Molly Sweeney*, a production that, apart from its thematic similarities, can be twinned with *The Devils* for its immense demands on the audience's capacity to listen and hear. What is at issue, for Dodin, is the devilry of egoism and control, both of which possess Frank, Molly's husband and Mr Rice, her ophthalmologist. Both men are driven by the hope of redemption at Molly's expense. Frank does so out of habit because, an incompetent man, he pursues hair-brained causes in order to build his own self-image. Rice becomes obsessed by the thought of redeeming his failed career and failed self-esteem by curing Molly's blindness. Molly turns out to be their experiment, their chance to play God. Rice operates on Molly's eyes, but what she 'sees' is nothing but a blur and nothing like the beauty that, unsighted, she had learned to see in her mind. Molly goes mad, and how and why she goes mad are the strong underlying motifs of the production. Dodin reads Brian Friel through Dostoevsky, and brings Friel so close to him that he might be embracing a brother.

All the verbal complexities of Friel's play were translated by Mikhaïl Stronin, Dodin's literary adviser, into a rather formalised Russian, which the actors adjusted into spoken language as they played so that the words would fit, as it were, into their mouths. Meanwhile, their subtleties concerning how, through a lifetime, Molly has transformed her disability into an asset, which Frank and Rice, seemingly well-intentioned, destroy, are conveyed through Friel's three intertwined monologues which Dodin orchestrates into three voices in an oratorio. A Moscow critic justly observed, when *Molly Sweeney* was performed at the Golden Mask Festival, that speech in the production is organised like a musical score and relies exclusively on intonation for its meanings (*Izvestiya*, 9 April 2001). The three actors – Shestakova (Molly), Kuryshev (Frank) and Semak (Rice) – sit in high-backed wicker chairs designed by Borovsky whose 'wings' screen them from each other. Only Shestakova occasionally moves to the front of the stage, slightly touching the few autumn leaves on it with her feet. The only other object in Borovsky's minimalist design is an empty swimming pool in the orchestra pit, into whose dank air – it contains more autumn leaves – Shestakova moves at the end of the performance. This is Molly's escape, in madness, from the demonic will of Frank and Rice. The actors produce, as most Moscow critics recognised, a feat of virtuosity and finesse and, in the words of one of them, 'demonstrate such a high level of craft that you understand why the Maly Drama Theatre of St Petersburg is called the Theatre of Europe and is considered to be the best Russian theatre' (*Moskovskiye novosti*, no. 15, 10–16 April 2001).

Chevengur: the absolute Idea

The problematics of the absolute Idea and the lunacy it generates resurface in *Chevengur*, although not in the tragic register of *The Devils* but in a surrealistic mode. The Idea here is a matter of blindness, of a blind Idea in that it leads nowhere, of blind faith in that it is categorical, and of the blind leading the blind in the sense that the Idea overwhelms everyone who is in contact with it in a chain reaction whose only finality is death. Dodin chose Peter Breughel's painting *The Parable of the Blind* to illustrate the programme for the production when it was shown in St Petersburg in September 1999 after its Weimar opening in February and performances in Gibellina in July. The significance of the illustration did not escape the Russian critics who, almost invariably, linked Breughel's representation of human folly to Dodin's programme note in which he refers aphoristically to people's quests for Paradise on earth. In fact, the image of Paradise, together with that of blindness, which, however, Dodin had not initially tied to Breughel, had been his major touchstones during the two-year devising and rehearsal period for the two-hour work.

The production was constructed from the 400-page novel completed by Andrey Platonov in 1929 but not published until 1989, Gorbachev having reha-bilitated the writer whose nonconformist, eccentric communism had led him to imagine his characters' vision of utopia in such phantasmagoric terms that it metamorphosed instantaneously, right there on the page as it was written, into a dystopia. Chevengur, the city of their dreams, which Platonov's characters make synonymous with 'communism', is actually nothing but a chimera pursued by a band of semi-literate vagabonds. Platonov describes them as 'orphans', suggest-ing that they had been literally orphaned by the 1917 Revolution and metaphorically orphaned by it as well, in so far as events had left them behind. They were effectively rejects and outcasts who had nowhere else to go but into their naïve outpourings about a better life. For them, Chevengur-communism is the place where the sun will do all the work while they bask in it doing nothing. This and similarly crazy notions are behind their dehumanisation. They scav-enge for food, virtually starve, lose all capacity for affection, tenderness and kindness and even all memory of these feelings, and finally commit mass suicide as any religious sect or bunch of cranks might do in preparation for doomsday.

The religious and the loony blur in Platonov's novel, making it extremely diffi-cult to catch the tone of his densely poetic style peppered with Biblical and folkloric archaisms, vivid neologisms and deliberate verbal jumble. His characters have such names as Dostoevsky and God, which, in Dodin's production, caused titters wherever it was performed. Or else they have odd-sounding names and follow even odder pursuits: Sasha Dvanov, who goes in search of his father the Fisherman who had drowned himself to see what was on the other side of death; Kopyenkin, who conjures up a horse out of his imagination called Proletarian Revolution (shades here of the horses of the Apocalypse) and is obsessed by his ideal love called Rosa Luxemburg; Chepurny, who invokes the perfections of Chevengur like a mantra and whose 'We have read nothing, but have achieved everything' is delivered in the production with the stupefying self-assurance of those who are vacuous or ignorant; and so on, in a group of ten Chevengurians united by their vision of beatitude and eternity. The tone found by Dodin for Chepurny's sublime line is detached, as it is for other dialogue that is similarly naïve but loaded with hidden ironies. Dodin's distance from his subject, which caused some Russian critics to respond lukewarmly while others observed that, because of it, he appeared to be 'writing a foreign history' rather than a Russian one (*Nezavisimaya gazeta*, 7 September 1999), stems from the non-judgemental approach taken by him during devising and rehearsal, as if objectivity was the only way into Platonov's strangely ludic text.

Rehearsals from St Petersburg to Weimar

In the rehearsals which I observed, Dodin once casually remarked that his production was 'even Brechtian' (Weimar, 10 February 1999) – a touch disingenuous since its content and perspective are far from Brecht. Presumably he was thinking about the production's very own type of distance-effect which gives off a dispassionate aura and is quite unlike anything he had done before. This outcome was reached through the company's usual channels for devising, namely, reading aloud and what I have termed 'research-during-play-into-play' by means of *études* and improvisations through which, also, dialogue is collated. Since the process is organic and cumulative rather than set to a plan, it is unpredictable and may look haphazard during any given slice of time. This is exactly how it appeared to me six months before the opening date in Weimar, when scenes, sketches, or smaller units for *études* that Dodin calls *mikroproby* (micro-tries) seemed to be performed in random order and disparate pieces of text were re-read here and there and glossed to find a connecting thread. If there was any rationale to the chopping and changing of what was to be played and when, it was certainly not visible to me.

However, what did become visible fairly quickly was that three episodes were the target of the work at hand. The first revolved around the Fisherman who drowned himself, and was eventually framed by Dodin as a prologue to the production. The second concerned the murder by the Chevengurians of the townspeople whom they call the 'bourgeois', this word perceived by Dodin and the actors as symptomatic of the way the Chevengurians imitated terminology they did not fully understand. The third involved a scene with a mother and a dead child. What was not so visible to my observing eye, and took the actors the remaining six months to discover, was the particular sense of these episodes, where they might fit in the stage sequence and, above all, how they were to be acted. As it turned out, all three proved to be pivotal to the work for narrative reasons as well as because their strength from the point of view of content could be adapted, without loss of substance, to the matter-of-fact, quasi-documentary manner that they eventually acquired.

Dodin's commentary at this stage of the process followed a *via negativa*, showing what he did not want rather than what he thought might be appropriate. Yet even the question of appropriateness was enigmatic since Dodin had not declared the key in which the stage composition might be written even if he yet knew what it might be. For example, the actors devised the episode concerning the killing of the bourgeoisie in various keys of their own, going from the major of bombast and action-packed heroics to an elegiac minor in which the citizens were 'murdered' by a gentle touch. Thus, the victims sat quietly on benches and, as they were touched by their 'killers', one by one, got up just as quietly and moved out of the playing space to suggest that souls were leaving their bodies. This *proba* had an ethereal beauty of its own, but, judging from Dodin's commentary afterwards, poetry was no more the goal than graphics. In what would be best described as a stream of consciousness, Dodin referred to witnesses' accounts of how people were taken away during Stalin's time and disappeared; similarly, to how Jews had been abused and beaten in Nazi Germany, which led to allusions to anti-Semitism in Soviet history. He also referred to Solzhenitsyn's *First Circle*, associating the Gulag denounced by the writer with the *lager* that the company had visited in Buchenwald when it performed *A Play With No Name* in nearby Weimar. This reference led to Kafka and to questions of how to perform the life of a cockroach. Talk of cockroaches, now a figure of speech for the despised and the humiliated – Kafka here joined elliptically to Dostoevsky – took Dodin back to Buchenwald and specifically, this time, to the showers that the company had seen in the concentration camp. Showers of this type, Dodin suggested, are where the Chevengurians could wash themselves after their extermination of the 'bourgeois'. The implied analogy with the extermination of the Jews and of the Chevengurian seekers of Paradise with the Nazis was instantly grasped by everybody, although the problem for the actors still lay in finding the 'right' way to transform comprehension into play.

It became clear from Dodin's talking method which, as we saw in the preceding chapter, he believes stimulates the actor's imagination, that the images he offered his company called for a starker, harsher performance idiom than they had envisaged to date. The advantage of having a 'common language' was that the actors were able to respond immediately to Dodin's evocations and perform differently during the next days when both the heroics and the poetry of their previous sessions ceded to a drier, tougher style of presentation. Six months later, by the time of the company's five-day rehearsal period in Weimar prior to the opening of the show, this style had settled in, although not entirely to Dodin's satisfaction. He was still guiding the actors to avoid slippages into gestural exaggeration, reminding them that the drama of what they were doing lay in 'the facts' (Weimar, 9 February 1999).

By now, the killing scene was like a sharp shot in a film, but not sharp enough, given Dodin's instructions to the actors to speed up their movements. In addition, he focused on the moment when Chepurny is suddenly trussed up in a black sack by his own gang while, almost immediately, his fellow murderers drag other black sacks on to the stage from the wings. The scene appeared to have passed muster when, in the final rehearsal before opening night, Dodin decided that its action – the actual 'fact' of extermination – was not clear. He replaced the black sacks with cellophane bags so that spectators could see the bodies tied up inside them. And this change in a scene that had already undergone such radical transformation since its gestation called for another change, that of showing *naked* bodies through the transparent cellophane. This grisly image accentuated the next one flowing straight on, which involved the Chevengurians emptying bags of earth on to the cellophane bags before dragging them out into the wings (and before the actors inside them suffocated!). At the eleventh hour, Dodin had found, at last, the routine brutality towards which his various associations must have been groping for two years.

The scene leads into another one that combines the same kind of routine and ruthlessness. No sooner do the Chevengurians kill their prey than they strip off their clothes and head down towards the showers where they wash themselves so naturally that killing and washing appear to be part of the same continuum. The showers had been hidden until then by Poray-Koshits's plexiglas platform, which tilts at different angles throughout the performance. During the Weimar rehearsals, Dodin returned to the association that he had made months before between Buchenwald and the Gulag, recalling how much the company had learned about such camps through sheer observation. His purpose was to stimulate his actors to show behaviour, externalise it rather than seek justification for it. Thus, he also told them to play 'in an almost naturalistic way'. In the light of the company's more usual working principles, which marry inward and outward impulses, this was a most unusual direction. Yet Dodin's allusion to naturalism explained to the actors how they could achieve the objectivity of 'facts', that is, perform without any interpretative intervention: no emotion, no empathy, no sympathy and no evaluation, only the deeds as such.

Dodin also reminded his actors, as he had already done in St Petersburg, to think of their characters as mentally ill. The image of madness dangled before them had obviously helped the actors to take their distance. They did so, however, by noting that, unlike *The Devils* with which *Chevengur* has a thematic affinity, madness here seemed impermeable, incomprehensible, too alien to be 'seized' by anything other than its external manifestations. The cross-pollination between productions which, we have noted, is a feature of Dodin's directorial method (however unconsciously it may happen), is not confined to the lingering influence of *The Devils* on *Chevengur*. What must surely also have spilled over into Dodin's thoughts on madness, albeit outside a political context, was *The Queen of Spades*, which he had begun to prepare some eight months before *Chevengur*'s premiere. That this cross-reference most likely did occur somewhere in his mind, as an aspect of his creative process, will be borne out by my discussion of Dodin's work on the opera in the last chapter of this book.

Several more details from the other two scenes will give us greater insight into Dodin's creative process. They are the mother and child and Fisherman scenes. The mother and child scene started in St Petersburg from psychologically charged versions figuring a small child in a pram. It was gradually pruned of empathy and, by Weimar, consisted of the skeleton of the story presented in a show-and-tell style that could be called 'Brechtian', taking up Dodin's prompt. In Weimar, Dodin set about removing the vestiges of sentiment that had begun to creep back into this scene. By the time he was done, the mother appeared as impervious to emotion as the Chevengurians, and as crazed as they in that she seemed unable to recognise that her child was dead. The real child used in early rehearsals had been replaced by the metaphoric 'child' of a bundle of cloth.

A similarly chameleon-like transformation occurred in the Fisherman scene that was to become part of the prologue to the production. The scene opens with the Chevengurians talking about art, and especially music, as the pinnacle of civilisation. During the St Petersburg rehearsals, the actors listened to music through earphones. In the course of their conversation, the Fisherman cast his line and pulled in a fish attached to his hook by the props manager participating in rehearsals. By Weimar, these signs of realism had vanished. The earphones, whatever their experimental and provisional character, had gone for good, and a fish in a bowl, although long and real, now had a purely symbolic function. This fish symbolised Christianity and humanity, as in Platonov's novel, while the bowl could be read as a symbol of utopia, one whose water was bloodied, however, when the Fisherman cut the fish's throat. Blood could be taken to represent the production's critical stance on this utopia based on bloodshed.

Cultural resonance and history

In any case, the production's critique is pre-empted by the structure of its prologue, which is a montage of voices coming over the top of the characters' dialogue about art. The montage contains fragments of a speech by Boris Yeltsin telling the country that everything is fine – and this on the eve of Russia's economic crash of August 1998. Bill Clinton then tells the world that he has not had sexual relations with Monica Lewinsky – and this just as the world was about to discover the opposite. Meanwhile, Arturo Toscanini sings his way through *La Traviata* – and this as he conducts an opera about lies in a medium, art, whose defining characteristic is fiction. The prologue-montage ends when the Fisherman walks fully clothed into the water and disappears under it, an episode anticipated by Poray-Koshits whose design holds a narrow canal of water stretching from one side of the stage to the other. The canal is also crucial for the production's conclusion when Chepurny, in his final act of utopian conviction, picks up a heavy stone and carries it into the water. He is followed by all the Chevengurians who, one by one, strip off their rags, take up a stone and walk into the water convinced that they, too, are now entering Paradise (Figure 6). This parable of the blind transferred to water closes when the plexiglas platform tilts forward and the earth on it falls down onto the bundles of rags that have fallen, as the platform tilted, to the front of the stage. When the last of the Chevengurians disappears, the water is drained away and a metallic grid rises up to show their stones. The rest might well have been silence, but for the audience's applause.

Dodin's *coup de théâtre* is somewhat heavy-handed, but is not without effect in what a Moscow critic accurately describes as a 'pitiless' work (*Kommersant*, 7 September 1999). And it contains, as does the whole work, traces of the multiple

Figure 6 *Chevengur* at the Golden Mask Festival, Moscow, 2000.

From water l. to r.:
S. Kuryshev, S. Kozyrev, A. Koval, A. Zavyalov (screened by O. Dmitriyev), N. Lavrov, A. Zubaryov, V. Seleznyov, I. Chernevich.

Photograph by Ken Reynolds, courtesy of Ken Reynolds.

idioms – expressionism, symbolism, psychological realism, epic realism, natural-ism, absurdism, melodrama – through which the devising and rehearsal processes had passed before Dodin distilled a surrealist essence from their mixture. *Cheven-gur*'s self-conscious contrivances – can surrealism exist without them? – take their model in the bizarre juxtaposition between the Chevengurian story and Toscanini's happily singing *La Traviata*. Moreover, Toscanini sings recurrently through the production and not only at its beginning and end. Although insistent, the music appears aleatory until you realise that Toscanini is rehearsing; further, that this rehearsal is a cryptic sign for the Chevengurians' 'communism'. Their 'communism', then, which Russian critics decoded specifically to mean commu-nism in Russia, is nothing but a rehearsal for a show that never came. The show could be called happiness, utopia, or Paradise on earth. Or, according to one St Petersburg critic, this utopia could be likened to a Russian Atlantis or the fairytale city of Kitezh – those mythical civilisations lost under water that belong to the 'endless story of illusion and disillusion' familiar to Russians (*Sankt-Peterburgskiye vedomosti*, 29 September 1999).

Dodin's personal disillusion was virtually complete by 1999. In his view, Russia under Yeltsin was run by a self-serving corrupt elite barely distinguish-able from its predecessors, and his wry reflection on Yeltsin in the prologue to *Chevengur* is a criticism, on moral rather than political grounds, of Yeltsin's abuse of the moral authority invested in the presidential office. Hence the parallel between Yeltsin and Clinton who, too, was caught lying. By the time the Maly showed *Chevengur*, not only had the Soviet Union ceased to exist, but Russia had undergone mutation into a market economy with little visible improvement:

> At the end of 1998, seven years of Russian economic reform seemed to come to a denouement in which the conditions of life were in many respects worse than when the new state began in 1991. The late summer financial crisis and currency collapse, which resulted in shortages and breakdowns in nearly every kind of transaction . . . were remarkable not only for the velocity and depth of the crisis, but also for the lack of surprise or outrage with which the crisis was met by the population. Russians had, tragically, been there before . . . Unfortunately, on the basis of meagre gains in efficiency, investment, and production, as well as epidemic crime, corruption, and social catastrophes including rising income inequality, poverty, and public ill-health, the Russian economy during most of the 1990s was a picture of despair even before the crisis of 1998. Moreover, despite recent improvements in growth, many negative effects of the transi-tion, such as corruption and the lack of the rule of law, continue unabated.
>
> (Barany and Moser, 2001: 135)

Dodin's moral high ground in respect of political leaders resonates with these realities and, apart from being recognised by his audiences, was shared by the Russian population at large.

Curiously – given the cultural resonance of Toscanini and *La Traviata* in Italy

– Italian critics ignored the possible significance of the rehearsal, but stressed the production's global relevance. In the words of *La Repubblica*, 'communism' refers to 'the mirage of a terrestrial paradise common to all totalitarianisms and fundamentalisms' (2 August 1999). The journalist of this left-leaning newspaper not only registers how ideological boundaries are blurred in *Chevengur* (the result, as we have seen, of Dodin's crossing communism with fascism during the production's rehearsals). He also updates them with a currently potent word, 'fundamentalisms', by which he links the Euro-originated '-isms' of the earlier part of the twentieth century (socialism, communism, fascism) to the religious (fundamental) '-isms' of its closing decades, when Islamic fundamentalism loomed large. If Italian critics, unlike their Russian counterparts, favoured worldwide sweeps in their political interpretation of the production, they narrowed their literary references to Europe alone: *Orlando Furioso, Don Quixote* ('Kopyenkin's Dulcinea is Rosa Luxemburg', *Corriere della Sera*, 19 December 1999, on performances in Milan), Hašek, Gogol, Orwell and Beckett. They made a good deal of Dodin's account of his emotion when he first visited Gibellina and saw there the immense, flat monument built to the victims of its 1968 earthquake. Indeed, how the earth just swallowed up an entire village without a trace was one of Dodin's main inspirations for the close of his production, where nothing is left but stones. Given the method of association by which Dodin proceeds as a director, the Gibellina earthquake could also have been a symbol in his mind's eye of the history of twentieth-century Russia: an entire country eaten alive, as it were, by its earthquake, which was communism.

The distinctive receptions of *Chevengur* in Russia and Italy are intimately bound up with these countries' different experiences of history and the way their literary touchstones vary accordingly. But this observation about the historical-cultural grounding of perception opens our eyes to the shifts in Dodin's *oeuvre* from a historically- and culturally-specific theatre to a theatre whose identity is not quite so deeply Russian. In other words, the fact that *Chevengur* was open to different emphases in Russia and Italy is not solely a matter of spectatorial perception, but has to do, as well, with Dodin's position in relation to his material. His aphoristic, emblematic approach in *Chevengur* gives the production its generalising power and is comparable to his project for 'universal' meaning in *Lord of the Flies*. *The House* and *Brothers and Sisters*, by contrast, are rooted in Russia and the Soviet Union no matter how much recognition and empathy they evoke in international audiences. The perceptible changes in Dodin's theatre of prose after *Brothers* lie in his adjusted focus from daily life (*byt*) to philosophical issues. Hence *The Devils*, although as Russian as Dostoevsky, is concerned with vast questions that are certainly Russian but also transnational as well, that is, comprehensible in any culture concerned with the laws of God and with the moral, as well as religious, implications of violence, including the violence of politics. Dodin's widened scope, in addition, involves his search for a varied aesthetic vocabulary. *The House*, *The Devils* and *Chevengur* are worlds apart in genre, form and style, as should be clear from the foregoing analysis of each.

Dodin's urge to cross national boundaries in his theatre preceded his actual journeys outside Russia. After all, *Lord of the Flies* was crafted before the Maly's first western European tour in 1988. Nevertheless, international touring gave the company a different air to breathe while broadening its horizons and opening up possibilities for it to receive such international honours as the title of 'Theatre of Europe'. And the implicit responsibility of such an honour is making a theatre that is Russian *and* European – a theatre, in short, that *aims* to be meaningful across peoples and cultures. Almost 20 years after *The House*, *Chevengur* had shed some of the nationally idiosyncratic qualities that define the former. It appears to have more in common stylistically, although not by subject or perspective, with Peter Brook's *Les Iks* (1975) than with the Maly's own repertoire. This is because the Maly's performance of destitution – whether seen directly as Chevengurian or in allegorical terms as the destitution of Gulag inmates – recalls the denuded and detached performance of terrible starvation in Brook's production. The echo is purely coincidental since neither Dodin nor his actors had seen *Les Iks*. What it suggests, however, is that, like Brook, Dodin and the Maly had to take a journey away from home to change home, that is, to discover what might be new for their theatre and also for their life. In the same instance, the journey enabled them to put their own history into perspective.

4   The student ensemble

Gaudeamus and *Claustrophobia*:
postmodernist aesthetics

An examination of the five complex novels behind Dodin's 'theatre of prose' –
Lord of the Flies being the simplest of them – shows just how remarkable their
refashioning really was in his incisive and succinct productions. Even *The
Devils*, whose length exceeds the normal working hours of a day, is an extraordinarily compact work. What is equally noteworthy is how seriously Dodin
took upon himself the role of a chronicler of his times who, through his particular kind of immediate, cut-and-cull performance writing, treated the past as if
it, too, were the present. The purpose was to remember history in the making.
Moreover, the censorship of *The Devils* and *Chevengur* had played tricks with the
past and cultural memory. *The Devils*, although available for some three
decades, had not yet acquired the patina of a classic. *Chevengur*'s very recent
appearance in 1989, after 60 years of suppression, made it a piece of new
writing imperatively to be explored for the theatre by a theatre whose hall-
mark was its voice of the now.

Its currency notwithstanding, this was the literature of an older generation
accustomed to the comparatively mild dissidence of Abramov's village prose.
Dodin was to turn, then, to the vanguard writing of glasnost and perestroika –
to Kaledin's *The Construction Battalion* – for the students training with him in
1989, who were to become the new generation of actors at the Maly. Kaledin
belonged to the popular *chernukha*, the 'black genre' that gave horrifying descriptions of everyday Soviet life, and which, by its excesses – scatological, sexual,
linguistic – 'opposed the ideologically driven writing contained in the avalanche
of journals associated with glasnost . . . This genre did not tolerate a "happy
ending", a moral rebirth or the eradication of evil by the authorities' (Epstein *et
al.*, 1999: 91). In a country that had abolished censorship in 1987, *The Construction Battalion*, written in the same year, had the distinction of being the only book
banned by Gorbachev's government, to be released in 1989. This was largely
due to its portrayal of conscripts in a construction battalion of the Soviet army
as a group of violent, racist, drug-addicted and alcoholic misfits who mirrored
the military that exploited them. The armed forces had always had peculiarly
close relations with the state, the Communist Party and society at large, providing protection to the first, assurance to the second and 'political socialisation' to
the third, while aiding the economy with the labour of its personnel (Barany

and Moser, 2001: 174–6). The construction battalions figured high on the list of labour-intensive operations.

Furthermore, the Soviet Union's superpower status had depended on the strength of its military on which huge amounts had been spent for decades (Brown, 1997: 159). It was unthinkable, at a time when the system was rapidly crumbling, to downgrade this institution any more than events themselves had already done. The army had lost a good deal of authority and prestige, both nationally and internationally, and was now joining the ranks of the poor. Not even glasnost could permit Kaledin's blow to its already shattered image, all the more because its plight reflected so badly both on the regime and the country as a whole. Dodin was to claim, during a reprise of *Gaudeamus* in Milan, that Kaledin's book, which had inspired the production, was the child of the war in Afghanistan (a ten-year struggle from 1979 to 1989) and expressed the army's violence and despair during that war (*Il Giorno*, 11 December 1999). Scholars of the Soviet Union have generally stressed the deleterious effects of the Afghanistan war on the Soviet army, some pointing out how it continued on its downward spiral after the war.

> Since 1989, the former Soviet army has lost an empire, an alliance, a country, a war, its identity, mission, funding, a large part of its personnel, weapons, social prestige, and cohesion. It may, in fact, be the former Soviet institution that has been the most devastated by the political and economic systemic changes.
>
> (Barany and Moser, 2001: 213)

Since the army was well on the way to its post-1989 situation before this date, it is clear why Kaledin's book would have had enough sting to be banned. The construction battalions were disbanded in 1990.

That Dodin should have found Kaledin's type of *chernukha* instructive for his students is a measure of the anger, even revulsion, he and many of his genera-tion must have felt towards the political system from which they had been alienated for so long. In the great instability of the late 1980s, with its anarchi-cal psychological climate of anything goes, the novella must have looked like the nightmarish outcome of the mad utopia dreamed up by Platonov in *Chevengur*, whose publication more or less coincided with that of *The Construction Battalion*. In view of Dodin's cross-referencing of his work, it would be reasonable to suppose that he tackled *Chevengur* with *The Construction Battalion* in mind, the one seen by him as the pre-history of the other. However, where *Chevengur*, the pro-duction, experimented with several stylistic modes, *Gaudeamus* centred on the absurdity which it was his students' task to find while devising, and caught the infectious fun and vitality of their inventiveness as they devised. The students' irreverence supplanted Kaledin's murky text, yielding 19 improvisations whose cheeky spirit was announced by the work's complete title *Gaudeamus (To all those beautiful years that our youth gave us)*. By quoting the medieval student song even jokingly, they also paid tribute to the rites of learning through which they were passing with this production. However, the 'beautiful years' of its title turned out to be duplicitous in that the production projected what should be the lot of the young rather than what actually was their condition: instead of being students, they were conscripts, and instead of enlightenment from the university, they received the lessons of the hardest school of hard knocks.

A few years later, when anticipating *Claustrophobia*, Dodin was to ask the eight student directors of the group to devise two pieces each with the actors, one as a ballet and the other as an opera, which they were also to direct. The students generally followed the devising, improvising and rehearsal procedures they had learned from Dodin, exploring the literature most in vogue in the early 1990s for its punch to the period. They experimented with *chernukha*, foregrounding the prose of its high priest Vladimir Sorokin, who deconstructed the legacy of the Soviet age, including whatever had been canonised by it from the pre-Soviet epoch. Sorokin was quoted in an interview as saying that he had no 'social interests', by which he disclaimed the political intentions that had been attributed to his writing: 'To me it is a matter of total indifference, whether it is the period of stagnation or perestroika, totalitarianism or democracy' (Epstein *et al.*, 1999: 276). Sorokin's punk attitude riddles his prose – in fact, is symptomatic of *chernukha* in general – and was scrutinised by Dodin and the students as he relayered their *études*. Whether their attempts at a critical appraisal of *chernukha*-type gratuitousness came off in the production is to be seen, but its raw material provided the impetus for devising of their own which involved extended dialogue scripted without any prompting from pre-existing texts. By the end of the process, a bundle of *chernukha* and *chernukha*-type remnants remained at the core of *Claustrophobia*: pieces by Sorokin, certainly, and by Ludmila Ulitskaya, a representative of the so-called 'new wave literature' or 'alternative prose' of the 1980s and 1990s, as well as by Venedikt Erofeyev and Mark Kharitonov, the first winner of the Booker Russian Novel Prize in 1992 for *The Line of Fate or Milashevichev's Chest*. All of these authors were at least a generation older than the student actors but clearly had spoken to them in an immediate way. The major input of the students in terms of the structural, more strictly directorial, decisions for the work probably makes it more their own within the co-authorship parameters of the Maly, than *Gaudeamus*, its pair.

Gaudeamus and *Claustrophobia*, although in line with Dodin's usual compositional methods, move towards a new aesthetics for the Maly that, given its features, can only be called postmodernist: absence of narrative, absence of characterisation, dislocation of pieces, fragmentation, montage, non sequitur, parody, pastiche, simulation and the techniques of citation, self-reference and reflexivity. Reflexivity, in conformity with a postmodernist check-list, is used in the productions for the purposes of self-mockery, which is coupled with the mockery of whatever might be imagined to be the 'other', or 'object', of its discourse. Add to this catalogue of postmodernist devices the 'cool' of non-judgement, of a self-consciously objectified, uninvolved stance, as typified by Sorokin who, after the advent of this trend in the arts in Russia, was taken to be a leading postmodernist in the country. The trend was not quite coterminous with its western counterpart, but was near enough to it in all particulars to be acknowledged as postmodernism abroad as well as at home. It could be argued that, by its extravagances, it even outdid its western homologues.[1]

One might well consider how postmodernist aesthetics are inextricably linked to their societal conditions of production which, in a sociological perspective, would be defined as the disintegration of social structures, the destruction of hierarchies, the loss of faith in institutions and authorities and the concomitant throw-back of individuals upon themselves.[2] If these sociologically identifiable tendencies were sufficiently strong in the capitalist world in the last decades of the twentieth century to spawn a postmodernist culture, they were magnified a thousandfold in Russia in the 1980s and 1990s, so much so as to make the western capitalist 'postmodern condition', as Jean-François Lyotard had termed it in his 1979 book with this title (never anticipating the effect his terminology would have, for it spread like wildfire), appear ludicrously tame by comparison with its late-communist/early new-capitalist manifestations in Russia. It is worth reflecting upon Pierre Bourdieu's analysis of end-of-century neoliberalism, which is so like sociological accounts of postmodernist society as to suggest that neoliberal ideology and its economic implementation are the underpinnings of postmodernism (1998: 95–119; 2001: 75–91); that, in fact, when used to describe late twentieth-century societies, 'neoliberal' and 'postmodernist' are synonymous terms. Russian new capitalism, albeit *sauvage* or unrestrained, has enough in common with western neoliberalism to generate relatively comparable conditions from which could grow much the same artistic species, making the notion of 'postmodernism' meaningful across the board.

In these circumstances, *Gaudeamus* could not help but look like a member of the postmodernist family, even if Dodin had not set out to be a postmodernist, nor coveted the label. Nor was he unduly influenced by anything thus classified. He had used, in *Lord of the Flies*, music by Schnittke, which was also soon to be described as postmodernist; and, being himself an avid reader, his reading of Kaledin exercised its influence because it was receptive rather than indiscriminately ingested. He wished, in *Gaudeamus*, to capture the mood of a culture synchronised at so many points with an anti-establishment youth culture with which his young students did not necessarily empathise, but which they could well understand. Fear of conscription to the army, with a war in Afghanistan, was part of this culture of the negative. It was a youth culture that went for broke – drugs, sex, brutality among its paraphernalia – and, while it was at it, derided its own antics because the young either saw no future or had none, and because derision, the psycho-emotional flipside of stylistic reflexivity, was the defence of the disempowered. *Gaudeamus*, from a stylistic point of view, was to refract this context kaleidoscopically. Its fractured form refracted content as well because Dodin had broken up his students' 40 hours of improvisations to highlight the production-making processes of the enterprise. If, for Dodin, theatre worthy of the name always retains signs of its making, *Gaudeamus* lay bare its devices as never before in his theatre. This radical exposure of the mechanisms of theatricality was to be surpassed only by *Claustrophobia*, and was not to be repeated to the same degree again. It was of the moment, for the young, who found that its physical demands became more difficult as they grew older (Irina Tychinina, St Petersburg, 26 April 2001).

Gaudeamus: **Chaplin in the Gulag**

The pronounced reflexivity of *Gaudeamus* is largely predicated on its comedy – burlesque, slapstick, sardonic and sultry, all of it brazenly in your face. It is not a comedy of character, since the characters have names but no psychology, but of situation and incident. Its prime target is the coupling of force and passive resistance in the figures of a hapless Major and a Junior Lieutenant and the equally hapless recruits under their command. And since there is no tension between them, only ridiculous situations, the bullying and the bullied elicit the same kind of laughter. This is particularly the case of the improvisation the students had developed from the theme of 'Don't get drunk!' Its tone is set by the Major, who pops up from a trap in the raked stage covered with fake snow and harangues boots lined up downstage, oblivious to the fact that they are empty. Their owners are sloppily in line at the back of the stage. The Major orders a soldier to straighten up, whereupon the offending pair of boots snaps to attention (Figure 7, overleaf). He thus suddenly discovers his mistake, turns around, momentarily stares at the soldiers and continues his lecture without drawing breath: they are not 'to get pissed', and if anyone does, they must turn their mate onto his side so that he does not choke on his vomit. When outside the trap, the Major repeats his commandment again and again, gesticulating forcefully and occasionally demonstrating with a soldier's head. The soldiers, meanwhile, are bored or diffident – one slumping his shoulders, another turning in his feet – their lack of discipline humorously showing up those brief moments when they march perfectly as one. The actors' virtuosic display in these vignettes of army control is in itself a source of laughter.

Traps are a focus of laughter from the very beginning of the production when young men run hither and thither and vanish, one by one, into black holes hidden beneath the snow. They continue to dive or fall into them throughout the production. Since the holes also signify latrines, the Major's unexpected appearance from one of them, his body visible only to the chest, makes its comical point about what, precisely, they are all in. The message is reinforced – redundantly, as happens in slapstick – when a soldier intones that he is 'shovelling shit' because the country needs it.

The exquisite farce of this episode is matched by two improvisations involving the Junior Lieutenant. The first shows him reading instructions from a rule book in his hand as he puts his men through a drill. They twist and contort their bodies in impossible positions, and end their parodic sequences with a parody of musical theatre when they perform the drill as a dance routine to a popular Soviet song. (Russian audiences invariably join in by clapping as the soldiers fall out of line and dance about the stage. Western European spectators are more reticent about participating in the fun.) The second improvisation shows the

Figure 7 *Gaudeamus* at the Maly Drama Theatre, 1990. A. Koshkaryov as Major Lysodor.

Photograph by V. Vasilyev, courtesy of the Archive of the Maly Drama Theatre, St Petersburg.

Junior Lieutenant reading again from his book as he divides the line of soldiers into Arabs and Israelis to drill them on the Arab–Israeli conflict. Humour is derived from such jokes as a Jewish recruit being told he is an Arab, from the zany dialogue arising from this situation, and from how mock combat, which is initiated verbally, is extended through push-up and weight-lifting competitions. Corny humour, it nevertheless succeeds in exposing racist and anti-Semitic remarks, while implying they are standard fare in the Soviet army. Of the three improvisations discussed, the ridicule of this one allows the least scope for complicity.

The minority issue, otherwise known as the 'national question', was of foremost importance when the Soviet Union began to break up, and Dodin drew attention to it in rehearsals in the hope of building a caustic sketch around it – that is, in addition to pieces touching on the problem of anti-Semitism. This materialised in the first improvisation of the production which concerns Kirimov, who is from an unspecified Soviet Central Asian Republic but is described with racist indifference as to his ethnic identity as an 'Uzbek clod'. In one of the last improvisations, Kirimov attempts suicide, which momentarily brings home the gravity of persecution. However, the first improvisation fundamentally plays for laughs, despite conjoining xenophobia with the initiation ritual by violence of the *dedy* ('oldies'), many of whom were known to be among the criminal elements of the Soviet army, not least of its construction battalions. It was thought that, despite prohibition, the army was unable to eradicate this extreme form of bullying; further, that in certain quarters it was even encouraged. The potential dread that the subject could have inspired is checked by the whimsical pathos of Oleg Gayanov's Kirimov, which includes a benign rather than malicious take on the character's accent when he speaks Russian. Moreover, Gayanov dissipates the sketch's sinister overtones by providing, by his innocent compliance, a marvellously deft foil for the Russian bully Popov.

Less deceptive are the lines of dialogue, song or poem – these forms are mixed in the production – which proclaim service to the Soviet Union, even though they are spoken hurriedly for comic effect. Still others, although relatively few, are altogether explicit in their intention. Such is the case, for instance, of the stanza recited by a character who dreams of emigrating to America: 'Farewell, you oafish land of Russia / A land of squires, a land of slaves / Adieu, contemptible descendants / And you, you servile common knaves'.[3] The actor speaks his poem defiantly, emphasising the word 'slaves' as he looks directly at the spectators so as to implicate them in his oration. The poem ends with 'Hello, America!' after which he begins to sing 'America' and, still singing, is forced down one of the traps at the front of the stage by his comrades. It is from below the stage that the whole company then sings 'America' with gusto – another example of the cut and undercut typical of the production.

Burlesque, if taken literally, can only be taken seriously, and this, together with unequivocally provocative fragments like the ones just cited, offended members of the audience during the production's first season in St Petersburg in 1990–1. Irina Tychinina remembers how people disrupted performances, shouting that the production was a disgrace, that none of it was true, that the company was dragging the country into the gutter, and so on, before leaving the auditorium (St Petersburg, 22 September 1998). Sometimes debates would arise in the middle of a performance and become so heated that a meeting could have been held there and then to discuss the issues. The actors simply continued to play through the turmoil, not allowing what they considered to be a right-wing backlash to hold sway. Almost always, in 1990, they were afraid to leave the theatre, so aggressively had some of them been accosted in the streets.

Tychinina remembers most clearly the political dimension of the attacks. But there was much else in the production, besides words and incidents perceived to be anti-Soviet, to incense spectators: obscene language, vulgar gestures, bared breasts, ostentatious drink, drugs and sex scenes, including a gang rape. All the sex episodes in the production are highly fragmented and are disconnected even more by snippets of music cutting in and fading out to parody them. Thus, most notably, 'Girl' by the Beatles several times breaks up an incident in which a man 'shares' his girlfriend. The incident is undercut additionally by a brief duel scene quoted from Tchaikovsky's opera *Eugene Onegin*. This pastiche of women's honour avenged is enmeshed in a series of embeddings when Tatyana, the 'Girl' girl, enters on roller skates dressed in a long, fur-trimmed red dress. Tatyana is the name of Tchaikovsky's heroine, who is modelled on the original in Pushkin; Pushkin's ironies lie in this scene beneath Tchaikovsky's romanticism. Clothes function as comedy: she had worn a red mini-skirt previously. Fantasy collides with reality in that the duel is Tatyana's dream of how she would like her lover to behave. She skates around her 'dead' man (the raked stage makes it quite a feat), scoops up snow into the water pitcher she is carrying and showers it over him as she speaks. Meanwhile, the opera continues, as disconnected from her monologue as its noble sentiments are from her ignoble situation and the equally ignoble insults she suddenly receives from her lover when he comes 'alive' and staggers up off the snow from his drunken stupor.

The anger vented by spectators in the theatre and the street also found its way into print in the pilot issue of the *Peterburgsky teatralny zhurnal* published within a year of *Gaudeamus*'s first successful tour in western Europe. A good part of the issue was devoted to the Maly, in recognition of its stature in the city, and, besides features on some of its established actors, included a full-length article by the journal's editor Marina Dmitrevskaya. The article is noteworthy not only for its exceptional animosity (newspaper reviews of *Gaudeamus* in St Petersburg at this time appear to be non-existent), but because it relates the production to Dodin's earlier work, which the critic had always admired. Dmitrevskaya argues that, while *Brothers and Sisters* was motivated by empathy, *Gaudeamus* is full of hatred. While, in *Brothers*, Dodin shared the fate of the nation, in *Gaudeamus* he dissociates himself from it. For example, the song 'I, You, He, She' (which was popular in the Brezhnev era) is delivered sardonically and the 'We' of the song's 'lovely family' is actually a distanced 'They', the miserable Russians, who are stuck in the latrines. Dmitrevskaya here refers to an improvisation in which the soldiers, who have been ordered to give samples of their faeces for testing, toss up dozens of match-boxes from the traps as they sing this song. The performers are invisible, which makes the dance of the match-boxes all the funnier. The dance is of no concern to Dmitrevskaya since her attention is exclusively on the song's verbal content and its associative links throughout the whole production: 'They', she stresses, are not only 'in the shit', but are 'nothing but shit' (Dmitrevskaya, 1992: 6–10).

Dmitrevskaya is equally hostile about the devices used to mediate attitudes towards women. Where encirclement in *Lord of the Flies* inspires concern for the victim, a similar device in *Gaudeamus* in the rape scene generates feelings of disgust. Yegorsha in *Brothers and Sisters* pulls Lizka by her hair, but his action is affectionate, teasing her in a scene constructed on multiple meanings. A similar scene in *Gaudeamus* is merely crude. (It shows a randy soldier who drags a woman by her wet hair around in a circle before she returns lust for lust.) Sex by coercion, Dmitrevskaya argues, is the only type of relationship envisaged between men and women by the production (although she ignores hints of homosexual coercion in it). This contributes to the wretched image of the Russian people reflected by *Gaudeamus* to Russians, let alone across the world. She regrets the Maly's long absences from St Petersburg but, while implying that the production's international success might be tied up with its prurient interests, stops short of accusing Dodin of pandering to western prejudices and tastes. Dmitrevskaya's allusions to the Maly's possible collusion with 'the west' presuppose that western audiences are homogeneous, which they are certainly not, and, to boot, that they are incapable of discernment – also not the case. Critics outside Russia, by and large male, were also uncomfortable about the production's depiction of women and sex, although it took a woman, Claire Armistead, in England in 1991 to put the case bluntly:

> The representation of sex as an overwhelming preoccupation of the con-scripts' life has its problematic side. While it might seem precious, in context, to complain about the portrayal of women as tarts and nympho-maniacs, the light-hearted treatment of a gang rape by a group of drugged soldiers is hard to take. One can only assume there is a satirical thrust to the scene which is lost on an English audience.
>
> (*Financial Times*, 16 July 1991)

Western responses, then, were not always compliant. Nevertheless, this review calls for several observations. First of all, the issue of what may have been lost is not cultural. It is not a matter of English lack of comprehension, but of stylistic misunderstanding, namely, there is no satirical thrust to the rape scene and it is meant to be hard to take. Secondly, the production is less inter-ested in 'tarts' than in brutes and, although open to criticism from a moral and gender point of view, has a postmodernist penchant for literal-mindedness. These stylistic nuances make a difference to how we perceive the production and allow us to note, in addition, that what is raw in one scene is counterbalanced by the sarcasm of another. Furthermore, the variety of hyperbole provided by its pieces cannot give the production unity of tone, whether of satire or of any other genre. Which is why the German critic who describes *Gaudeamus* as a 'Gulag Circus' that combines Chaplin and Solzhenitsyn (*Neue Zeit*, 25 September 1992) is on the right track. In actual fact, he does not go quite far enough, since there is more of Chaplin than Solzhenitsyn in *Gaudeamus*, given its boots scene, the Arab–Israeli scene, the giggly girls, 'dead' rivals, mock sentiments, roller skates, and so on. It is Chaplinesque, as well, in its swift and sharp turnabout from one tone to another, say, from the horrible note struck by the rape in the shadows to the next, which is the magic of red balloons floating up from the black holes in the stage and filling it up entirely. These balloons represent the drug-induced state of the characters. In some performances they are multi-coloured to denote a psychedelic 'trip'. Whatever their colour, they are always popped, as happens at parties, and their sound doubles for machine-gun fire, its serious underbelly emerging from the scene.

Perhaps the most hyperbolic sketch of them all concerns a mutual seduction on a piano. It begins when a grand piano tied up by ropes descends from the flies. It develops through the actors' skilful tugs and slides across its lid, and reaches its climax as the lovers sit astride the piano and play Mozart's 40th Symphony with their toes, first searching for the notes, as if sounding each other out, and then gathering confidence and speed as they go. The piece ends with panache as they blissfully perform a *pas de deux* on the piano's lid while the piano swings back up to the ceiling, the symphony playing full blast from a recording. It is an amazing metaphorical transposition of a love scene, charming, dangerous, exciting – every bit a display of that 'stunning flair' and 'virtuosic artistry' (*The Independent*, 15 July 1991), 'unrivalled theatrical artistry' and 'physical virtuosity' (*The Observer*, 14 July 1991) and 'theatrical brio' (*Daily Telegraph*, 17 July 1991) which English critics noticed in the production as a whole and applauded, even when they remarked that *Gaudeamus* 'sometimes delights a little too obviously in its own theatrical virtuosity' at the expense of its content (*The Guardian*, 13 July 1991).

While the question of content had bothered a number of reviewers in London in 1991, it appeared to be of minor importance to their colleagues five years later, when *Gaudeamus* was on its regional tour. Once again, these critics enthusiastically praised the company's virtuosity, but perhaps the shock of Russia's upheavals had worn away, leaving them less aware of the production's allusions to national affairs. One critic, who, by contrast, anticipated substantial content, was totally unimpressed, thinking there was nothing much to the production at all (Newcastle *Herald and Post*, 22 May 1996). However, rather like Dmitrevskaya, this critic mistook one genre for another, expecting a serious play when the play was mock heroics. Dmitrevskaya's critique, moreover, was of a different order. She was judging from the inside, with an insider's awareness of national catastrophes and sense of identification with a national culture. One could add that, because of the latter, she responded with a hypersensitivity that is ultimately out of kilter with the production's verve. Its pungency is its very own way of dealing with such catastrophes and of fighting back against the sense of obliteration and despair precipitated by them. This, at once a stylistic and emotional ploy, is very much in the manner of Chaplin.

Hybrids and crossovers

The discussion of genre in these pages leads to the fundamental point that the greatest originality of *Gaudeamus* lies in its mixture of genres by which it forms a hybrid genre of its own. It combines circus, vaudeville, movement, dance (ballet and all sorts of other idioms), opera (including lip-sync arias), choral singing, liturgy and jazz band, which makes a sudden appearance at the end when the students pop out of the holes with the brass instruments they had learned for this production and blast out a rousing finale. And, as we have already noted, *Gaudeamus* combines poetry and prose. In its use of the genre of mock heroics, it develops the latter's propensity for citation, making what might be called a citational genre that is part of the general mix. Thus, for example, Hamlet's 'To be, or not to be', which is recited at the beginning by one performer in a hole, and then is picked up by others, is an item all on its own, delivered as a quotation of a quotation that is not quite a speech. A second example of the 'Gaudeamised' *Hamlet* returns towards the end of the production. Here the line is 'Halt, who goes there?', which is relayed between the Major and the soldiers, who sing it low in chorus. The chant developed from their quotation is about a 'foreigner's jet' flying over the motherland they must protect. Its effect is dual: that of a nonsense rhyme chanted for sheer pleasure and that of a soft moment which is all the more touching for the amassed absurdity and violence preceding it. At the same time, this quasi-classroom recitation, like the first example from *Hamlet*, is the remnant of lessons and rehearsals left behind to show from what the production had been made.

For all its clever mixing and blending, which suggests that no particular element dominates, *Gaudeamus* is nevertheless marked by its crossover from theatre to dance, dance ultimately providing the main reference for its composition. There is barely an improvisation of the 19 available that does not contain or merge into a dance or dance-like piece, however small. Besides the examples already given, there are a march that merges into a waltz, and vice versa, and a skirmish that merges into flamenco; a soldier poses in a ballet position to dream a dream, while four women dance an ethereal ballet in white night-shirts; a soldier catches buckets thrown up from the holes in a short, sharp dance of cleaning the latrines; a husband and wife dance a waltz, soon joined by soldiers who take up their turn with her in a crescendo of movement, giving the impression that the whole stage is dance. The longest dance sequence is a minuet to Boccherini – one of the soldier's dreams invented by the students which was kept for the production, not least because it is quite moving by contrast with the crude realities of all the soldiers' daily existence. It is danced by the soldiers in uniform as a *corps de ballet* with candles, which they place in a large circle around the stage. The candles light up a couple who

Figure 8 *Gaudeamus* at the Théâtre des Salins Martigues, 1995. N. Kromina and Y. Kordonsky.

Photograph by Ken Reynolds, courtesy of Ken Reynolds.

dance the minuet among them as a ballet (Figure 8, overleaf). The whole group swings into a dance when the woman changes partners and dances with each of the men.

The most unexpected dance sequence might well be the ballet *enchaînement* that develops out of the choral 'Halt, who goes there?' In this sequence, the soldiers perform *ports de bras*, *attitudes* and jumps on the spot perfectly together while they recite their 'foreign jet' poem/song, the beauty of this ballet class (cum army manoeuvre, cum joke on ballet training) enhanced by the mist-like penumbra of the stage. Speech in dance is an integral part of *Gaudeamus* and takes the production, propelled by its dance dynamics, into dance theatre – and this before Dodin was to discover and fall in love with Pina Bausch's *Tanztheater* during the Maly's first tours abroad.

Dance theatre involves hybridisation, and *Gaudeamus*, by its complex hybridity, belongs to a distinctive strain of late twentieth-century theatre/dance/performance to which the 1960s counterculture in the United States had contributed through such experimental artists as Meredith Monk, Richard Foreman and Robert Wilson. All began making a lasting impression on western Europe from the early 1970s. Wilson probably did more than any of his compatriots, save those coming directly from postmodern dance (Wilson comes indirectly from it), to influence European perception as to what could be achieved by an 'impure', boundary-breaking 'theatre'. At the European end, Pina Bausch was very much a part of this transformation (witness her enormous success in France in the 1970s) to which she brought the history of German dance theatre – Mary Wigman, Laban, Jooss – none of whose peculiarities were in conflict with transatlantic experiments in hybridity. Russia, for her part, had her own history of generic mixing which dated from the Revolutionary avant-garde but had gone underground, only to sprout shoots here and there until they could grow freely, once more, after perestroika. Dodin's work with his students takes up this experimental skein and carries forward the principle of dance-in-theatre that he had made vital to his training method to make it fundamental for *Gaudeamus*. It is crucial, as we shall see, for *Claustrophobia*. By carrying the principle forward, the student productions do far more than incorporate dance elements. They change identity, dance being sufficiently instrumental in that change to determine their new identity.

These remarks suggest that the appropriate artistic frame of reference for Dodin's innovations is broad and international rather than one confined to a narrow definition of the theatre or to a narrowly national conception of it. This frame would become broader still if it included the major contemporary choreographers (let alone those who are not well known) who increasingly think and work like theatre directors. Bausch is a pioneering example of the past 40 years, but one could hardly ignore today, on Europe's fertile ground, the choreography of William Forsythe with the Ballett Frankfurt. Forsythe has turned the genre of ballet inside out by incorporating speech, by opening up his procedures to view, by assimilating parts of rehearsals in his choreographies, as well as such accidents as the fire curtain falling during a performance, and, among other things, by giving his dancers space for their own invention and improvisation. Take, from the numerous examples available, *Artifact* (1984), *Impressing the Czar* (1988) and *Eidos: Telos* (1995). Given his key position in the context of crossed genres evoked here, Forsythe cannot be put aside even though the similarities between Dodin and Bausch are more pressing for my argument. Bausch's dance theatre has the same capacity for capturing a polyphony of performance events in one hybridised fragment as occurs in *Gaudeamus*, the 'Halt' piece being a case in point. In addition, only her dance theatre – *Arien* (1979), *Two Cigarettes in the Dark* (1985), *Tanzabend 2* (1991), *Das Fensterputzer* (1997), *Masurca Fogo* (1998), to give representative samples – plays so freely with the crossover from dance to theatre as to destroy the distinction between them. One might say that Dodin simply alternates the pieces, his crossover going from theatre to dance.

There are, as well, strong similarities between how Dodin and Bausch work. Both stretch their performers' physical and psychological limits. Both play with sound, rhythm and inflection, paralinguistics rather than semantics providing sense. Both use sound to stimulate the body to explore steps, their possible combinations and their organic link to utterances, although sound and movement are not presumed to have to co-ordinate in a narrative or illustrative kind of way. A hiatus between the sense made by movement and the sense of utterances occurs in the 'Halt' piece in *Gaudeamus* and is certainly how Bausch achieves many of the unpredictable effects of her choreographies. Dodin's facility for crossover is partly due to his method of crafting productions on and through his actors, which is nothing if not choreographic, as was observed in my second chapter. Both Dodin and Bausch favour improvisation, experiment, and trial and error, and construct their compositions out of the material devised during the exploratory process. Most of this is true of the choreographic process developed by Forsythe who, unlike Bausch and very like Dodin, responds passionately to the 'vertiginous thrill of exactitude' provided by ballet – borrowing the witty, reflexive title of one of Forsythe's choreographies.

Yet while their methods have much in common, there are significant differences, one being particularly relevant for this discussion. Bausch turns her dancers' personal experiences (which also surge from their unconscious) into the very subject matter of performance, however complex their route through the choreography may be. Dodin, as we have noted previously, relies on his performers' personal experiences (which also surge from their unconscious), but these are stimuli for artistic invention rather than the stuff of invention itself. The only exception to Dodin's usual method is *Claustrophobia* in that it actually does relay autobiographical material *à la* Bausch. Dodin had asked his students to improvise on their impressions of foreign countries and of Russia after their return, and compare them (post-show talk at the Nottingham Playhouse, 22 May 1996). They were to create dances and operas from these impressions, dance essentially speaking for the west and opera for Russia. However, the process ran its course in such a way that most of the operatic parts of *Claustrophobia* intertwined with dance in some form and usually ended in dance, with or without words.

Claustrophobia **as choreography**

The production's set by Poray-Koshits captures the fact that *Claustrophobia* is led by the dance through and through. It is a white studio with a barre on stage right and five arched windows to stage left, below which are several white radiators. The studio tapers slightly inwards towards the back, where there are two white doors. It is the exact replica of Dodin's studio at the St Petersburg Academy, but could be an old-fashioned dance studio anywhere in the world. Into this light, graceful space runs one dancer, then another, then another – five all told – each one taking position at the barre or in the centre to perform ballet exercises. The exercises continue in silence in the harmony between movement and space and continue when two men in long black coats waft in through the windows and begin to speak. They are ghosts of the past, who evoke the building's illustrious history. (This was once the school of Mandelstam and Nabokov.) They are also shadows of the present, who explain that prostitutes, pimps and homeless drunks and beggars now live behind the studio's back wall. These men, who have been travelling (black berets and scarves suggest France), are 'Ubiquists' – 'organisms which can adapt themselves to any conditions', as one of them defines the species; and 'Ubiquists' might just as well be synonymous with 'Russians', since these figures introduce the production's scenes of Russian life. The time, one of them tells us, is shortly after 'the routing of the communists', thus after August 1991. Dialogue is uttered as one Ubiquist walks along the barre and performs small balletic movements on it. The other sits on the floor, as any dancer might when resting. Meanwhile, the silent dancers have changed places and sit on the window-sills holding natural poses which, here and there, become simple movements of the arms, lifted to accompany pieces of the Ubiquists' speech. The whole is accompanied by a piano played behind the back wall of the stage.

From here on, for one-third of its duration, the production is a choreographic suite. It features a man in a transparent lilac dress on pointes who, after a solo, partners a heavy woman in ballooned pants on pointes to the familiar theme of the film *Paris-Texas*. Cross-dress, cross-gender and cross-sex mix, and with a smile, as happens in Bausch's work. Single dancers and dancing couples fill out the duo with a seamless medley. Ballet merges with the Charleston, the can-can, line dancing, rock, jaunty jigs from musicals and athletic swirls on skateboards, all to a musical miscellany that is meant to denote the western world. This wordless choreography runs into a circle before it breaks up to introduce a long, energetic monologue – a chemistry lesson to recalcitrant students. Dodin here returns to the ballet-lesson motif of the opening, pitting a new series of elegant barre work against a very different kind of learning. As the teacher belts out her monologue and vigorously writes chemical formulae on the walls – here is Russia with a vengeance, the scene is saying – her male 'students' continue their dance on top of the barre, or hook their legs on the barre, head down, or do somersaults, or stand on their heads at the back of the class. Her female 'students' dance various steps, or lounge about in various poses, or sit on the floor or on the window-sills, as dancers do in rehearsals. Dodin's technique of skilfully weaving traces of his rehearsals into his compositions dates back to his early work with the Maly, as we have seen, but its pronounced character in *Claustrophobia* is on a par with the reflexivity of Bausch and Forsythe. Dodin firmly takes his place, then, in the crossover trends of the late twentieth century.

The lesson is to two different texts by Sorokin on the subject of Soviet/post-Soviet science and sex, and it is blatantly part of the *chernukha* genre. The teacher's diatribe against one of her students goes through several phases of sexual excitement before she takes down her hair, climbs up onto the window-sill, and sits with her legs wide open. By now she has begun to attack his slovenly appearance. The scene ends when she puts her hand into his trousers to straighten up his shirt and discovers that he has ejaculated. Black farce turns into balletic eroticism when the teacher suddenly leaps across space into the arms of a newcomer while her student rolls out of sight. The suite continues as dancers come in from the windows to haunting Georgian music for wind instruments. One by one, they take off their tops and dance in free form. Despite the criticism they had endured at home, the ensemble must have been emboldened by the world success of *Gaudeamus* since there are far more exposed breasts here than in the preceding work.

As they dance, the Georgian music merges into 'On the Hills of Manchuria' which other actors play in a brass band as they step in through the windows. (By choosing 'Manchuria', the younger generation cracks a joke about *Brothers and Sisters*, where this waltz was first used.) The instrumentalists dance too, until this long sequence tails into mimed instrumental play. Silent dance and silent music are then broken by a violin played by a woman who walks in from one of the back doors – a relatively rare entrance since the actors usually come in from the windows. Later in the production, they come in through the holes they have torn in the plaster walls. These acts of vandalism are 'Russian', as distinct from the production's 'western' acts. (The walls are mended after every performance, one of the actors being a skilled plasterer.) Walking through walls is stunning, but then action in *Claustrophobia* is always polyspatial and never more daring than when its performers slide up and down the pipes hidden along the walls, appearing to be walking vertically on walls.

The remaining two-thirds of the production contain several opera-like scenarios in which Russia comes out a dismal second to the 'west'. They are not purely experimental, since nothing in Dodin's work – rehearsal or production – is ever only a matter of style; style, for him, is at the service of life discovered through the theatre. Thus, the histrionics of opera in *Claustrophobia* serve to show up the cruel life of Russia which, in the production's optic, has hardly changed at all after the counterattack to the August 1991 coup. Yet much had been expected of that attack, hailed by 'political leaders around the world, and academic observers . . . as a historical victory for Russian democracy' (McFaul, 2001: 160). Expectations, where politics were concerned, had been dashed. Yeltsin and his allies' 'failure to institute new rules of the game for the political system created and perpetuated ambiguities in the distribution of power' which contributed greatly to the repolarisation of politics in Russia that 'eventually toppled the First Russian Republic' (ibid.), its fall occurring on 3–4 October 1993. These are precisely the two years of *Claustrophobia*'s gestation for its commissioned opening in Paris in January 1994. By this time, the actors had more than once experienced a sense of dislocation on their return home, and the country's political instability only exacerbated their feeling of cultural shock. Dodin was to put the issue in these terms when *Claustrophobia* toured Britain in 1996:

> For the first time, these 20-year-old actors saw another style of life and another kind of culture. And the more they saw, the stronger their impressions were on returning to Russia. They saw old things under a new light.
>
> (*Financial Times Weekend*, 18–19 May 1996)

The old things were ugly, judging by the production's selection of scenes of mendacity, spite, resentment, aggression, selfishness and cant. A long recitative based on Ulitskaya's text on the poor (*The Chosen People*) is delivered by a one-legged beggar in front of a church to a feeble-minded girl who has been sent there to beg by her mother. The recitative develops into a hysterical aria before subsiding under the syncopated rhythm of people's bickering voices in a group meant to represent a queue (extracts from *The Queue* by Sorokin). The performers, bunched up for musical reasons like the chorus in opera, soon change their score into a syncopated chant of 'Me, Me, Me!' to put egoism in a critical light. The scene glides into another when a broad swing comes down from the flies. Audiences discover to their amusement that the body lying on it is Lenin's embalmed corpse, which 'doctors' promptly treat using brass instruments for stethoscope, drip-feeder, thermometer and whatever else besides (Figure 9, overleaf). This was Dodin's idea. It was the students' idea, on the other hand, to send Lenin and his wife singing up into the clouds and back down again to sing and swing side by side. The text – rather, libretto – by Igor Konyayev, one of the directors who also performs in the production, is danced and sung by Lenin and 'Nadya', Nadezhda Krupskaya lovingly called by the diminutive of her name for satirical bite. Dance sequences without words, to a Mozart piano concerto, move in and out of the chain of snapshots. They are mock-elegiac, with pointed toes and curved arms, or angular and pelvic, as if inspired by some form of contemporary dance. The section ends to the toll of bells as guards, in an imitation of the changing of the guard at Lenin's tomb, lightly goose-step from the back doors while Lenin and Nadya's airy dance blends in with their march. All exit to conclude a montage which, by contrast with much that is 'oafish' in preceding sections, stylishly buries an old culture. In fact, what is also buried is an old politics and the 'cult of the personality' that went with it.

The ugliest scene by far concerns a husband and wife who cook *pelmeny*, a Russian type of ravioli, right there on the swing used for the Lenin sequence. Once again, the text is by Sorokin. To cut a long story short – and the scene is

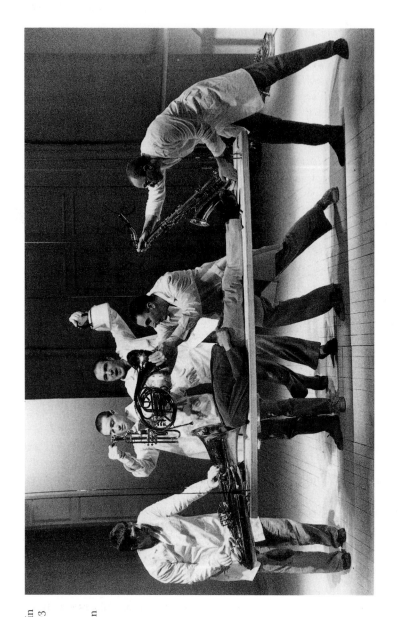

Figure 9 Curing Lenin in *Claustrophobia* at the MC93 Bobigny, Paris, 1995.

Photograph by Ken Reynolds, courtesy of Ken Reynolds.

far too long – the husband changes for dinner into his army uniform and ends up on the swing-table, urinating into the bowl they had previously used for mixing meat, held up to him by his wife. Several incidents indicate that he beats her. This purportedly quintessentially 'Russian' scene of social and moral 'back-wardness' – *pelmeny*, vodka, drunkenness, patriotic sentiment, patriarchal husband, subservient wife – is interrupted by a choreography known by the ensemble as 'The Parisian'. It is danced by a woman in black tights and leotard who is joined shortly afterwards by a *corps de ballet* dancing along the walls (Figure 10, overleaf), to a medley of songs sung by Edith Piaf. Stereotypical Russia meets a no less stereotypical France. Similarly banal images and *longueurs* return towards the production's end in a scene on anti-Semitism, borrowed from *Gaudeamus*.

Claustrophobia's critical reception – Moscow observing

Claustrophobia was received in France to the fanfare of the *Saison russe* and, although the occasion encouraged backslapping, critics were genuinely bowled over by the production. They admired its mixture of genres, fire, intelligence, commitment (*Le Monde*, 21 January 1994) and the way it pulled together all the qualities of the troupe (*Libération*, 20 January 1994). All concurred with *Libéra-tion*'s assessment that the 'actors' vitality went completely against the pessimism of their subject matter', the critic from *Le Quotidien de Paris* going so far as to say that the production left people feeling transported, exalted and free (25 January 1994). All discussed the production's concern with history as it was happening, and all supported unreservedly its capacity to face up to the worst of a society in disarray.

Two years later, when *Claustrophobia* opened its British tour at the Notting-ham Playhouse, critics were no less appreciative of its stylistics – its 'patchwork of Pina Bausch-like dance, opera, acrobatics and dialogue' (*The Independent*, 24 May 1996), or, in the words of the *Daily Telegraph*, its 'eclectic mix of drama, dance, music, operatic recitative and sheer spectacle' (23 May 1996). They were no less aware of its gaze on contemporary history, although some worried about which bits belonged where, whether to the pre- or the post-perestroika period (*The Independent*), or how this two-year-old show had been 'overtaken by recent events' (*The Guardian*, 25 May 1996). Performances in Glasgow did not arouse qualms about historical accuracy: this was 'a show about post-communist Russia' (*The Times*, 2 June 1996) and the 'fragmented chaos of contemporary Russia' (*The Scotsman*, 31 May 1996).[4] The impact of the production, whether in Nottingham or Glasgow, never failed to elicit strong sentiments from the critics: 'too nihilistic to be moving, perhaps, but a theatrical *tour de force*, wrenching shape and meaning from chaos with a level of artistry, an almost casual, creative brilliance, that leaves audiences gasping' (*Scotland on Sunday*, 2 June 1996). Even so, Michael Billington from *The Guardian* was concerned about its 'structural amorphousness' and Paul Taylor from *The Independent* felt that it was 'too impressionistic and structureless for its own good'. Billington added: 'As a

Figure 10 'The Parisian' in *Claustrophobia* at the MC93 Bobigny Paris, 1995.

Photograph by Ken Reynolds, courtesy of Ken Reynolds.

guide to the new Russia, it is a sketchily impressionistic piece crying out for an authorial vision.'

The only critic to stand out against the general adulation was Alastair Macauley from the *Financial Times* when reporting on the London leg of *Claustrophobia*'s journey. *Claustrophobia*, in his view, 'looks like a very thorough plunge into western Eurotrash' and is 'laden with Euro-clichés', being 'all too like many pieces made by Pina Bausch for her Dance Theatre at Wuppertal' (5 June 1996). He concludes, supported by a list of astutely chosen examples: 'Nobody doubts that life in modern Russia must be culturally grim, and *Claustrophobia* confirms that. But it is not a work of art.' Since Macauley is the critic who wrote with such passion and lucidity in both 1994 and 1998 about *The Devils*, it is imperative to record how he compares *Claustrophobia* with the earlier production: 'On the 1994 evidence [of the Maly's British tour], the Maly performers are at their best in character acting: above all in revealing both social surface and spiritual essence, as in Dodin's superlative three-part staging of Dostoevsky's *The Devils*.'

Critics in France had at no point queried the structure of *Claustrophobia* or whether it failed to deliver character acting or lacked an 'authorial vision'. Nor had they asked about its historical placing or questioned its negative view of Russia. The difference between English and French critics on these points may have something to do with the strong tradition of text-based and realist and psychological theatre in England and the more pronounced development in France during the past three decades of physical theatre, 'total theatre' and an inclination for international experimental theatre/dance.[5] That said, Macauley is not mistaken when he argues that character acting is a strength of the Maly (which elsewhere he compares with English character acting). Nevertheless, *Claustrophobia* is constructed according to different criteria, and the central question is why they necessarily apply.

The 'why?' of it was problematical in Russia, as the 1994 special issue of the *Moskovsky nablyudatel* (*Moscow Observer*) on the *Saison russe* showed. The journal was something of a summing up after the event, and included extracts from the French press about the Russian productions, as well as articles by Russian specialists on the French productions of Russian plays during the season. Its editor, Valery Semenovsky, refers to the scepticism of certain Russian critics towards the Maly's success in Paris – and its international renown generally – arguing that such scepticism was based on two main factors: first, the lack of information as to what this success meant in terms of the standing and quality of the theatres where the Maly performed (how, he asks, did a provincial theatre in Brighton compare with a prestigious venue in the capital?); second, the Maly's absence from home, 1994 virtually being a year-long journey abroad. Dodin, he asserts, extols the virtues of the Russian theatre-home, but the Maly Drama Theatre is 'a house on wheels, a house on call, a house that is not for us' (Semenovsky, 1994: 6). Anatoly Smeliansky writes in the same journal that the few Russians who had seen *Claustrophobia* in Paris unanimously insisted it was made for export, 'for them, but not for us'. It was a special kind of product into which assumptions as to what would please the foreign public for whom it was intended were necessarily built (1994: 10).

There is a hint of defensive insularity about these reports, as there was two years earlier when Dmitrevskaya had sceptically surveyed the international success of *Gaudeamus*. Criticism now of *Claustrophobia* was based on similar objections. Semenovsky denounced *Claustrophobia*'s vision of life in Russia as a life in the sewers. Further: 'Dodin thinks, as do the French, that *Claustrophobia* is the mirror of the Russian revolution. And I think: it is time to stop giving diagnoses of this country' (Semenovsky, 1994: 6). Of course, Semenovsky was speaking against a turbulent political background, since barely a year had gone by after 3–4 October 1993, the date that burned in everybody's mind, when more than 100 people died in the armed conflict between the president and the parliament. This was the second major uprising after August 1991, and the event spurred western scholars to observe that 'the last time Moscow had endured such violence was during the Bolshevik takeover in 1917' (McFaul, 2001: 207). By mid-1994, when the *Moscow Observer* went to press, Russian failings were being aired daily in the Russian newspapers and on television, and Semenovsky was most probably thinking of these attacks on the Russian self-image when he chastised Dodin for his interpretation of Russia's woes.

By contrast, Smeliansky's critique is focused more on the organisation of the work than on its possible psychological, sociocultural, or political implications. He repeats the diagnostic idea floated by Semenovsky, arguing that *Claustrophobia*'s 'artistic diagnosis' is inaccurate. Russia's frontiers are no longer closed and Russians today are not afraid of claustrophobia, but of a life that has no limits, nor a past or a future. The production is cold and its young actors' performances cannot compare with *Gaudeamus*, which was full of the joy and freedom of creativity. The texts by Ulitskaya and her peers are monotonous and all alike. The production's foul language lacks emotional charge, nor is there any 'human necessity' for it. It was all very well for spectators in Paris to be enthusiastic about *Claustrophobia*, but all they saw was pictures. They did not hear what the words were saying, which had to be considered in any evaluation of the production. The individuality of his actors was the most valuable quality of all of Dodin's theatre, since it gave his productions the multiple hues loved by his audiences. This had gone. One had to acknowledge how the world's theatre capital (that is, Paris) had taken to the production, but his, Smeliansky's, heart had not taken to it (1994: 10–11).

The drubbing Dodin received from the *Moskovsky nablyudatel* was counteracted by his St Petersburg champions, notably by Yelena Alexeyeva, who praised the actors for their readiness to break the customary silence held in Russia over sensitive national matters (*Chas pik*, 1 March 1995). She also claimed legitimacy for *Claustrophobia* by arguing that it dealt, from a contemporary point of view, with the theme of the sins of the fathers inherited by their sons which pervades classical Russian literature.

The debate thus raised continued after Russian audiences had had a chance to see the production. Two issues of the relatively widely read *Ekran i stsena* covered the case (Nos. 43 and 46, November 1995). The production's advocates focused on artistic issues – the troupe's virtuosity, vitality and capacity to dance, sing and encompass any performance genre – while its attackers concentrated on its subject matter and outlook, both judged to be totally negative. Critics in this aggressive camp took the opportunity to demolish *Gaudeamus* while they were at it, maintaining that it was deeply inappropriate – 'unwatchable', in fact – 'in the context of the war in Chechnya where blood, not urine or faeces, was being spilt'. By the time this attack against *Gaudeamus* was launched, the war in Chechnya had been fought for one year and had begun to look like another Afghanistan. The war was a highly contentious issue in Russia, dividing families, let alone the nation, on political, ethical and ethnic grounds, and casting doubts on Yeltsin's leadership, even among those who had been his most ardent supporters. *Claustrophobia* was lumped together with *Gaudeamus*, and innuendoes regarding national self-esteem, which had traversed the pages of the *Moskovsky nablyudatel*, returned. The idea that *Claustrophobia*'s terrible tale about 'us' had not come from foreigners, but from 'ourselves' – this was its worst feature – was stressed most of all in *Vechernyaya Moskva* (11 November 1995).

The most ferocious criticism, which was also a personal attack on Dodin, was to be found in *Vecherny Peterburg* (30 January 1995), and can be summarised briefly as follows. *Claustrophobia*, like *Gaudeamus*, had taken the Maly into a dead end. It was a clinical diagnosis of what had been constructed as a 'sick' situation full of people who, when not sick, were simply beasts. The production's experiments amounted to nothing more than mere aestheticism, which could hardly be relevant to 'Russia's bitter fate'. In any case, Russians had had their fill of 'home-grown apocalypses' and of the 'poetics of disgust' of such authors as Sorokin and Kharitonov who, moreover, were now out of date. The production had used this disgusting poetics for the sheer hell of it, not as a cry from the heart.

Apart from giving us a clear idea of the Russian critical reception for *Claustrophobia* and *Gaudeamus* in 1994–5, this synthesis opens up a number of important issues. One of them concerns the role of the theatre in society which, in Russia, irrespective of the demolition undergone by the country, had not been obliterated. The theatre was still thought to have the power of appraisal, illumination, guidance and criticism, even though the criticism offered by these productions went against the grain. The fact that the critical response was visceral meant that the theatre still mattered, whatever else was happening to it – commercialism, trivialisation, co-option and even opportunistic internationalisation, of which Dodin stood accused. Yet, that Dodin's embrace of international visibility should have been interpreted as a cop-out, or a sell-out, or a commercial deal testifies to how deep the insecurity within the profession and in society at large had become. It could be argued, in addition, that such interpretations came from within a society unaccustomed to a market economy and, consequently, to the idea that theatre works might have to enter the competitive environment to survive at all. The malice of much of the criticism indicates that personal rivalry and jealousy must also have played their part.

There is, as well, the issue of how conditions, particularly when they are on the edge, influence judgement as to what the theatre can or may be allowed to say and do. The reactions that we have witnessed could only have come from the gut with such immediacy in a period of great vicissitude when the stakes were played for all or nothing, every day. It is surely disturbing that in times of such great stress, suspicion overrides generosity and good sense. Dodin never doubted the advantages to the Maly of travel, over and above the fact that it helped his company economically. Travel, in his eyes, was never mere globe-trotting, let alone a compromise of his ideals for the company. Travel allowed the Maly actors to take a broader, more intelligent, view. It gave them the opportunity to sift through, compare and evaluate the information flowing from the Russian media and, by exposing them to different ways of life, gave them the scope to observe, think and learn, all of which had refined their work (Paris, 8 April 1994). As for the argument that *Claustrophobia* was a gratuitous exercise in disgust, Dodin contended that the ability of young people to explore the devastations of their life was a sign of resilience and, therefore, of hope for the future (Nottingham, 22 May 1996).

5   Chekhov in an age of uncertainty

The Cherry Orchard was also part of the *Saison russe*, but escaped the vitriol poured by the *Moskovsky nablyudatel* on *Claustrophobia*. A short article in the journal ironised malevolently about Dodin's 'seriousness', but is itself so totally unserious as to warrant no further mention. The critics in France responded courteously, *Le Quotidien de Paris* alone in its exuberance (8 April 1994), while *Le Figaro* grumbled that this was a 'soulless' Chekhov, the last thing to be expected of a Russian company (7 April 1994). The British critics were enthusiastic, noting its brevity (two and a half hours without intermission), ensemble playing, 'Russian ease in large emotion' (*Financial Times*, 15 April 1994) and 'comic inflection that Chekhov so desired' (*The Guardian*, 16 April 1994). They generally felt that they were rediscovering Chekhov, the *Financial Times*, for example, declaring that 'this staging is less naturalistic than most British productions'. *The Independent* asserted that the production 'splendidly renewed your sense of the play's formal daring and perfection' (16 April 1994). *The Cherry Orchard* was met with equal praise in Amsterdam and Hamburg in 1995.

In view of the offensive taken by the *Moskovsky nablyudatel*, it is refreshing to note how relatively warmly the production was received by the Russian press, first in St Petersburg, where it was performed in the autumn of 1994, and then in Moscow one year later when the company took five productions to the capital, offering the whole gamut of its achievements, as had been done abroad. *Vecherny Peterburg* (12 October 1994) stressed how all the characters in this 'mature production' were bunglers (Firs's description of Yasha) who were putting an end to their illusions – a painful process not unlike, the reviewer implies, the experience of the majority of Russians in the present.

The feeling that *The Cherry Orchard* responded to the current situation was echoed later in the season by a thoughtful analysis in *Smena* (no. 28, February 1995) which pointed out how Ranyevskaya and Gayev's 'refugee' condition applied to every Russian, as did 'twenty-two misfortunes', Varya's epithet for Yepihkodov. The reviewers noticed approvingly, among several of Dodin's innovations, the principal role played by Firs (observed also by the French critics) and – something fundamentally lost on all critics outside Russia – the production's re-evaluation of Lopakhin. Soviet clichés had cast him as a vulgar merchant and the reviewers would have kept this in mind when they commented on the different kind of importance Dodin had attributed to him. In effect, Dodin had reconsidered Lopakhin in the light of the prevailing insecurities of the early 1990s and saw in him a man of moral, psychological and spiritual substance who, rather more adept than his friends in the struggle for existence, was nevertheless like them in his lovingness, vulnerabilities and desire to hold on to the mirage of plenitude. Furthermore, Dodin had taken note of Chekhov's remarks on how Lopakhin was central to the play (Benedetti, 1991: 171) and had placed him as near the centre as the equipoise of his construction and the Maly's ensemble ethos would allow.

Moscow critics were subsequently to have similar perceptions, most agreeing with *Nedelya* that the production was neither a triumph nor a failure but an 'inventive, very worthy show' (no. 30, 1995). The esteemed Moscow critic Natalya Krymova, in a favourable overview of the Moscow season for the Petersburg *Nevskoye vremya* (13 January 1996) was not quite sure about *The Cherry Orchard* and deferred to the Moscow Art Theatre expert Inna Solovyova who, well disposed towards Dodin's production, had remarked that it was 'dry' by design. This was so, according to Solovyova, because Dodin had kept in mind how tired the play had become from having been pulled apart over the years for new interpretations (*Nevskoye vremya*, as above). Solovyova might well have been thinking of how eager these new interpretations had been to avoid the ideological shadows cast on Chekhov since the 1930s.

Significantly, it was a Petersburg critic Nina Rabynyants who, in the next theatre season, and unlike her peers in respect of *Claustrophobia*, took the broader view by rejecting solely Russian criteria for assessing the production. Rabynyants put *The Cherry Orchard* in an international context by referring to the productions by Brook, Strehler and Efros to whose standards, she believed, Dodin's had measured up in Paris (*Nevskoye vremya*, 26 October 1994). Critics in Paris were quite scrupulous about avoiding comparisons, although many of them had reviewed these earlier masterpieces. Theatregoers certainly swapped notes on their memories of Strehler's white, airy *Cherry Orchard* at the Odéon in 1976, Brook's spare 1981 'carpet show', and the on-edge, 'Picasso' production brought by Efros to Paris in 1985 (Shevtsova, 1978: 43; 1983: 85–91; 1989: 294–5). Peter Stein's subtle 1992 Berlin production had also become a landmark in terms of which eager spectators oriented their reactions to Dodin (Stein was generally much admired in Paris). The importance of the terrain did not have to be articulated to be remembered, although Italian critics, when *The Cherry Orchard* was performed at the Nuovo Piccolo Teatro in Milan in 1998, could not refrain from alluding to Strehler's superb production. So iconic was it to them that they tended to stencil Strehler's work over Dodin's and draw the latter in ways more suitable for the former, even though they had recognised the difference between the two productions, including how Kochergin's dark design was the antithesis of Luciano Damiani's for Strehler.

Dodin was aware of these re-visions of Chekhov: Strehler's, which he had seen on video, probably being the closest to his sensuality and Brook's, which he had seen in Russia, to his sense of craft. However, factors intrinsic to his *oeuvre* rather than extrinsic ones connected with his admiration for other directors or, for that matter, with his distaste for hoary Soviet stereotypes, account for his approach to *The Cherry Orchard*. The production was prepared in parallel with *Claustrophobia* and *A Play With No Name* which, although held back so that the other two could move forward, was worked on sporadically during the same period. A number of the *Claustrophobia* actors rehearsed *The Cherry Orchard* – Nikiforova (Dunyasha), Tatyana Olear (Anya) and Kuryshev (Trofimov) – while, in reverse, several older actors rehearsed *A Play*, planned for the young ensemble. This cross-movement was a natural way of integrating the latter in the company. Furthermore, as became clear in hindsight, a trialogue had grown between the three productions around the theme of house and home, explored more than a decade ago in *The House*. Then, the guiding idea was that house and home had been neglected. Now, they were appropriated and/or razed to the ground. In *Claustrophobia* they are wilfully vandalised by the Ubiquists. In *The Cherry Orchard*, seemingly invisible hands, discernible only to the most vigilant spectators, gradually break away bits of the decor indicating a house until the spectators realise with a shock at the end that nothing but a skeleton remains. Besides which, Lopakhin had bought the lot.

In *A Play*, Anna Petrovna, Chekhov's prefiguration of Ranyevskaya, is about to be dispossessed and Dodin hears in her voice the leitmotif of impending homelessness that he believes runs through all of Chekhov's writings. It was only after this production had returned to Russia from Weimar in 1997 that Dodin strengthened the links he had made between Chekhov's first and last plays. Instead of ending the production with images of drowning, as had occurred in Weimar, which deflected attention away from the house motif, he closed it with a reference to dispossession in a flashback where the characters, now ghosts from the past, gather together in what was once a home.

The disembodied hands of Dodin's *Cherry Orchard* speak volumes about his interpretation. Not for him the 'plight of the dispossessed gentry' which had been the focus of concern at the Moscow Art Theatre, Ranyevskaya flanked by 'Lopakhin's practical materialism and Trofimov's idealistic reforms' (Senelick, 1997: 71). Dispossession, for Dodin, is not a matter of jostling class positions, but of uncontrollable circumstances whose invisible work is so merciless that Ranyevskaya, Gayev and their entire household bow down before them. The protagonists' personal weaknesses play their part: Ranyevskaya's devotion to her lover in Paris, which means her mind is where she is not; Gayev's inhibitions, which block his capacity to act (hence his awkward 'cupboard' speeches, their motivation in inhibition astutely perceived by Sergey Bekhterev); their lack of pragmatism and common sense; their infantilism, which Dodin brings to the fore, highlighting it against the infantilism of the remaining characters, Varya, Firs and Lopakhin excluded. But, regardless of personal responsibility, all individual agency is subordinated to powers of such might that they become impersonal, scattering cause and effect and blame. Dodin does not gentrify Ranyevskaya and Gayev. He aligns them with ordinary Soviet Russians who, having been dispossessed after 1917, have had to endure the 'shock therapy' applied in 1992 of price liberalisation and wholesale privatisation (Gill and Markwick, 2000: 139). This lurch into neoliberalism and its accompanying precariousness saw many Russians in search of homes once more, literally and figuratively. Once again, as in his work on novels, Dodin's strong sense of the present infiltrates his reading of this classic of Russian and world drama.

Looking back from the end of the twentieth century to its beginnings, Dodin appears to see nothing but uncertainty, and detects much the same sensation in Chekhov. The phrase 'age of uncertainty' is the landowner Glagolyev's for Platonov who, in his view, 'typifies' the age. Slowly, not always consciously, Dodin was to use it as a tuning fork for both *A Play* and *The Cherry Orchard*. However, the state of uncertainty, as he and his actors heard it, is internal as well as material and tied as much to people's sense of their lives as to the circumstances beyond their control. Its internal rhythms were played subtextually in *The Cherry Orchard* and only openly in *A Play*. They were to be central, albeit accented differently, in *The Seagull* in 2001.

Dodin's emphasis in *The Seagull* on group interaction in the face of personal uncertainties is different both from the traditional view that foregrounds the romantic triangle Nina–Trigorin–Treplev and such radical interpretations as Efros's 1966 *Seagull*. In the latter, Treplev was the sole protagonist and was identified as an authentic artist crucified by the harshness and hostility of all those around him. Conceived during the renewed repression of the Brezhnev years after the mitigated 'thaw' of the Khrushchev period, this Treplev was to be a reference for another interpretative landmark, the visually beautiful but mild-mannered version by Yefremov in 1980, involving the destruction of the artist by oppressive power. Dodin's cultural memory was awake enough to remember the effect of the productions by Efros and Yefremov (Efros's was banned after a short run) and the motive force behind them in the given political context. Nevertheless, repression had given way to a licence after 1991 that, like opened flood-gates, had swept everybody up, causing major upheavals in which the freedom of artists was no longer in question. Dodin's *Seagull* deflects the issue away from art and Treplev's concern with 'new forms' to one that might be termed 'life forms' or the 'How?' of living.

The Cherry Orchard: the loss of house and home

The set is a composite one suggesting a group of triptychs, icons, screens, windows and darkened mirrors in which, on occasion, are reflected the silhouettes of the characters flitting by. Branches of white blossom are attached to these shapes and are lit by small lamps from behind. A chandelier hangs in the centre. It is lowered during the transition from Act III to Act IV into a small oval pond which is a figurative tombstone for Ranyevskaya's drowned son. There is a seat beside the pond, and a small round table and two chairs opposite, a wash-basin to stage right, a cupboard hidden at stage left, and a secret alcove hidden in the central triptych. Exterior and interior – orchard, park, garden and room are caught in one. The front space is quite narrow, domestic and intimate; and the floor, because it dips further back in a bow-shape that lifts the left and right triptychs, makes movement up and down it a touch perilous, albeit useful for gathering speed. The crescendo of speed is important, for instance, in a scene constructed by Dodin to express Anya and Trofimov's burgeoning love: Varya chases Anya and Trofimov in the shadows while they hide from her and play hide and seek with each other, the secret alcove serving as a focal point for otherwise quite violent zigzag movement. The form of this arbour/edifice is rather majestic, its colouring sepulchral, its mood gentle.

Birdsong fills the theatre before Dunyasha comes in briskly with a candle, her tempo setting the production's pace. Dodin here nods to Chekhov, acknowledging his impossible request that Act IV should run for no more than 'twelve minutes *maximum*' (Benedetti, 1991: 189) and his legendary complaints about Stanislavsky's elaborate sound effects for his plays. The birdsong is simple, though bright and persistent. It posits the season and the time – spring and the small hours of the morning which, although on the cusp of the dawn, are still of the night: 'the train was two hours late' (Gayev) and 'we waited and waited' (Dunyasha). The song, moreover, declares that this nocturne, with its waiting – a metonymy for what is to come – is not meant to be a dirge. A similarly crystalline image of time and tone is to be had from the flowering branches, the prompt, once again, from the text: 'three degrees of frost this morning, but the cherry is all in bloom' (Yepikhodov), which recalls the day, by association and contrast, when Anya 'went away in Lent, when we still had snow' (Dunyasha).

Imperceptibly, as the hands of time and misfortune overwhelm the characters – no one is spared, not even the ostensibly victorious Lopakhin – the blossoms fall in petals of snow on the ground. They will be seen distinctly in Act IV in the emptied space, where the skeleton/scaffolding suggests that the house will be knocked down (Figure 11, overleaf). The cycle of seasons will have run its course towards winter, and the inhabitants of the house will leave for nebulous, precarious, or reluctant futures. Lopakhin and Pishchik are the only members of this group construed as an extended family whose future appears financially and psychologically secure. The actors show by their voices and gestures throughout the act that the question for their characters now is not how to survive together, but how to survive on their own, and this task will separate them forever. Even Lopakhin, whom Igor Ivanov plays as a resolute man – with the delicate feelings Trofimov supposes go with 'fine hands' – is not convinced he will see them 'next spring'. Ivanov repeats these, Lopakhin's last words, thoughtfully (not repeated in Chekhov) with doubt creeping into his voice.

And Dodin ignores Chekhov's last stage direction. There is no sound of axes chopping down the cherry trees, only silence before and after Firs (Yevgeny Lebedev), in a recall of the opening scene, enters with a candle and lies down on the seat to die. Lebedev varies his performance. Either he puts the candle on his chest in a sign of Russian orthodox funeral rites before it clatters to the floor, or he blows it out before he sets it down on the table. Whichever way he plays it, Lebedev holds Firs's stillness and silence long enough to leave the audience in

Figure 11 *The Cherry Orchard* at the Odéon-Théâtre de l'Europe, Paris, 1994. End of Act IV. Design by E. Kochergin.

Photograph by Marc Enguerand, courtesy of Marc Enguerand.

momentary uncertainty: Firs could have been asleep, waiting for a slower, more cruel end.

In that synergy typical of the Maly, the designer delivers the sense made by the director and the actors of the play's temporal and narrative sequences and how they relate to its characters and their actions. The spatial-visual details of Act I anticipate the dramatic resolution of Act IV. Or, put differently, Act IV is already contained in Act I, spatially-visually and in terms of action and argument. The events in between develop the story. The whole is sober – neither elegiac nor lyrical, despite Tatyana Shestakova's emotionalism for Ranyevskaya in Act I; nor rough, though Natalya Akimova (Varya) and Anzhelika Nevolina (Charlotta) blurt out their characters' anxieties in Act IV. Akimova's speechless, sudden fall to the ground, after Lopakhin fails to propose to Varya, is keen, like a knife in a bloodless wound. When it happens, it seems that lethal sobriety like this was just about everywhere below the surface, ready to strike.

'Now time'

With Firs dies the memory of a whole way of life, when people and orchards were productive, and cherries were dried, preserved and made into jam, while the surplus was sent away to make money. Lebedev, in a magisterial performance of Firs – slightly unsteady on his feet, muttering, devoted, dignified – gets plenty of mileage out of these lines on cherries in Act I, forecasting his reminiscences of 'forty or fifty years ago' in two exchanges in Act II, which are key to the production in so far as they focus its attitudes towards the past seen from the perspective of a bleak present. The first involves Firs recalling his rejection of 'the freedom', by which he means the liberation of the serfs in 1861. Ivanov's Lopakhin ironically replies that serfs were flogged in those 'good days'. The second is a laconic exchange between Firs and Gayev after the sound of the 'breaking string' from the sky which Dodin, taking Chekhov at his word, conveys literally as such from the back of the stage. Firs recalls a similar sound 'Before the misfortune' and, to Gayev's 'Which misfortune?' replies 'Before the freedom'.

In both dialogues, but the second in particular, Lebedev calculates his timing for maximum recognition of his meanings. Audiences, especially Russian audiences, seize them instantly for, behind Firs's words and through that 'bivocality' or double-voicedness, so powerfully conceptualised by Bakhtin (1981: 304–5; 326–7), is a critique of retrograde attitudes to the 'freedom' announced by the dissolution of the Soviet Union in December 1991. In other words, the dialogue has both a surface and a subtextual value and is updated by implication: Firs's implicit homily on serfdom has the ring of an implicit homily on communism, the latter having been denounced as another form of serfdom by liberals of all kinds in the wake of 1991. That the audience affirms the update and undermines Firs's speech – on the surface, innocent – is communicated by its laughter of recognition. By contrast, Firs's account of the estate's cherry industry is not undermined in the slightest, whether it is viewed from within the world of the production which, primarily through Lopakhin, endorses the value of such industry, or from the end of 1991, which foreshadows renewed faith in industriousness as a means of self-help and the return of private enterprise, whether accepted as part of 'shock therapy' or not, in a neoliberal Russia.

These updates position the production in relation to 'now time', but rely on spectators who can fill in from the inferences made by them. The same holds for Lopakhin, who has a touch of the New Russian businessman about him. However, Ivanov, instead of playing to type, focuses on the inner man who, regardless of his accountant's notebook, has a gift for sizing up people and situations with sensitivity, Ranyevskaya first among them. Lopakhin also has a poet's imagination for creating worlds, which is why Ivanov relishes his speeches on growing poppies, building dachas, and so on, and why an exasperated, down-to-earth Varya, who is cruelly exposed to his gaze, cannot appeal. Even Lopakhin's jubilation over his purchase of the cherry orchard is connected by Ivanov to his fancy – first the can-can, then a Russian dance, then embraces from Ranyevskaya and kisses for her – all of it free and easy, nothing greedy or vulgar, or merely practical or materialistic in the Moscow Art Theatre mould. Ivanov, when preparing the role, thought compassionately of how Lopakhin only had 14 years left (that is, from 1903, when Chekhov finished the play) before his entrepreneurial drive would be quashed and his wealth appropriated (Paris, 9 April 1994). This is the iceberg below the tip of his performance, the invisible source of the affection that infuses it and makes the production a little less 'dry'.

Trofimov, too, is shaped affectionately, and is anything but a mouthpiece of 'idealistic reforms' or revolutionary fervour, whether caricatured or endorsed, the second alternative having shaped the Moscow Art Theatre tradition. He is the decent boy next door whose occasional over-earnest and naïve commentaries need to be dealt with sensibly. Witness how Shestakova slaps down Kuryshev's drivel about being 'above love', her tone of voice implying that she could well be wiping Trofimov's nose. But he has backbone and will work for himself and others regardless of his stated cause because he is a good person. You could trust him with your daughter, says Kuryshev's performance, which is why Ranyevskaya accepts him for Anya.

By underplaying the social aspects of character for the idea that these are all 'good people' for whom things went wrong, Dodin appears to shift the emphasis from historicity (and thus the sociohistorical circumstances of behaviour) to notions of time and life as transcendentals, as 'Time' and 'Life'. This is suggested in the ball scene of Act III, where a chain dance weaves in and out of the corridor mirrors, now reminiscent of a maze, and runs through the entire act. Most of the characters, together with newcomers who play the guests, dance in this chain that breaks into waltzing couples before it links up again and continues its motion. Early on, Charlotta plays one of her magic tricks by sweeping in and out dressed as a gigantic witch. (She is on the shoulders of an actor who is hidden beneath her skirts.) The chain and the music stop only near the end of Lopakhin's speech on how he bought the orchard. Dodin here changes the order of Chekhov's lines to show Lopakhin in command: Lopakhin orders the orchestra to play again *after* it had stopped, not during its tuning up, as occurs in Chekhov. Once the dramatic turning point has been marked, the dance changes from a graceful one danced on tip-toe to a noisy dance with knees lifted and toes flexed. Time and again during the last rehearsals in Paris, Dodin urged the actors to 'let the chain flow, the dance flow, quietly, quietly, quietly on your toes, let it flow, let it flow, like life, like life flowing away'. It would be difficult, given how this idea underlies Dodin's direction, not to see the qualitative change for the worse in the dance as an indication of a qualitative change in the life of all the characters in the future. Yasha's plea to Ranyevskaya to take him away with her to Paris, while Pishchik asks her for a waltz, seems all too incongruous in this ebbing away of life (Figure 12, overleaf).

But here is the nub of the tension in the production which, in its early performances, I took to be its unsettled and 'unresolved air' (Shevtsova, 1997b: 317). It is implied, notably through Ranyevskaya and Gayev, that life runs its own course and nothing much will change it. Hence these characters' lack of agency. Viewed from this angle, the invisible hands destroying the house are the hands of Life-Time itself. By the same token, enough undertones and overtones arise, from which it may be inferred that these invisible hands are the hands of history. In which case, they are also the concrete hands of 1917 and beyond. The third line of vision involves the way forward, which lies with Lopakhin, Trofimov and Anya who are agents of action capable of determining their own destinies. Yet their departure is brusque, with nothing joyous about it. All of these strands are open, not quite connected, and carry several views through the production which its sobriety tends to obfuscate.

Farce with a revolver

Dodin leaves room in this productive irresolution for comedy and, mindful of Chekhov's description of his play as a farce, creates unadulterated farce in Act II. His purpose is facilitated by reverting to Chekhov's original text instead of using the one Chekhov had adjusted for Stanislavsky, which is the canonical *Cherry Orchard* that we know today. Stanislavsky, with Chekhov's agreement, had transferred Charlotta's 'autobiographical monologue to the top of the act' from the end so that he could conclude Act II with a tender scene between Trofimov and Anya (Senelick, 1997: 70). His reshuffle entailed deleting the exchange between Charlotta and Firs that followed her monologue. Dodin, by bringing Charlotta back to her original position at the conclusion of the act, is able to end it on a strong note and dovetail her solitude and lack of identity and belonging – the subject of her monologue – into his theme of dispossession. This repositioning also allows him to construct a strong whimsical-farcical scene in keeping with the tenor of the act as a whole.

Dodin had already allowed more space than is usual for Charlotta's conjuring in Act I, which, besides Chekhov's card tricks, feature a trick with a burning candle and another with a dove. His additions to Act II strengthen the weight

Figure 12 *The Cherry Orchard* at the Odéon-Théâtre de l'Europe, Paris, 1994. Act III,

l. to r.: N. Pavlov, Y. Lebedev, T. Shestakova, N. Lavrov.

Photograph by Marc Enguerand, courtesy of Marc Enguerand.

he gives Charlotta's role. She 'magically' extracts a cucumber from her pocket and eats it while talking with Firs. She pulls a handkerchief out from somewhere on Firs's body which she attaches to her glasses and wears on her nose, looking as if she has put on a gas mask. She talks on, while Firs – deaf – mutters at cross purposes. Apart from the comic bonus to be had from ending the act with Charlotta, Dodin is able to get a structural one out of it as well. For her last trick, Charlotta fires her hunting rifle into the air. Confetti cascades from it, and music and dancing begin. Dodin's cantilena principle goes into action as the ball scene flows in.

There are additional benefits from Dodin's return to Chekhov's original intentions. By moving Charlotta back to the end of Act II, he is able to begin it with Yepikhodov (Arkady Koval) singing and playing a guitar. Yepikhodov's music starts in the shadows and continues when he and Dunyasha are on the seat side by side. Dodin makes some minor cuts to Chekhov's dialogue so as to make this scene a cameo of flirtation in a pure French-farce style. Equally, he removes Charlotta from this scene and her lines ('These people sing horribly . . . phew! They're like jackals') are uttered by Yasha (Nikolay Pavlov) who is half-hidden in the central alley, as if spying on the lovers to make his moves. Dunyasha, on the pretext that she is cold (her line interpreted differently from the norm), sends Yepikhodov off for her shawl so that she and Yasha can kiss hotly. They stop hurriedly as Yepikhodov returns, his shoes squeaking as they had done in Act I, to the audience's delight.

Once they are prepared, Dodin does not stint on all these ingredients of a farce. Yepikhodov pulls out his revolver with a flourish and trips against the edge of the pond. The revolver flies into the water. Yepikhodov dives into it head first. His legs are perpendicular for a while before he comes up, holding an old iron in his hand. Taking a deep breath, he dives back in, which actions he repeats once more before he comes back up, waving his revolver in the air. Every time he is under the water – spectators only see his perpendicular legs – Dunyasha and Yasha kiss away. They pull apart as Yepikhodov comes up, and repeat their scenario as he repeats his. Wet clothes, dripping water, squeaky shoes, and his song sung without his guitar, but which Yepikhodov waves about (his revolver is now tucked into his pants), close a brilliant piece performed by all three with brio.

Spectators cannot be expected to register Dodin's textual reconstructions for the purposes of his production. None of the usual paratheatrical channels – programme notes, press releases, interviews – inform them of what lies below the visible tip of the work on the stage. It is not certain whether *The Independent* critic was aware that Dodin had bypassed the canonical playtext and that his renewed sense of 'the play's formal daring and perfection' was, in fact, based on a recovered play. Nevertheless, Dodin's adventurous staging would have been enough to persuade spectators that they had found something they had not realised before.

The 'life of the production'

My analysis is of *The Cherry Orchard* in its Parisian and mid-1990s Russian seasons, and several remarks on later performances will suggest the course the 'life of the production' had taken. By the end of the 1990s, the production had matured with its time, not always well. Its farcical elements were firm, but the unresolved tension that had hung over it, leaving it suspended on an interesting question mark, had given way to something more clear-cut. Nowhere is this more evident than in the Ranyevskaya–Lopakhin relationship, where a voluble, fraught, defensive and self-justifying character not there in 1994 is played by Shestakova to Ivanov's frustrated and angry Lopakhin. Is it that the actors had become irritated with their characters and partners? Was Ivanov, for instance, impatient with Ranyevskaya's procrastinations in the face of a chance to save her future? After all, she could have financed her life in Paris with the sale of the orchard. Was Shestakova bent on excusing Ranyevskaya for failing to be a free agent, an individual who acts? (Shestakova is quite vehement on Ranyevskaya's 'What can I do?' about her lover.) Had both actors – with Dodin – become dissatisfied with the idea that circumstances were like a 'broken string', whether of Life or the Revolution – a bolt from the blue that could not be controlled? Did they think, instead, that house and home were a matter of personal responsibility, in the manner of Ivanov's Lopakhin, and that *taking* responsibility was a way of combating uncertainty? Further, did they think that his species had not become extinct in 1917, but could be regenerated in themselves – indeed, in all citizens, which Russians had at last become even if the communist legacy and the country's sustained economic depression still made Russia a 'weak civil society' (McFaul, 2001: 320)? I would hazard a guess that the answer is 'Yes' to all these questions.

It was established in the second chapter that a Maly production's maturation is in symbiosis with the actors' development as human beings. How rapidly changing social developments in the late 1990s shaped the actors' work in the production can only be a complex issue, involving individual psychologies that are well beyond the capacity of this research. On a directly observable social level, a knot of national traumas before and after August 1991 had been internalised by most people in their individual way, and the financial crash of August 1998 might well have seemed like the last straw. It may not be possible to offer more than generalities about how exasperation with the government and the fresh quotidian anxieties brought by that crash affected, say, Ivanov's increasingly angry, even strident Lopakhin who wants solutions to be found and Ranyevskaya to act. Current preoccupations, while bound to be in the human being who is the actor, do not necessarily translate into the semiotics of the production. What is semiotically embodied in its 'life' after 1998 is a more tendentious *Cherry Orchard*, perhaps in reaction to the cumulative stresses leading to the economic breakdown in August that year. The desire to end uncertainty, with Lopakhin's pivotal role more evident than before, possibly also explains why the momentum of the chain dance, that symbolic dance of life of 1994, had dropped, drawing the eye to the prosaic representation of people just dancing at the back of the triptychs.

A Play With No Name: drowning or adrift

This play was found, without a title page, after Chekhov's death and was not published until 1923 when it appeared as *Platonov*, after its main character. It is Chekhov's first surviving play – possibly completed by 1881, when he was 21 – and as long as *Uncle Vanya*, *The Three Sisters* and *The Cherry Orchard* put together. A 'monstrous melodrama' (Rayfield, 1997: 80), it 'least accords with any conceivable stereotype of Chekhov's work' (Hingley, 1992: xi), but contains all of the themes of his major plays. Dodin believes that Chekhov crammed his already considerable life experiences into it and, despite its extravagances, showed a surprisingly mature understanding of people. The work was already that of a doctor who could not pretend that a cancer was a blister, its objectivity foreshadowing the severe world view of his last plays (Weimar, 9 July 1997). Dodin went so far as to claim, when *A Play* was performed at the International Chekhov Festival in Moscow, that it was one of the most penetrating works of world drama, concerned with the eternal, tragic rift between people's ideals and their fate (*Kommersant*, 6 May 1998). He was not prepared to give it a name because, like life, it could not have one.

For all its oddities, the play has had a distinguished production history, which includes its first appearance in English in 1940 as *Fireworks on the James* at the Provincetown Playhouse. It was billed in New York in 1975 as *A Country Scandal*. Its first British production was as *Don Juan (in the Russian Manner)* in 1959 at the Nottingham Playhouse. In 1960, George Devine and John Blatchley directed it as *Platonov* at the Royal Court, with Rex Harrison in the title role. It was performed at the National Theatre in 1984 in the free adaptation *Wild Honey* by Michael Frayn, and in 1990 as *Piano* by Trevor Griffiths. Griffiths was inspired by Nikita Mikhalkov's 1976 film *Unfinished Piece for Mechanical Piano*, which is a montage of the play and of several short stories by Chekhov.

Jean Vilar revised the play for the 1956 Théâtre National Populaire production, *Ce Fou de Platonov*, and performed the leading part. His undertaking prompted its discovery in Britain and continental Europe, Russia included, where it was performed in Pskov in 1957 as *Platonov*. Giorgio Strehler directed it in 1958 as *Platonov e gli altri*, which lasted until two o'clock in the morning to great acclaim. Otomar Krejča staged it in 1974, Chéreau in 1987. Other productions in eastern Europe include two in Moscow, the 1991 *Without Patrimony* and the 1993 *Platonov*, when Dodin was already at work on *A Play With No Name*, and a St Petersburg *Platonov* in 1996. Several, besides Dodin's, including one from Poland, were at the 1998 Chekhov Festival. More recent productions in western Europe include Paris and David Hare's adaptation as *Platonov* in London in 2001.

Chekhov's text condensed

An outline of the plot of this unfamiliar work is necessary to appreciate the diamond production Dodin cut out of Chekhov's rough material. Everything happens at the country estate, in a hot southern province of Russia, of Anna Petrovna, a young widow with whom Platonov, an impoverished landowner turned schoolmaster, has been having an affair unbeknown to his wife Sasha. He meets up again with his old love Sofya, who has married Sergey, Anna's stepson. When Sofya knew him as a student, she imagined him to be a Byronic hero who would fight for just causes, but realises how little he has done with his life. Maria Grekova, a scientist, who first hates and then loves Platonov, appears on the scene. She is the butt of Platonov's sexist jokes, among them his jibe that she extracts 'ether out of fleas'. Platonov, who is aimless, feckless and frustrated, strings these four women along, but without any real sign of will-power in his philandering.

Anna Petrovna is deeply in debt to several local landowners and financial dealers. Among them are Vengerovich and his son Isak, and Glagolyev, who courts Anna and through whom she hopes to save her estate. A fireworks scene on the river is a turning point in the sequence of events. Platonov, whom Sofya has more or less persuaded to run away with her, has an assignation with Anna on the night of their flight. Meanwhile, Sasha, who discovers Platonov's infidelities, attempts suicide twice, once by throwing herself under a train, and the second time by swallowing matches. She is saved the first time by Osip, a horse thief who, together with Vengerovich and Isak, plots to murder Platonov, and on the second occasion by Triletsky, her brother, who is a doctor and attracted to Grekova. To cut it short: Osip is lynched by peasants; Glagolyev forces Platonov to admit his affair with Anna, and leaves for Paris in despair with his dissolute son Cyril; Anna loses her estate; Grekova, who brings a charge of assault against Platonov, drops her case at the last minute; Platonov contemplates shooting himself; Sofya, who discovers at the end that Platonov will not, in fact, run away with her, shoots him dead. There are 20 characters, all but three of whose speeches are long, though in the everyday language characteristic of Chekhov.

Dodin cut out nine characters and the subplots dependent upon them, and, after countless *études* and *proby*, turned in a production of four hours with a short interval. Thus, he cut Isak and the murder subplot around him, which involves scenes where Platonov humiliates him with anti-Semitic and otherwise belligerent talk. Similarly, he cut the Triletskys, Sasha's father and brother, who in Chekhov dance attendance on Anna and complicate the Anna–Platonov plot. Sasha's brother is doubly irrelevant because Dodin dispenses with Sasha's attempted suicides. Dodin also deletes superfluous landowners so as to concentrate on Glagolyev's relations with Anna. This has the additional advantage of throwing Anna's relations with Platonov into relief. Anna and Platonov, then, are a clearly defined couple, set off by a series of permutations and combinations of couples that provides the production with its relatively compact structure: Platonov and Sofya, Sofya and Sergey, Platonov and Sergey, and so on. The nine characters cut by Dodin are replaced by nine who play servants and conveniently function as stage-hands. They speak relatively little or not at all, their principal role being musicians of a jazz band that plays right through the performance, the actors' musical training here shining brilliantly.

Nevskoye vremya asserted that Dodin used the band like a chorus in relation to the protagonist of a Greek tragedy and, in doing so, had realised Meyerhold's dream of recovering a model destroyed by Chekhov's drama in which there no longer existed a dramatic centre (21 January 1998). The observation is perspicacious in that it picks up a new feature of Dodin's work – pride of place accorded to one character. What must be added, however, is that Dodin does not allow the performance of a central character to overshadow concurrent performances. In other words, structural centrality is not presumed to replace actorly centrality, that is, the primary importance of play by all, which gives ensemble playing. The jazz band is the perfect instrument to render Dodin's thought concretely. Whether it serves the purpose of a chorus is a moot point, but it is indubitably an element of the stylisation loved by Meyerhold and which combines with Dodin's Stanislavskian focus on character and acting, the two historical mainstreams of Russian theatre fusing in this work.

Dodin's pruning concentrates the production's themes: aspiration, hope, the loss of hope and disillusion, which are exemplified by all the characters, especially by Platonov; homelessness (Anna Petrovna, and Sasha and her child after Platonov's death); fatherlessness (Platonov orphaned by drunken parents, his child with Sasha abandoned by him); spiritual destitution (Platonov, Sofya); abandonment (all the women); exile (Glagolyev); shattered subjectivities and identities (all, but condensed in Platonov). Uncertainty is the core theme because this state is endemic to all the others. Uncertainty is also the temper of the times when the term 'age' is accentuated in Glagolyev's 'our modern *age* of uncertainty', which Dodin, following Glagolyev, takes Platonov to typify. The fact that Platonov *typifies* ensures his structural and thematic centrality.

What he typifies is transmitted through water and jazz. Water is Dodin's trope for life and its wash and waste, and for the characters' floundering in it, some staying adrift, some barely hanging on. Platonov as good as drowns in it. Associations with the river Styx are there to be made, and the big-band sounds of 'Down by the Riverside', which the actors play approximately half-way through the performance, add to these associations even as they jest about the setting, since the water represents a river on Anna Petrovna's estate. Jazz, a modern genre, is Dodin's trope for the 'modern age' interpreted to refer not to the time when Chekhov allegedly wrote his play, but to the twentieth century.

Water – with nowhere to go

There are four spaces for performance: the ground, which is covered in sand; two wooden platforms, one above the other, whose stairs and banisters on the first floor suggest a bath-house or dacha; a mass of water slightly below ground level in which are immersed the supports of the building that also suggest a pier. The water is a performance space going *in depth* in that actors continually emerge from it, talk or play instruments in it, or dive under it. Its importance is made clear from the opening scene when Anna (Shestakova) swims in the water and talks with Platonov (Kuryshev), who sits on the sand elegantly dressed in white. He moves a figure on the chess-board by the water, as if continuing a game he had begun last summer. Almost all the characters are in the water at some point, or are in and out of it most of the time, as happens for Anna, Sofya (Irina Tychinina) and Sergey (Oleg Dmitriyev). Sofya and Sergey lovingly swim around in it, or are parted by it when they plunge into it out of anxiety or pain. Sasha throws herself spectacularly into it in despair from the rail on the first floor of the construction; and her tragedy is comic. Grekova (Natalya Kromina) does a whimsical flip into the water after one of Platonov's insults – a loopy gesture from a character played eccentrically throughout. Water also features at the top level where, already estranged, Sofya and Sergey stand naked under showers. Other characters wash here as well, but to suggest the heat of the summer and the south. All of these washing events are theatrical inventions, none featuring in Chekhov's text.

But it is Platonov who is an amphibious creature, more in the water than out of it. He strips before diving, or suddenly dives into it fully clothed – 'bizarre' actions done quickly to suggest they are motivated by stresses from within. Water, especially in the second half of the performance, is his refuge, the only place to go when he has nowhere to go, an emblem of his alienation from others and himself. He sinks more and more into the water, delivering some of his most savage and desperate lines from it, all of which is brutally undercut when Sergey, who jokes about his wife sending him off to fish, lifts Platonov out of the water. Platonov, the 'fish' caught, is ensnared in a huge net (Figure 13). This powerful image of helplessness has its correlations in scenes that follow where Platonov, half-naked, slips and slides down the stairs near the pier, or is immersed in the water, his whole body, his face and eyes in particular, suggesting exhaustion. When Sofya shoots Platonov, his long, half-naked body sprawls along the stairs face downwards, his head touching the water, his arms lifeless – indeed, a fish beached, or a man who has drowned. The feeling of emptiness engulfing the stage is relieved when rain falls.

The production's closing cruel image emphasises one individual's fate whereas so many more had been implicated in it. Dodin felt that Platonov's sprawling body did not 'look right' from both a thematic and a compositional point of view (St Petersburg, 24 September 1998). On his return to St Petersburg, he found a solution to the problem he had perceived in Weimar in an incipiently sentimental image of harmony, of family and friends around a table behind the curtain of rain. This image reappears in different configurations between black-outs, like photographs flashing by, or cinematographic shots. The effect is that of an afterimage, when you realise that the cumulative images presented with Chekhovian objectivity had, in fact, added up to a tragedy. Dodin brought this revised version to the Barbican in London where *The Guardian*'s Michael Billington

Figure 13 *A Play With No Name* at the E-Werke, Weimar, 1997. O. Dmitri-yev and S. Kuryshev.

Photograph by Ken Reynolds, courtesy of Ken Reynolds.

remarked that 'this breathtaking production . . . discovers in Chekhov's earliest play unmistakable intimations of the febrile uncertainty and spiritual angst that afflicts Russia today' (11 June 1999). Dodin believes that Russia manages to magnify to the extreme the afflictions of the contemporary world (Weimar, 9 July 1997).

Jazz – with multiple voices

The witty paradox of this production is that it does not sound like a tragedy. It begins with jazz in water and Sidney Bechet's 'Bonjour Paris', which also ends the first part but leaves the music suspended mid-phrase (indicating interrupted business). Bechet's piece begins the second part and ends the show, thereby writing its signature on the production. In each instance, Platonov-Kuryshev and Sergey-Dmitriyev double as jazz players. They are up to their chests in the water, the first on trumpet, the second on clarinet, while the whole band, arranged on the different levels, is in full swing (Figure 14). Arresting visual and sonic effects like these are to be had throughout. For example, when the band plays 'Cherry Pink and Apple Blossom White', Kuryshev joins in unexpectedly, playing his trumpet while he swims around. At another moment Tychinina-Sofya joins a brass trio leading 'Love's Last Word is Spoken'. She runs out of the water as Sofya, reappears at the top deck as if she were still Sofya and then suddenly goes out of character when she puts a trumpet to her lips and plays the song. At this point the crooning tune turns sharply into satire because the image to which it is played is Platonov caught in a net.

Swing picks up the blues, Gerry Mulligan, Scott Joplin and the cool jazz of Dave Brubeck as well as pieces like 'Brazil' and Piazzolla's 'Libertango'. There is also a variety of classical music serving various purposes. Mendelssohn's 'Wedding March' is a prelude to a dinner scene on the sand where a toast is called for Sofya and Sergey. (The scene is prepared with a touch of whimsy as the musician-waiters, who have set up trestle tables and covered them with white cloth, go around on each other's heels, each one putting out one utensil – spoon, knife, fork – or whichever plate or dish had been assigned him.) Grekova-Kromina, who is insulted by Platonov, articulates her internal agitation through a quirky waltz by Shostakovich, which she bashes out on a piano standing beside the showers at the top level. Sasha plays a violin instead of speaking her emotions, while in a simultaneous scene below her Platonov makes love to Sofya on the sand. Elsewhere Sasha sings a phrase of the blues in a gravelly voice when she ushers her husband in off the veranda – a comic moment to show she is aware that Anna Petrovna is outside, waiting in the night for him. Glagolyev and Anna Petrovna sing and play a duet from *La Traviata* on the piano and use their parody bivocally to give the scene at least two meanings. One concerns Glagolyev's relationship with Anna: he loves her, but she merely flirts with him. The other is a mocking aside about this relationship: the audience knows, as Glagolyev does not, that Anna is misleading him.

Figure 14 *A Play With No Name* at the E-Werke, Weimar, 1997.

Photograph by Ken Reynolds.

Music, as is evident from these examples, replaces words, behaves like language, and contributes in all kinds of other ways to the production's heteroglossia. Besides jazz and opera, it involves cabaret and folk songs, which are sung, intoned or hummed; also Russian Romances, which are sung softly in chorus. Musical genres clash. Sometimes a merger is made out of the contradictions, as happens when a particularly soulful Romance by Glinka blends in with Joplin's 'Ragtime', the two played for a while together. The musical intelligence of the Maly's teachers is especially admirable in these moments of polyphonic 'cacophony', in Bakhtin's sense of 'cacophony', where the 'voice' of music holds its own against the production's other 'voices', that is, its dialogue, dance and spatial and visual dynamics.

This multi-voicedness is seen to greatest advantage in a fireworks scene which Dodin embellishes more than seems possible from Chekhov's text. An explosion of fireworks sets off a carousel of lights that turns madly to 'Brazil'. Meanwhile, all the actors follow their own track. Everybody, male and female, plays an instrument of some sort – brass, string or percussion. Some pass rapidly from one instrument to another. Everybody dances something at some time during this stretch – waltz, Charleston, tango, samba, bee-bop, twist – or marks it out elliptically by arm and hand movements. Osip (Igor Chernevich) juggles torches of cascading light as he imitates a tight-rope walker on the veranda rail above the water and – an old circus trick – careers over it pretending he might fall in. Sergey, who is wildly dancing, has a similarly dangerous torch strapped to his chest, which shoots out, releasing fireworks and sexual innuendoes in one blow. This is a spectacular coda to an extended party syncopating the production's philosophical themes.

The heteroglossia of the production permits intertextuality within it so that one genre, say *La Traviata* (by which Glagolyev and Anna Petrovna play out their own operatic love story), changes the way another genre is heard, say the Dixieland jazz preceding it. Most striking of all, however, is the way Dodin overlays the musical collage and the dialogue, the one always imbricated in the other so that not only do music and speech play simultaneously, but speech rises above the music and is clearly heard without being shrieked or yelled. As we saw, Dodin rehearsed dialogue to music at full blast, precisely with this goal in mind. The whole is an extraordinary feat. Its complex weave of different dialogues – music and different actions happening all at once – allows spectators to pick and choose what they will listen to and watch. It has a filmic quality about it except that, instead of a roving camera selecting pieces for you, your eyes and ears take in the whole while they choose a part for central focus. A similar process of multi-focality occurs in William Forsythe's choreography, whose pertinence for Dodin's work we have already noted; that of Merce Cunningham might now also be cited as relevant. Yet the point of the comparison is to indicate that Dodin's is a rather more complex process because it is multi-focal *and* multi-vocal and, as such, supersedes the achievements of dance while, at the same time, contributing something of great potential to the theatre. Sadly, he has not taken this venture any further at the Maly to date.

With *A Play*, Dodin honours both his performers and several creators who have marked him, notably Federico Fellini, Pina Bausch and Peter Brook. The production's eccentric, exhibitionistic and surrealistic strokes – for example, Platonov playing his trumpet in the water – recall *La Dolce Vita*, as do its themes, regardless of their source in Chekhov. Platonov is arguably a Marcello figure, a figure adrift who, like Marcello, no more belongs to the *dolce vita* than to anywhere else. Anna Petrovna in top hat and tails for her party also recalls Fellini. Pina Bausch pays tribute to Fellini in *Tanzabend 2*, which Dodin had seen in Paris in 1994. Her subversion of established steps and gender roles specifically with reference to Fellini is evident in *A Play*. Brook's *Mahabharata* is honoured by 'intertextual' citation in the candles that float on the water towards the end of the fireworks scene. Dodin also 'ghosts' Fellini, Bausch and Brook in *A Play* because their work confirms in various ways that the 'age of uncertainty' diagnosed by Chekhov a century ago had set in.

The Seagull: love in solitude

Water is Dodin's chosen element for *The Seagull*; the play's lake has emblematic value for the production in much the same way, and with similar implications, as the river does in *A Play*. Furthermore, for Dodin, this is the lake where all the estates in Chekhov's writings could well have been set, and where his characters' lives slip away through their fingers; Chekhov's term 'comedy' for his play is nothing but an expression of fear that he might be thought a melancholic because of his tuberculosis; what is comic in it is our smile of recognition at ourselves (Palermo, 7 October 2001). Poray-Koshits's design is, duly, a variation of the one he had constructed for *A Play*, but here the water is enclosed or not at will by a metallic grid covered in green grass that rises from below the water to give a lawn. The stage-length platform behind the water holds a cupola whose frame and incomplete walls suggest a decaying gazebo in front of which Nina (Kseniya Rappoport) performs Konstantin Treplev's play (Aleksandr Zavyalov). This shell also suggests Treplev's abandoned theatre, to whose strange appearance reference is made in Act IV, as well as his room in the same act when Zavyalov attaches pages of Treplev's manuscript to it to indicate his character's growing activity as a writer.

The makeshift, booth-like stage on which Nina performs is in the cupola, its presence marked below in an oddly displaced way by a row of stiffly starched white sheets pegged to a line. The grass ramp goes down so that the lake separates Nina from her spectators. She delivers Treplev's long monologue with her head protruding through a hole in a diamond-shaped white curtain, brightly lit from behind. Her white painted face and dark curly hair, which is teased out like the head of a Gorgon, evoke symbolist art – perhaps a painting by Vrubel or a scene from Meyerhold's production of *The Fairground Booth*. Over and above its visual impact, the image makes sense both of Arkadina's term 'decadent' for her son's work and his own 'new forms', and, at the same time, situates their words in the debate on modernist aesthetics at the turn of the century.

The whole is an ascetic space with few objects besides the pages on Treplev's walls or the papers he sticks by way of arranging seating on the benches facing his stage at the beginning of Act I. The actors sit on them for the play within the play with their backs to the audience – a reference to Stanislavsky's founding production for the Moscow Art Theatre, as noted by critics when *The Seagull* was given its world premiere at the Theatre Olympics in Moscow in June 2001. And the benches have several other uses, notably as a bed for the sick Sorin in Act IV. The most important objects, however, are bicycles which, if not featured in Chekhov's play or usual in productions of it, were not unusual, Dodin claimed, in Chekhov's time (St Petersburg, 25 April 2001). The characters, notably Nina, Trigorin and Masha, ride these bicycles around the ramps of the stage as if, in fact, they were riding around the lake. Nina, who always comes to the estate on a bicycle (which replaces Chekhov's horse), holds on to it in her dialogue with Treplev in Act IV. Trigorin goes fishing on a bicycle and a bicycle features in a good deal of his dialogue with Nina. Shamrayev, when he refuses Arkadina horses in Act II, creates humour by speaking of horses while dumping a bicycle in high dudgeon onto Sorin, who is sitting on the grass. Elsewhere, in an image that could well be associated with the characters' entanglements, bicycles are piled up in a heap, their wheels turning. For all their scenic novelty, they have great thematic significance, as will be clear shortly.

The production's soundscape is the antithesis of the flamboyant music of *A Play*. It is composed of rustles, shivers and tinkles most of which are produced by the actors when they pass by and run their fingers through the various wind chimes attached to the cupola. On occasion, actors lightly drum their fingers on the wooden shell or the shelf running to both sides from it, as occurs when Arkadina (Shestakova) counteracts Trigorin's plea to be released from her in Act III. Whatever the occasion may be, the actors write the percussive score as they go, improvising differently in different performances. The sound of pegs being pulled off the line or falling to the ground is also written into the score, as is the crackle of starched sheets, none of it sounding more intensely than when Arkadina wrenches the sheets off the line in panic in Act III to wrap around Sorin, who has a sudden dizzy spell. There was talk during rehearsals in St Petersburg of a harpsichord being placed in the left corner of the space above the water to be played for percussive effect as well. Eventually Dodin dropped the idea, preferring to experiment with objects as sound-making instruments.

Song was also reduced to a minimum. The actors had rehearsed a waltz-song about a seagull by a minor nineteenth-century composer V. Grodsky, which was allegedly one of Chekhov's favourite pieces. Dodin had unearthed it in a music archive and, at the end of April 2001, virtually on the eve of the production's Moscow opening, was still planning to use it quite significantly, intoned by the actors. By the time the production was ready to be shown, he had taken the barest fragments from it which were half hummed so as to be as unobtrusive as possible in a score built on the slightest of sounds. By contrast with *A Play*, this music, like this production as a whole, was intended to be simple, natural and untheatrical – like life, Dodin observed in rehearsals, running its normal course.

Hope without hope

For all the effectiveness of Nina's appearance and speech, the production does not give dialogue about art and the theatre any particular attention. What takes precedence are the emotions underlying the dialogue, which have little to do with either; and this is the production's most radical departure from established *Seagulls*. When Treplev downgrades Arkadina's 'routine' theatre in Act III, the argument that ensues between them calls into play a whole host of feelings, among them Arkadina's fear of losing Trigorin, Treplev's of losing Nina, Arkadina's sense of guilt towards her son and his longing to recreate the intimacy he had with her as a child. Dodin commented more than once in rehearsals that Treplev recalled the ballerinas with whom he and his mother had had tea, not because he remembered the ballerinas, but because he still savoured the times when he could be close to her. In other words, Dodin was finding ways to inspire the actors trying the role to look beyond the text into the heart of their character and find there Treplev's hunger for love – love for his mother, uncle, Nina, all of it intermeshed. Accordingly, Dodin instructed them to tone down their effusiveness. Treplev, in his view, was not driven to emote since he knew his feelings and thoughts well, and they simply kept recurring as familiar preoccupations. Hence his suggestion, for the encounter between Treplev and Nina in Act IV, that Treplev be focused inwardly on his love for her and not outwardly in response to her words.

Similarly, Dodin suggested that the issues concerning writing and public success inherent in the dialogues between Treplev and Arkadina, Nina and Trigorin and Sorin and Arkadina were of secondary importance by comparison with the great pool of love at stake between them all. They were, then, to be noted simply, unstressed rather than highlighted, even though Treplev's self-love as a new writer 'sucked him like a snake' in Act I, regardless of the fact that he was a 'manly kind of person' (St Petersburg, 24 April 2001). Similarly, Nina's talk of the theatre in Act IV and questions as to whether she was a good or bad actress were taken to be peripheral to the central issue of unrequited love – Nina's for Trigorin, and Treplev's for her. However, Dodin wanted this suffering to be muted. Consequently, in rehearsals, he trimmed away the expressiveness of the two women playing Nina, controlling her closing speeches, which he never saw as monologues but as continuous conversations that Nina had had with Trigorin, and with herself, and was now having with Treplev. Dodin:

> We don't know whether Nina will make it in the theatre, but we do know that she has been going around this lake for some days, crying and giving vent to her pain. She has gone through her emotions, and does not need to let them all out now, as if for the first time.
>
> (25 April 2001)

Nina's scene with Treplev was conceived as a continuation of those invisible scenes around the lake and was consistently performed with the momentum of such. Dodin was adamant, above all, that it should not be performed as a mad scene, with Nina as a kind of Ophelia, as happened frequently on the Russian stage (Palermo, 7 October 2001). Nor should Nina be fused in any way with the seagull that Treplev had killed, which, in his view, was a weakness of productions that saw Nina's lines as delirious ('I am a seagull . . . No, that's not it. I am an actress'). There was no such character as 'the seagull' and, if the bird signified anything, then it symbolised the hope in which all the characters lived (Palermo, 6 October 2001). In performances of the production's western European premiere in Palermo, Rappaport, accordingly, performed Nina's concluding speeches virtually monotonously, giving her voice a business-like, determined tone – this Nina *was* going to succeed – that occasionally sounded mechanical and a touch self-consciously flat, in a postmodernist fashion. Zavyalov rose to the challenge by discreetly suggesting that his character, who had lived in uncertainty as to whether Nina would renounce her love for Trigorin and return, now knew that he lived completely without hope. His slow, deliberate motions for Treplev tearing up his manuscripts before he leaves to shoot himself articulate Treplev's hopelessness. Clearly, Zavyalov had remembered Dodin's comment, when they had rehearsed Treplev denouncing Trigorin in Act III, that Treplev should not weep over his disappointments, 'not be small and without strength' (St Petersburg, 25 April 2001). Zavyalov had wept at the time and had moved everybody in the rehearsal room deeply by his *proba*. His intensity ceded to the Spartan quality that gradually took over the production.

Of the principles that emerged from Dodin's rehearsals, the most important for the production are three: emotional reserve, as indicated above; unaccentuated diction so that speech is natural, conversational, and does not allow pointed value judgements as to what is said about whom; relational attentiveness so that the energy flows between the characters, weaving bonds of love and affection between them. What is most unusual about Dodin's production is how both the actual and the potential conflictual elements between the characters are held in check or erased so that even Treplev's animosity towards Trigorin comes out as far less aggressive than in traditional interpretations. Its surprising turnabout is due to Dodin's realisation that

> we could not open the work with its usual key . . . Treplev is usually played as a neurasthenic, Trigorin as some kind of Don Juan, Dorn as an old cynic, Arkadina as an *actress*, a *grande coquette*, whereas, as she says, she is 'a woman'; she is a lover, a mother and a sister who loves and is loved.
>
> (Palermo, 7 October 2001)

The new key with which the Maly unlocked the work gave, as well, a caring brother and sister relationship – with a surprisingly compassionate Sorin (Koval) – of the kind evident in *The Cherry Orchard*. Trigorin (Kuryshev) is created as a solid, agreeable and open personality whose dissatisfaction with his own writing is truly sincere. His allusions to Tolstoy and Turgenev, although inspiring smiles, were never tossed off in rehearsals as funny lines.

A revolver without a shot

The Maly's radical character reorientations were perceived with interest by Russian and Italian critics alike, although the latter appeared more doubtful about Zavyalov's physical credibility as Treplev who 'twenty years older than the character seems like the brother of the mother' rather than her son (*La Repubblica*, 9 October 2001). Dodin, for his part, was struck during the creative process by Zavyalov's freedom in the role, as noted in chapter 2. This not only convinced him that Treplev was not a mandatory *jeune premier*, but also sensitised him to Treplev's country origins to which Zavyalov's rustic appearance was suited. Thus, he also interpreted Chekhov's hint in Act III to the letter when Arkadina, by way of reference to Treplev's father, calls her son a 'Kiev shop-keeper'. Shopkeepers, as Chekhov knew only too well from his own father, were one generation away from peasants – a point of social history that helped Dodin take Treplev out of his young, romantic, urban mould.

The production's emphasis on love also means that there is nothing carping about the relationships between Polina (Akimova) and Shamrayev (Gayanov) and Polina and Dorn (Semak). The latter relationship is traditionally played as a covert adulterous affair. Here, the love between them is transparent, tactile and so disarmingly genuine that no one, on stage or off, is put out by it. This includes Shamrayev who, although taciturn and despotic, appears to realise that love might have a calling greater than its participants – an attitude evident in moments when Gayanov enters, as if Shamrayev had unexpectedly come upon them, and looks at them quickly, knowingly, but without reproach. In addition, several affectionate strokes and glances between Gayanov and Akimova suggest that this husband and wife have a sympathetic understanding of each other. It is precisely this kind of tacit bonding between all the characters that transcends their various agonies: Polina's awareness that she and Dorn are ageing and, *carpe diem*, should openly declare their love; Trigorin's abiding, warm respect for Arkadina, which tears away at his realisation that Nina's love offers him a second chance to show some character and, perhaps, even to become the writer of his dreams; Sorin's deep love for his nephew whom, for lack of money, he cannot help; Sorin's joy in Nina's presence which, at Dodin's suggestion that he might well be in love with her, is played on a note of regret for opportunities that never came. In these and many more instances, familial unity and personal desire cohabit, open to view. As a Moscow critic put it: 'Here there is no life in the wings . . . Everybody knows everything about everybody else' (*Nezavisimaya gazeta*, 15 June 2001).

The one thing they may not know is whether Masha (Tychinina) is Dorn's and not Shamrayev's daughter. The audience, however, is given hints that she may well be, starting from the last scene of Act I, when Masha speaks of her closeness to Dorn and her alienation from Shamrayev. The intimacy between Masha and Dorn is implied by their physical proximity when sitting on the lawn, and their smallest gestures and glances. (Elsewhere Dorn glances at her frequently, as if keeping his eye on her.) But the more telling details are the unexpected ones, such as the familiar way in which Dorn throws away her cigarettes, or the exceptionally familiar gestures of threatening to clip her on the ear for smoking, or touching her gently on the head which, when Treplev is present, appears to be a comforting gesture. Most evocative of all are the scenes including Polina when all three sit together, lie or lounge about on the grass in what looks like a happy family group. This image would have been cloying but for the detached perspective of the whole production.

Dodin associates Masha in particular with this horizontal axis. Thus, Tychinina opens Act I by coming in to lie down on the grass, from which position ensues her dialogue with Medvedenko. She is in a similar position in her discussion with Medvedenko at the beginning of Act IV. In the first case, Tychinina replaces Masha's traditional irritation with Medvedenko with indolence, in the second with affection, which is reciprocated by a confident Medvedenko rather than the brow-beaten one of comic versions of him. In another instance, she pulls a flask and two vodka glasses out of her pocket and sets them on the grass. She then sits down and proceeds to drink the vodka, her legs astride. These lightly humorous touches link allusions in the text to Masha's surreptitious drinking – except that here it is open – and to her unrequited love for Treplev. All in all, Tychinina plays Masha as an appealing, centred and grounded character, which is an uncommon interpretation and, in this way, fixes the spectators' attention on her. Even her voice has gone into a lower register, Galendeyev, on Dodin's instigation, having helped Tychinina to change its timbre so that Masha's voice could give the emotional key of the whole production from the moment she speaks.

A soft kind of gravity imbues the production. It gets rid of the stereotypes and 'banalities of Chekhovian theatre', as noted particularly by *Kommersant* (15 June 2001), and affirms – in the words of *Il Manifesto* – that there is 'so much love about, but always for the wrong person' (7 October 2001). Yet, because there is so much of this love, even loving in solitude has the power to sustain people, as is made explicit by the actors' presence on stage when they are not involved in a scene. The actors sit or stand and watch the action – echoes, certainly, of themselves in rehearsals. However, they play the embodied thoughts of the characters who are speaking and are thereby presences in their lives, as people do, indeed, live in other people's thoughts. The only character for whom such embodiment provides no comfort whatsoever is Treplev. No shot is heard when he shoots himself, out of sight. Spectators know of the deed from Arkadina's frozen silent scream. The intuition of love has told her what Dorn refuses to tell her at the end.

The closing scenes of Act IV run counter to expectations, not least because they are packed around an unpredictable lotto scene 'bordered' at the front by Sorin's body lying on a bench and covered to the neck by white sheets, like a corpse. The scene is played with the actors pedalling continually on immobilised bicycles fixed in a row facing the audience in a bicycle rack fastened to the metal grid (Figure 15, overleaf). Some – Shestakova-Arkadina especially – pedal increasingly furiously as Masha, who sits on the floorboards rather than on a bicycle, calls out the numbers and they respond. As the actors pedal, the water, now a sickly greenish colour, rises and laps about the wheels. Four signifiers come together: *wheels* turning and *riders* going nowhere, a *game* of chance and rising *water*. The water is symbolically charged, as in *A Play*. The remaining symbols are just as clear, even trite: the game of chance is Life, and the wheels are the wheels of Fortune and of Time. The coupled Life-Time returns from *The Cherry Orchard* to suggest that love might be the answer for an age of uncertainty. But *is* love all you need? *The Seagull* suggests that love is all you've got, even when it leaves you solitary, alone, on a bicycle built for one.

A networked world

Dodin's world view seems to have undergone a radical shift with *The Seagull*, in so far as the space open for the larger sociohistorical and cultural issues in the Maly's productions over 15 years has here been encroached upon by family and domestic issues, the issue of love itself being perceived as a family matter. It is tempting to see, reflected in this, a worldwide trend at the turn of the present century, whose uncertainties have led committed and concerned people to abandon the public sphere and seek refuge in the private one, where interpersonal, affective relations seem the only certainty possible in a world of shifting sands. Even then these relations are under siege because of the confusions, dissipations and instabilities of what Bourdieu calls the 'precarious society' (1998: 95–101), Bauman the 'liquid society' (2000) and Castells the globalised 'network society' (1996–8), the latter nevertheless having a more optimistic outlook than his fellow sociologists. Given that Dodin and the Maly have been free of an iron curtain for more than a decade, there is good reason to suppose that their exposure to the networked world in Castells's most comprehensive understanding of the concept – that is, as global economic, political, social, technological and cultural intermesh – into which Russia, too, has been networked, has worked on them and been woven through their theatre.

There is another shift in *The Seagull* which is an aspect of the exposure in question. The Maly's previous international exchanges essentially concerned directors, for example, Pasqual, Lavaudant, Donnellan. *The Seagull* for the first time involved an international designer, Chloé Obolensky who, among her professional achievements, counts some 20 years of costume and stage design with Brook's Centre Internationale de Créations Théâtrales. Obolensky had created the costumes for Dodin's production of *The Queen of Spades*, first in Amsterdam in 1998 and then, with considerably modified costumes, for its reprise in Paris in 2001. Obolensky brought to *The Seagull* her characteristically unpretentious, elegant lines, dressing the actors in costumes styled for them according to how they inhabited their roles. The result was a delicate palette of beige, off-white

Figure 15 *The Seagull* at the Maly Drama Theatre, 2001, Act IV.

l. to r.: I. Tychinina, S. Kuryshev, T. Shestakova, P. Semak, N. Akimova, S. Bekhterev. *Foreground*: S. Kozyrev as Sorin.

Photograph by V. Vasilyev, courtesy of the Archive of the Maly Drama Theatre, St Petersburg.

(Trigorin's suit), off-black (Masha's black 'in mourning for my life'), various pastels and an occasional stronger colour (a sky-blue, ample scarf for Arkadina's travel cloak in Act IV). The exquisite cut of the clothes gave Masha and Nina long jackets, Nina soft shirts and skirts, Polina fine sleeves and flowing skirts, and loosely falling outfits for the men, including a loose, not quite peasant shirt for Treplev. There was nothing more than a *souvenir* of period costume in the garments, as Obolensky described her aim (St Petersburg, 25 April 2001), and their visual harmony added to the intimacy between the characters desired by Dodin, however fragile their grip on their world may be.

The Seagull suggests that, a decade after the major historical turnaround of 1991, Dodin and the Maly, while conscious of the burdensome weight of history, have put it aside to meditate, instead, on their own fragility and how they should cherish the ties between them. By doing this, they may well be following the pattern discerned by political analysts who claim that civic groups in Russia have become increasingly uninterested in public affairs (McFaul, 2001: 320), mainly owing to disappointed expectations and people's preoccupation with survival in a 'harsh market' (Gill and Markwick, 2001: 250). The production feels, in that auratic, atmospheric way which eludes reasoned analysis, that its makers have lived through a prolonged crisis and are now in its subdued aftermath. Although the Moscow critics varied in their response to it, they generally saw the production as controversial without thinking to raise controversy over it. The febrile sociopolitical circumstances in which, ten years earlier, *Gaudeamus* had provoked debates in the theatre and attacks upon its young performers in the streets, and which, by mid-decade, had fuelled abrasive reactions to *Claustrophobia*, had become the crisis management of the rest of the decade – a feature of the global 'network society' – bringing with it what might be called precariousness fatigue. *The Seagull* creates a space of quietude in this fatigue, where characters who play the role of thoughts in other people's lives also look at other characters as if they were the witnesses of their lives.

Where will the Maly journey from here, from this quiet sadness, this fall-out from precariousness fatigue? The next play of its Chekhov cycle is *Uncle Vanya*, scheduled for 2003. Only then will it be known what route the warmth of Dodin's reading with the Northern Stage Ensemble in 1999 will have taken when the whole world is poised on the brink of uncertainty, terrorism and war having made it so.

Part III
Dodin at the opera

6   Dodin directs opera

Dodin's playful experiments with opera in *Claustrophobia* changed character when he turned to the genre and staged Strauss's *Elektra* at the Salzburg Easter Festival in 1995. This co-production with the Maggio Musicale in Florence, where *Elektra* was performed in the following year, was played by the Berliner Philharmoniker under its chief conductor Claudio Abbado. According to *Die Welt*, the Philharmoniker's tonally luxuriant rendition of the opera justified its reputation for being the best orchestra in the world (10 April 1995). Dodin was accompanied in his prestigious debut on the operatic stage by David Borovsky and Jean Kalman who were responsible for set and costume design and lighting. Kalman was already a lighting designer of repute in lyrical as well as dramatic theatre, including work with Deborah Warner, Robert Lepage, Stein and Brook, not least the latter's *Impressions de Pelléas* (1992) based on *Pelléas et Mélisande* by Debussy.

Borovsky and Kalman were to be part of Dodin's team for the next three operas he was to stage by 2000. Shostakovich's *Lady Macbeth of Mtsensk District*, conducted by Semyon Bychkov, followed *Elektra* at the Maggio Musicale Fiorentino's Teatro Comunale in April 1998. Then came *The Queen of Spades* by Tchaikovsky, also conducted by Bychkov, with De Nederlandse Opera in Amsterdam in December 1998. This co-production with the Maggio Musicale Fiorentino and the Opéra National de Paris accordingly went to the Teatro Comunale in April 1999 and the Opéra Bastille in October of the same year. Having entered the repertoire of the Paris Opéra, it returned there in February 2001. Chloé Obolensky now designed the costumes and changed them to suit the different singers of the Paris edition. Dodin's fourth opera was Tchaikovsky's *Mazepa*, premiered at La Scala on 21 March 1999, the great cellist Mstislav Rostropovich conducting in Milan's great house. It was La Scala's very first production of *Mazepa*. Costumes, this time, were by Luisa Spinatelli, Strehler's erstwhile collaborator, Strehler himself having had a long and often stormy relationship with La Scala.

Dodin's fifth opera *The Demon* by Anton Rubinstein (1875) to Lermontov's poem (1841) was performed in January 2003 at the Châtelet in Paris by the Mariinsky Theatre (Kirov) and conducted by Valery Gergiev. *The Demon* belonged to the *Saison russe* of opera and ballet with which the Châtelet theatre marked the tercentenary of St Petersburg. It was part of the programme of larger celebrations in St Petersburg in the spring of the same year. The Châtelet was, of course, home to Diaghilev's *Ballets Russes* whose operatic repertoire did not, however, include the then-popular *Demon*. Strauss's *Salomé* is Dodin's sixth opera, planned for the Paris Opéra Bastille in October 2003, conducted by James Conlon.[1]

Ancestral vendetta in *Elektra*

Dodin's entrance into the battlefield of opera was a public but not blazing critical success, the Germanophone press either withholding judgement or dishing it out negatively. *Die Welt* (10 April 1995), at one end of the scale, notes that *Elektra*, for Dodin, is a world of blood, hatred and revenge, given the heaped corpses on which Elektra dances in triumph at the end of his production. *Wiener Zeitung*, at the other end, observes that Dodin directs a tragedy that never happens. Borovsky's suggested amphitheatre and a sectioned wall (the palace in Mycenae, where the action takes place) is part of Dodin's attempt at modernising the opera, which does not work, especially because it is 'a kind of scenic oratorio' that fails to move the audience (11 April 1995). Furthermore, no tragedy occurs in the orchestra pit either, since Abbado fails to bring out the electricity of Strauss's magnificent score, passing over 'exciting detail with shocking superficiality'.

Critical opinion was of a different order in Florence a year later, all reviews being nothing less than exultant, no superlative being too exalted for the orchestral playing – its full-bodied sound, incandescence, 'intensity of communication greater than in Salzburg' (*La Nazione*, 7 May 1996). Eulogies were piled on the soloists' singing, as on their characterisation, both musical and dramatic. In fact, close attention was generally paid to the relationship between the pit and the stage. *Avvenire* commented on the convergence between the music and the *mise en scène* (7 May 1996), *Il Tempo* on how Dodin's intentions harmonised perfectly with the score (7 May 1996) and *Il Giorno* on the 'unity of conceptions' between Dodin's 'crude and emotional modernity' and the 'compact violence' of Abbado's musical direction (8 May 1996). *Il Gazzettino* spoke of the 'impressive tension and dryness of Dodin's direction' (7 May 1996), which in the eyes of another was a 'quasi-timid correctness' (*L'Arena*, 7 May 1996). For *La Stampa*, however, the matter was one of an apt sobriety from which the singers had learned a lesson: thus, they refrained from 'overloading a score already extremely rich in effects and perspectives' (7 May 1996). By making this observation, *La Stampa* showed that it had noticed, more than any other newspaper, the importance, for the coherence of Dodin's production, of the disparity between abandoned orchestral playing and singing and a controlled *mise en scène*.

All in all, the Italian critics wrote very much from the premise that opera was both a scenic and musical phenomenon and a singing feat that would not work without good acting. Several of them offered acting details. For instance, the critic for *Il Mattino*, while lukewarm about the overall effect of Dodin's staging, pointed out that Karita Mattila played Chrysothemis in a less infantile way than usual; similarly, that her stronger characterisation in relation to Deborah Polaski's indomitable Elektra produced a 'confrontation between complementary psychologies' (7 May 1996). This was seen as a dramatic bonus. Dodin had indeed sought a dialectic between Chrysothemis and Elektra, between the human warmth of the one in her desire to live and have children and the pounding obsession with vengeance and death of the other. Just as astute on direction was *Il Gazzettino*'s critic who stressed that the singers performed as if they were actresses in dramatic theatre. He noted, as well, that their awareness of play together with Dodin's 'impressive tension and dryness' were 'the results of Dodin's experimentation with the Maly'. The fact that this critic made the link between Dodin, stage director, and Dodin, opera director, is highly significant, since turning opera into genuine theatre is *the* central issue for Dodin, as for numerous directors comparable to him of the twentieth and twenty-first centuries.

The Italian critics, like their German and Austrian counterparts, also remarked on the unflattering lighting, 'squalid atmosphere' and 'unwashed, old-looking clothing' (*La Repubblica*, 5 May 1996). However, more than their counterparts, for whom these elements were tokens of 'modernisation' (*Wiener Zeitung*, as above), they saw them as Dodin's way of unifying the mythical past of Greek tragedy with a menacing present (*Il Tempo*, as above). Publicity before *Elektra* opened in Florence may have been influential, for it had indicated that Dodin's interest lay in world affairs rather than in psychoanalysis, thereby warning the critics who assumed the latter provided the norm for interpretations of the opera. Such an assumption rested on the fact that Hofmannsthal's 1909 libretto for Strauss, like his poetry, was generated by the Vienna of Freud's theory of the unconscious and Krafft-Ebing's theory of sexual pathology, and Elektra was taken to be a prime candidate for both. Critics had been additionally forewarned by Dodin who had been quoted as perceiving the opera in terms of 'the ancient, ancestral blood vendetta that still exists today . . . in Northern Ireland, Bosnia, Palestine and Chechnya' (*La Stampa*, 4 May 1996). He was to make a similar type of association, when rehearsing *Mazepa*, between Peter I's war against Ukraine – one of the subjects of the opera – and the current wars and 'ethnic cleansing' in Bosnia and Chechnya (Milan, 19 March 1999). Mazepa, the leader of the Ukrainian revolt, was likened by Dodin to Radovan Karadzic 'who fought for Serbia's independence, but covered his country in blood' (*Corriere della Sera*, 22 March 1999). In other words, irrespective of how critics interpreted him, the turn of mind intrinsic to Dodin's work with the Maly, which has as its touchstone the contemporary world, shapes his work on opera.

Opera as 'a musical *dramatic* art'

By his understanding that opera should be qualitatively equal to the theatre, Dodin joins Stanislavsky and Meyerhold, the founders of the modern opera.

Like them, his interest in opera arises from its immense capacity for drama and theatrical expressivity and its inventive combinations of the various elements – orchestral music, song, dialogue, scenography, event, narrative, thought content, and so on – that characterise the genre. When rehearsing *Mazepa*, Dodin claimed that opera had two main advantages over the theatre. First, its musical notes generate great power of a kind actors find much harder to achieve with words. Second, its musical resources combine with everything that the theatre can do, thereby expanding possibilities unavailable to the theatre (Milan, 16 February 1999). Opera for Dodin is a 'musical *dramatic* art' where the musical is predicated on the dramatic and cannot be separated from it. His view has prompted Dodin to treat singers as actors so that they shed the bravura style of conventional opera, where notions of what is operatic mean 'ostentatious', 'exaggerated', 'heroic', among other descriptions that have been fuelled by 'grand' opera and have stuck to it. By shedding excess and approaching sung dialogue as if it were speech, singers were to be singing actors – the imperative of a musical dramatic art. Like the actors of his own company, they were to avoid stereotypical projections and develop their individuality. They were to find nuances of character, situation, action and, above all, of interaction and inter-relationship between all participants, which were fundamental to serious ensemble acting.

Dodin's aim to elevate opera to the standards and potential of the theatre is shared by prominent stage directors, living or recently deceased, who have ventured into this domain. Each has his or her trademark. Strehler, for instance, who was a major reformer of the opera, sought lyrical ease with dramatic effort-lessness – a magic of the stage that belied the contrivances going into it. Wilson – calculated, deliberate – continues to make artifice a salient operatic principle, shorn, however, of vulgarity. There is Brook's concision and simplicity, Warner's narrative spine onto which she fleshes dramatic conflict, Sellars's skill in bringing America into Mozart, that is, in making opera speak in contemporary tongues, which is a taste he shares with Dodin; and there are more – Stein, Lepage, Ronconi, Serban are also in this group. Individuality notwithstanding, all strip away the residual trappings of pre-modern opera to facilitate its capacity for being a 'total art' of the theatre which, as well, shuns time-warp and follows the rhythms of its times. That all were schooled in the dramatic theatre (Wilson's hybridised theatre included) and, in most cases, still work in it, distinguishes them from directors who are primarily, or even exclusively, directors of opera.

One more feature needs attention, and that is the fact that these directors have had to challenge the 'operatic' practices of opera houses from the vantage point of their habitus as shaped by their working theatre world. Bourdieu's 'habitus' is the most appropriate term for the intricate interweave of a way of seeing, being and doing which arises from the concrete, material conditions of a specific practice and is concomitant with it (Bourdieu and Wacquant, 1992: 96–110; Bourdieu, 2000 [1972]: 256–85). Put in the terms of my discussion, this means that a theatre director's values, attitudes, mind-set, prospects and perspectives – the mental constituents of habitus – are all rooted in the physical practicalities of his/her work, which are the technical, socioeconomic, political and institutional constituents of habitus. When coming into opera, his/her habitus encounters and frequently comes into conflict with the ingrained habitus of opera practitioners, who cherish and reproduce the values of their practice. This is so whether they are soloists, chorus singers, conductors, managing directors or administrators, the whole institution of opera being, as Dodin puts it, 'an extremely heavy machine to move' (Milan, 19 March 1999).

Dodin's involvement with opera shows that this machine, with all its complex mechanisms, is engaged when the questions of style and delivery pertinent to dramatic theatre operate as *musical* dramatic theatre. These questions are especially urgent, as Brook's and Strehler's experiences have demonstrated, when directors' ambitions for opera are so deeply integrated with the theatre elaborated by them that they clash irreconcilably with the ambitions and expectations of opera houses. It is well known that Brook turned his back on such houses to produce his own type of chamber opera at the Bouffes du Nord, a theatre set out and run according to his specifications. Strehler, when he finally obtained the Nuovo Piccolo Teatro in 1997, a new, larger and better equipped space than the historical Piccolo, planned to open it with Mozart's *Così fan tutte*, the culmination of years of commitment to staging opera as he staged plays. Strehler, had he lived longer, would probably never have set foot in La Scala again. Dodin, to date, has sought liberty for opera in traditional houses, regardless of their top-heavy machinery. Equally, and like Wilson or Sellars who continue to work in them, his direction impinges upon and questions the 'schemas of perception, thought and action' of a group habitus (here, of opera professionals) that 'guarantees the conformity of practices and their consistency across time' (Bourdieu, 1980: 91).

The most important of Dodin's objectives concern acting, singing, music, the chorus, the role of extras and the structure of ideas, theme, plot and action. Let us start with acting, which must replace 'operatic posturing' – the words of Julian Rodescu, who sings the priest in *Lady Macbeth* and who, in rehearsals, was struck by how Dodin had led the singers into their 'inner being' to find the substance of the words they sang (Florence, 16 April 1998). Dodin's goal is to transform posturing so that voices, bodies and spatial relationships have dramatic meaning rather than virtuosic or exhibitionistic impact, or purely ornamental value. Meaning, for him, is tied to characterisation, and *Lady Macbeth* provides an example of how Dodin viewed this connection through the seduction scene crucial to the opera's plot and outcome. The scene's protagonists are Katerina, the merchant's wife who is 'Lady Macbeth', and Sergey, a workman in her husband's flour-mill. Jyrki Niskanen, in the role of Sergey, at first reverted to the stock gestures that cling to a melodramatic 'lover', as he freely acknowledged when Dodin remarked that Katerina would hardly allow a lover of his type into her bedroom. Dodin: 'Why would she let you in when you are just as likely to dance the can-can, gesticulating like that? You are moving about without showing you have understood her desire and are used to fulfilling your own' (25 March 1998). The task for Niskanen was to draw a character from Shostakovich's composition and not, as Dodin put it on another occasion, from *The Merry Widow*. Dodin, when Niskanen tried too hard: 'When an actor always demonstrates, I realise that he is not thinking anything, merely demonstrating.' His emphasis at the Maly on thinking is here also seen to be a necessity for acting in opera.

Dodin's second main point concerning dramatic meaning involves co-ordination between acting, stage action, orchestral music and singing. However, the co-ordination he aims for is between *distinctive* rather than subordinate processes which merely echo each other. Dodin's idea is that 'we do not demonstrate the music. We have to go across the music with our own independent action' (25 March 1998). What this indicates is that the stage neither mimics nor illustrates the music, but 'says' something of its own accord. The same holds for the music which, since it also says plenty independently, does not need pictorial explanations. Time and again during the rehearsals not only of *Lady Macbeth* but of all his opera productions, Dodin would point out how the musical articulation might be best served when the singer-actors do nothing at all. The principle of non-doing is especially valuable, in his view, when orchestral interludes fill the space, as happens in *Lady Macbeth*. He urged soloists to sit still here and just listen to the music. When the music is driven by a particular emotion or tone – rage in *Elektra*, irony in *Lady Macbeth* – he asked soloists to juxtapose it (calm against fury, for example, or seriousness against irony) so as to bring out one against the other and connect them through their opposition. Vocal delivery in such cases is not a matter of rivalry between concurrent forces or even of outdoing them (by singing louder, for instance), but of riding along with them.

The difficulty of how voices are to be heard is nevertheless a real one, especially as Dodin, like Brook and Strehler before him, prefers a more intimate sound, a mode of singing as if it were spoken dialogue. While this transfer from the theatre is integral to the natural rather than bombastic style of acting for opera envisaged by all three directors, it poses the problem of how soloists can sing 'naturally' (and not strain or belt out sound) in large auditoria and against a full-scale, rich orchestra like the Berliner Philharmoniker. This difficulty, eventually considered by Brook and Strehler not worth fighting, sent them into the alternative spaces of the Bouffes and the Nuovo Piccolo. Dodin first tackled it in *Elektra* by working from the inside of the characters so that the soloists' voices sang from within. His strategy could be described as funnelling the power of the voice, which checked its extroversion but did not dampen its sound; and he was to develop this strategy further while exploring various other solutions, as will be apparent in chapter 7 on *The Queen of Spades*.

A similar theatre principle leads Dodin to use the chorus as actors who are a complete part of the stage action instead of ancillary to it. The chorus in grand opera has great musical importance, not least because its mass voices contribute to the colour, power, dynamics and logic of the music. However, it is often inserted awkwardly into the stage action, is often an encumbrance to the events taking place, and is used to fill up 'empty' spaces with extra bodies as well as to fill in gaps between scenes. In addition, the chorus is used purely pragmatically when it provides extras to carry out actions. Most of the chorus's ostensible functions are thus detrimental to dramatic and theatrical logic. By making the chorus a veritable character, whether in one body or broken into several characters by individuals or groups, Dodin, in a kind of synaesthesia, hopes to make the musical logic appear on stage rather than emanate solely from the pit and to the ears alone. Supernumeraries, who are hired by opera houses as required by directors, are used by him with special care as to their dramatic purpose and meaningfulness for that particular opera in its entirety.

Finally, though centrally, is the issue of structure, which includes the clear organisation of plot sequences so that their themes and the ideas explored through them are intelligible and persuasive, this being part of what makes opera a dramatic art. Structure, in Dodin's case, sometimes means restructuring – a practice he carries over from the Maly – and is particularly apparent in his *Queen of Spades*. Yet his commitment to theatrical cohesion relies on the conductor and musicians working together with the stage rather than subordinating it to the exigencies of their score. Borovsky observes shrewdly that musicians treat their scores as texts and, consequently, are especially cautious about anything that appears to 'tamper with' them (Paris, 8 October 1999) – a view, one might add, not unlike that of literary scholars as regards the written word. Borovsky also notes that stage directors who do not have a musician's bias towards scores dare to take a freer approach to them since they are not hampered by notions of the 'sacrality' of the notes and of the markings on the page for musical interpretation. This having been said, such liberty requires agreement with and support from conductors, the *maestri* who are in charge of the scores.

Lady Macbeth of Mtsensk District: Eros in a chain gang

With *Lady Macbeth*, Dodin returns to the Stalinist universe behind *Brothers and Sisters*, but now in a horrific vein. The libretto, written by Shostakovich and the Leningrad poet Aleksandr Preys, is an amended version of Nikolay Leskov's 1864 story. Katerina Ismaylova, who is stifled, bored and sexually unfulfilled, conceives a passion for the virile Sergey, a new workman in her husband Zinovy's flour-mill. At the end of Act I, when Zinovy is absent on business, Sergey comes to her bedroom. Katerina at first resists him, but then succumbs to his entreaties. At the beginning of Act II, after one week of love, Boris, her father-in-law, who also decides to take advantage of Zinovy's absence, catches Sergey climbing out of her window. Boris has Sergey flogged. Katerina poisons Boris with rat poison in the mushrooms she regularly prepares for him. Here, as in earlier scenes, Boris asserts his patriarchal tyranny, thereby compounding the motives for his murder. The ghost of Boris haunts Katerina. Zinovy returns, beats Katerina, and the lovers strangle him. In Act III, Katerina and Sergey marry, but not before Katerina suffers violently because of her crimes and is denounced by a self-seeking 'shabby peasant' to the local police. The police interrupt the wedding, handcuff the couple and lead them away. Act IV shows them among a group of convicts exiled to Siberia. Sergey, angry and resentful that he has lost everything, takes up with another convict Sonyetka. When Katerina discovers his betrayal, she hurls her rival and herself into the icy river, where they drown.

Shostakovich was sympathetic to Katerina, seeing in her origins in Leskov the 'tragic portrait of . . . a talented, clever . . . woman perishing in the nightmarish conditions of pre-Revolutionary Russia' which he framed in a 'tragi-satirical' opera (Shostakovich in Fay, 2000: 69). Most of the opera's satire comes through its iconoclastic orchestral score, including orgasmic trombones for the first sexual encounter between Katerina and Sergey and rumbustious passages for a scene at the police station reminiscent of the music for *The Keystone Cops*. Shostakovich had, in fact, composed as well as played the piano for silent films and cleverly drew on his experience in these and other scenes. Sullen sounds leading to a coarse, ironic waltz reveal Boris's lust, while orchestral galops in scene endings and interludes lampoon their subject matter. Such deft musical strokes for characters, themes and events show how the music carries 'semantic association' (Fanning, 1995: 157) which, in addition, bring forward the 'nightmarish conditions of pre-Revolutionary Russia' referred to by Shostakovich to his own nightmarish time of writing.

Above all, these strokes show an unerring dramatic sense which, although idiosyncratic to the composer, had been encouraged by Shostakovich's contact with Meyerhold. He had been inspired by Meyerhold's productions, had been a pianist for several months in 1928 at the Meyerhold Theatre and, in 1929, wrote the music for the director's production of *The Bedbug* by Mayakovsky. The opera was completed in 1932, opened in Leningrad in 1934 and two days later in Moscow where it was directed by Nemirovich-Danchenko, and outlawed in 1936 after the unsigned editorial 'Muddle Instead of Music' in *Pravda* on 28 January had accused Shostakovich of musical abominations ('the din, the grinding, the squealing' – Fay, 2000: 84). The editorial thrashed him, equally, for upholding dramatic formalism, alias 'Meyerholdism', while combining it with 'the coarsest naturalism'. The work was not even rehabilitated in 1956, after Krushchev's denunciation of Stalin, leaving it 'the most notorious cultural casualty of the Stalinist period' (ibid.: 197). When it finally reappeared in Moscow in 1963, it did so in Shostakovich's reworked version under its new name *Katerina Ismaylova*, with a new opus number to differentiate it from his earlier composition. In 1979, the 1932 score resurfaced in the west, becoming the 'legitimate' version for subsequent stagings. It is with the opera's heavily charged history in mind that Dodin approaches the work, taking its 1932 original and imbuing it with the atmosphere of the reign of terror of the 1930s. *Lady Macbeth* had presaged the terror, but what were then only forebodings resonate, for Dodin, with the knowledge of the period that came afterwards, the worst having surfaced after glasnost.

The Stalinist terror

The fact that oppression is omnipresent in Dodin's *mise en scène* is evident from the very start when Katerina, who is on an upper level in an enclosed balcony, sings of how she cannot sleep. Only the upper part of her body and her arms are visible as she holds several pillows close to her for comfort. Her placement, posture, distance and scenic context indicate that her freedom is restricted. Boris, below her, sings an almost parallel monologue in which he upbraids her for being useless both to the household and the business. Worse still, she is childless after five years of marriage, although Katerina insinuates that the cause is Zinovy's impotence. The scene is taut and with minimal gesturing, Katerina's agony and Boris's acrimony being conveyed first and foremost through the intonations of the voice.

How Boris incarnates patriarchy is especially pronounced at the end of this opening scene when Zinovy, whom he browbeats for not controlling Katerina enough, takes his leave. In the libretto, Boris forces Katerina to say farewell on her knees. Dodin has her prostrate on the ground at Zinovy's feet. Her abasement is meant to be shocking, all the more so in hindsight after the production has shown how strong-headed and assertive she is. Dodin insisted during rehearsals on Katerina's strength of character and, consequently, asked Karen Huffstodt, who sings the part, to avoid servile behaviour of any kind and any temptation to make her shrewish or shrill, particularly in her relationship with Sergey. This general rule applied as well to a scene like the second one where Zinovy's workers, Sergey among them, fool around with Aksinya, the Izmaylovs' cook. Sergey taunts Katerina, who has come upon the incident, urging her to wrestle with him. This scene, according to Dodin, is frequently misinterpreted as providing comic relief, whereas it is actually brutal since Aksinya is essentially molested by these men and Katerina demeaned by them.

Most of all, however, Dodin's advice to Huffstodt regarding Katerina applied to the last act, where Sergey uses her cruelly before he jilts her. Shrewishness and shrillness, he commented, were inappropriate for a woman of tragic stature who had been thwarted at every turn, had pursued true love and, notwithstanding her crimes, was a casualty of oppression. The production shows accordingly how Katerina's domestic oppression, starting with Boris's humiliation of her, is a mirror image of the clerical, police and sexual oppression to which she is also subjected. All are images not only of a patriarchal state but a police state, as Act IV, with its harrowing tableau of deported convicts, guards with rifles and Alsatian dogs, unequivocally demonstrates.

The upper space inhabited by Katerina at the beginning of the production signifies her space of happiness, to which she clings desperately enough to commit murder. Sergey makes his way along this elongated balcony to seduce her and they make love behind the 'wall' of the balcony, invisible to the audience as the music takes over the stage and narrates, mimics and parodies the erotic event. A swaying lamp that sways as long as the music plays humorously tells the audience all it needs to know. The light of the lamp is picked out by an additional shaft of light cutting across the scenography which looks like a flat canvas, all its contours having vanished into the penumbra. The light/dark dichotomy of Kalman's lighting always manages to keep a cavernous space below the balcony, which is associated with Boris, within the gaze. It is a threatening space from whose shadows Boris prowls out to spy on Katerina and where Dodin has him take out a poisoned rat here and there from among the sacks of flour. By linking Boris visually with rats (Katerina calls him a 'rat'), Dodin allows spectators to make a moral judgement which, as was evident from several of his brief asides during rehearsals, applied just as well to the 'shabby peasant' police informant whom he associated with the informants of the Stalinist terror.

Borovsky's constructivist design, likened pertinently by *La Repubblica* to a 'bunker' (22 April 1998), is made up of sheets of greyish wood. Light is cast on them differently to give a variety of greys, steel grey becoming the dominant shade in the last act. The design remains unchanged in the first three acts, and its compilation of angles and planes suggests the inside walls as well as the impenetrable outside of a house. These walls include the cellar where the lovers bury Zinovy and the room where they marry (a garden in Shostakovich's libretto). At the same time, they sketch out the flour-mill in whose 'courtyard' stands a construction looking ominously like a scaffold. Ropes hang from it to which extras who play workmen attach sacks and manipulate them up and down to give the illusion of a working mill, although Dodin tends to use the ropes for theatrical effect rather than naturalistic detail. Thus he builds the scene where Sergey and the other workmen molest Aksinya around their swinging on the ropes, virtually across the whole stage. Yury Khamutyansky, the Maly's circus teacher, had trained soloists, chorus singers and extras how to swing safely, and had taught the latter how to lift heavy sacks without injuring themselves.

A door on ground level at the centre of this set is skilfully used for atmospheric effect. A bilious light shines through it when the door mysteriously opens to suggest that Katerina sees Zinovy's ghost. Katerina and Sergey glide through it, looking stunned, on a low, narrow podium to the front of the stage for their wedding, Dodin having urged the singers in rehearsal to imagine that their characters were going to their execution. The priest who marries them walks heavily through the same door and, during the ceremony, mistakes a bottle hidden in the folds of his robes for a Bible. Dodin here picks up the sarcasm of the music to create a grimly comic micro-scene. The door is also a nodal point when the police barge their way through it, crowding the narrow space Dodin had designated for the ceremony. The whole scene, which Dodin organises by layering micro-scenes, as is typical of his work with the Maly, is structured with pristine clarity to counter the commotion of the music. Yet, although not mirroring the music, its combination of what is visually and kinetically mocking, hideous and strange – recalling Meyerhold's idea of the grotesque – is consistent with the caustic-grotesque quality of the music.

Borovsky's design changes for Act IV. The scene change is effortless in that the walls slide away to expose the walkway which had been hidden by the parapet of the balcony. What had looked earlier like the tower of a mill now resembles the watchtower of a prison or a concentration camp – Buchenwald, perhaps, which the Maly had visited when both *Chevengur* and *Lady Macbeth* were in preparation. The whole, however, with its guards walking up and down in grey Soviet-style uniforms and holding police dogs on leashes refers to a Soviet labour camp. The steel grey of the tableau, besides creating the impression of icy coldness in which the gang of convicts huddle for warmth, intensifies the sense of fear evoked by the images. The tableau is pitiless in the manner of *Chevengur*. It seems intolerably harsh because of the contrast with the music which, from the very beginning of the act, has exchanged satire for tragedy. Furthermore, the chorus now sings in full force the tonalities and melodies taken from Orthodox liturgy and old Russian folk songs. So moving are the music and song that they are almost overwhelming by the time Katerina throws herself and Sonyetka into the river. Since he anticipated the music's emotional impact, Dodin chose the simplest means for the death of the two women. Thus Katerina and Sonyetka seem to disappear behind the convicts, and only a shaft of livid light indicates their fall.

Comparably simple means serve Dodin's treatment of the chorus of convicts who are grouped together on a platform shaped like a raft, about as wide as the stage. As Act IV opens, the platform rolls forward from the deep space used for manoeuvring scenery behind the stage to indicate by a theatrical device rather than realistic movements that the convicts had been walking from a great distance. The singers first appear standing, which during rehearsals they had found normal enough. However, many of them had vigorously resisted Dodin's attempts to have them lie down straight afterwards. The libretto notes that the chain gang has arrived at a resting place and Dodin's aim was to have the singers go down at different moments, some on their sides and others flat on their backs or bellies. The singers had found this decidedly odd, arguing they could not sing from recumbent positions, they would not be heard and could not be seen, and, in any case, it was not common practice. The point of referring to their objections is not anecdotal but to show just how ingrained a habitus may be, which blinds singers both to the potentials open to them for singing and to the dramatic justification for certain actions. In the event, after some bickering (they also contested several other acting directions from Dodin), the chorus singers did what was asked. The result in performance was an extremely powerful scene to the eye and the ear, in which the grey mass of horizontal bodies hugging the ground suggested infinite sorrow, time eternal and death made all the more tragic by its anonymity.

The musicians were rather more open to suggestions that disrupted their normal practice. With Bychkov's agreement, Dodin had the whole orchestra lifted up, while playing, to the level of the stage. This occurred for some of the more ribald or strident orchestral interludes where brass instruments were particularly important. Not only did Dodin's ploy valorise the sound, which exploded into the audience, but it also showcased the sound-makers, who were usually holed up in the pit. It gave music in a 'musical *dramatic* art' the dramatic role of a character. This was precisely where the music could fully say what it had to say without actors illustrating or repeating it. The Italian press greatly appreciated the production's perfect co-ordination between the stage and the score, 'the immediacy and vivacity with which so many characters were fitted into the drama' and how such scenes as the police interrupting Katerina's wedding and the final singing scene of mourning (indeed, with the singers flat to the ground) were 'a measure' of Dodin's 'genius as a man of the theatre' (*La Nazione*, 22 April 1998).

L'Unità saw in Katerina's fight and destruction 'a heroine of our time' (23 April 1998). For *Il Messaggero*, the '"true" protagonist of the drama' was the people of the last tableau, a 'symbol of ragged and unhappy humanity' (23 April 1998). It could be said that, with *Lady Macbeth*, Dodin continues his 'theatre of prose' in so far as, whatever general idea of humanity may be extrapolated from the opera, he is still writing, with performing bodies, the history of Russia. *Lady Macbeth* received the coveted Premio Abbiati from Italian critics for the best opera production of the year.

Mazepa: love and war

Pushkin reworked by Tchaikovsky

The libretto by Tchaikovsky and Victor Burenin is based on Aleksandr Pushkin's 1828 narrative poem *Poltava*, concerning the battle that occurred in this place in 1709. It tells of the military commander Mazepa whose plans for the independence of Ukraine from Russia involve plotting against Peter the Great and rallying Ukrainian support behind Charles XII of Sweden, Russia's enemy, in order to defeat the Russian army.

A love story is intertwined with these historical events. Mazepa falls in love with his god-daughter Maria Kochubey who, notwithstanding the 45-year age gap between them, reciprocates his love. Maria's parents refuse Mazepa's request to marry her, and the couple elopes. Kochubey, who swears vengeance for his daughter's reputation and his outraged pride, informs the Tsar of Mazepa's treachery. Peter refuses to believe him and, deceived by Mazepa's intrigues, executes Kochubey instead. Maria finds out about the execution from her mother, but too late. Maria goes out of her mind. Mazepa and Charles XII are beaten in battle and flee the land. As fate would have it, they stop for rest at Kochubey's ransacked house where Maria suddenly appears, like a spectre, and Mazepa discovers her madness. She disappears into the night. Mazepa and Charles ride on.

The poem is thought to be long-winded, contrary to Pushkin's usual brevity. It is a hybrid form interlacing epic and lyrical qualities, third-person narrative, monologue, and dialogue written as if for a play, with the names of characters prefixed to speeches which sound as if they were meant to be spoken rather than read. It may not be exquisitely crafted like *The Bronze Horseman* (1833),

Pushkin's second epic on the life and times of Peter I, but it has enough verve to attract a composer of Tchaikovsky's stature, and its hero was legendary. The historical figure Mazepa, it must be remembered, captured the imagination of various creative minds, among them Voltaire, Byron, Hugo and Liszt. There were also 'popular' manifestations of interest such as the equestrian show *Mazeppa* [sic] *and the Wild Horse* performed at Astley's circus in London in 1833.

The libretto in three acts and six tableaux differs significantly from Pushkin's poem. Act I, which is invented entirely by Tchaikovsky, shows Maria first with a chorus of girlfriends inviting her to join them and then with Andrey, her play-mate from childhood. Andrey does not exist in Pushkin. Andrey, who does not know of Maria's feelings for Mazepa, confesses his love. This introduction is fol-lowed by Mazepa's arrival for festivities at Kochubey's house for which scene Tchaikovsky writes a boisterous *hopak* – one of several folkloric components of the opera. Kochubey's wife Lyubov and Iskra, his loyal companion, are present, as are Andrey and sundry guests. Mazepa asks for Maria's hand but is rejected. A quarrel ensues. Mazepa fires a shot into the air, which brings his guards rushing in. Maria is forced to choose between her parents and Mazepa, and leaves with the latter to general consternation. The second tableau shows Kochubey with Andrey, Lyubov and his followers and servants represented by the chorus. Kochubey writes a letter to the Tsar denouncing Mazepa's treach-ery and sends Andrey, whom he thinks of as a son, to the monarch with it.

Act II, in three tableaux, is rather more complex in terms of situation and characterisation. The first tableau opens with Kochubey, who has been impris-oned by Mazepa, interrogated by Orlik, Mazepa's henchman. Orlik attempts to extract false confessions from him, along with the whereabouts of his money. The second tableau shows Mazepa disturbed by the idea that he will execute his old friend but nevertheless resolved to do it. Mazepa is also tortured by the fact that to kill her father is to betray Maria and, as if to exonerate himself of his bloody deed, demands from the unsuspecting woman a declaration that he is dearer to her than her father is. In addition, he insinuates to Maria that he will soon rule Ukraine. She is beguiled by the prospect, not least because she supports the cause of national independence. Before Mazepa leaves, he reas-sures her of his love and asks her forgiveness, a request whose meaning, under the circumstances, she cannot hope to understand. Exit Mazepa and enter Lyubov, who has braved his guards to plead with her daughter to save Kochubey's life. Maria eventually grasps the enormity of everything her mother tells her, and the two women run out. The third tableau starts with the execu-tion, to which the women arrive just as the axes come down on the heads of Kochubey and Iskra. The finest lines in this act, with their focus on the psycho-logical, emotional and political intricacies at play, come almost directly from Pushkin and prompted Dodin to observe that Tchaikovsky's music was better when he composed directly from Pushkin's verses than when he and Burenin modified and added to them (Milan, 18 February 1999). This convergence between Pushkin and Tchaikovsky is an instance of the dramatic intelligibility which Dodin believes is essential for a 'musical *dramatic* art'.

Act III, in one tableau only, is the aftermath of the battle. Andrey seeks Maz-epa to kill him. Mazepa and Orlik – not Charles XII, as in Pushkin – are in flight, Peter's army at their heels. Maria appears and, not recognising Mazepa, sings some of the most powerful verses of Pushkin's poem about how she was tricked into believing that a wolf's head was her father's, and how the old man before her cannot be Mazepa since he is horrible to behold and has whiskers covered in blood. Orlik urges Mazepa to hurry, or else they will be caught. Mazepa abandons Maria. Meanwhile, Andrey has been shot by Mazepa. As Andrey lies dying, he sings to Maria of his love for her. She is oblivious to him in her madness and, mistaking him for a child, sings a lullaby as she rocks his head in her lap. This is a purely Tchaikovskian invention, full of human and melodic pathos. Pushkin would never have entertained even the idea of such a heart-rending ending.

Dodin rehearses Mazepa

Dodin wanted to bring out the tragic force in *Mazepa* and give it the clean, sharp focus of ancient tragedy. This meant deleting, with Rostropovich's complete agreement, all the opera's picturesque components, that is, the *hopak* from Act I and several verses for chorus and soloists in that act, and an episode in Act II with a drunken Cossack and peasants. Dodin then divided his produc-tion into two parts, placing the interval after the second tableau of Act II, after Maria and Lyubov leave. His primary purpose for putting the break here was to sustain the tension between the characters until it reached its resolution – pre-cisely as the term is used in music – in the women's realisation that Kochubey cannot be saved. Dodin's idea that mother and daughter come to this realisa-tion was not prompted by Tchaikovsky but grew out of the sense that he had been constructing for the scene – demonstrating the notion of 'dramatic intelli-gibility' referred to above. Dodin felt that his chosen break gave the two parts some sort of equilibrium, the last act in Tchaikovsky being inordinately short compared with Act II. His structural solution was also determined by the fact that he totally ignored Tchaikovsky's scenic directions, which indicate that the curtain is to fall after the first tableaux of Acts I and II, and between the acts as well, following conventional operatic practice. Dodin wanted to eliminate these ruptures because of his conviction that story, movement and emotional drive must run without interruption until an interruption becomes an absolute dra-matic necessity.

The same cantilena principle affects the relationship between the stage and spectators in that their attention is held on the performance instead of straying from it as a result of the closing or opening of the stage curtain, or the dimming of the lights for scene changes, or simply having intervals between acts. The fact that Dodin transgressed generic 'rules' was particularly evident in how the man-agement of La Scala responded to his intention of doing away with curtains altogether. This included the curtain that, in a house as tradition-bound as La Scala, is supposed to open at the very beginning of the production and 'announce' the work, and closes the production and 'announces' the performers before they take their bows. While La Scala simply ceded to Dodin as regards the opening scene – no curtain, with spectators looking at Borovsky's stage design before the performance begins – it was less pliable as far as taking bows was concerned, arguing, once again, that calls without curtains belonged to *prose* theatre, but not to *lyrical* theatre, *not* to opera.

All this would appear to be trivial were it not for the fact that it illuminates the extent of the challenges brought by dramatic art to opera and the habitus of the people working with it, even down to the smallest details. That La Scala maintains its links with old rituals more than most opera houses today only accentuates the critical artistic issues that arise when changes to rituals are made. This was the case with Dodin's timing of the interval. Until the dress rehearsal, he placed the interval after Maria and Lyubov leave. The management suggested that he bring forward the interval and place it at the end of Act I, as would be expected by La Scala audiences. Not being fixed in his ways – since he believes that everything in the theatre is a matter of experimenting – he agreed to see how it would work.

Several major consequences followed from this reorganisation. Instead of being nearly symmetrical, the dramatic weight shifted to the latter part of the work. Second, the cantilena principle was condensed in the latter part. As a result, it built up intensity right until the end of the execution, instead of stopping at the Maria–Lyubov scene, as had happened before. Third, the Maria–Lyubov scene changed character radically, from one working on internalized tension to a scene of overtly expressed urgency. Dodin's original purpose was to show the fatality of events. Thus, when the women sang 'Let's hurry', their actions did the exact opposite. Instead of hurrying out, they slumped into stillness on the floor, with Maria more or less paralysed by her dawning realisation that she had unwittingly played a decisive role in her father's death. The interval was to come after the tragic image of an unalterable situation had been impressed upon the spectators. Dodin's modified version, the one performed for the public, required Maria and Lyubov to take both the text and the music literally and to hurry and run out into the wings. This was dramatically effective and exciting, if rather more predictable than the stunned inertia and minimal outward activity that Dodin had rehearsed and intended.

It is worth pausing over the Maria–Lyubov scene a little longer because it admirably demonstrates the principle of the respective integrity of staging and music. In rehearsals, the mezzo-soprano in the role of Lyubov (Tatyana Gorbunova) had some doubts about the validity of Dodin's idea that acting at the end of this scene should be at a minimum. She pointed to the turbulence of the music, arguing that it compelled bigger gestures and a bigger voice than Dodin seemed prepared to allow. To which he countered that the music was doing all the necessary work anyway, and that if the singing and the acting repeated it, one of these elements was superfluous. It was not difficult to deduce that the whole point, as he saw it, was to make nothing superfluous.

Furthermore, his desire to play down rather than to play up vocal and dramatic expression was consistent with his approach to the beginning of the scene. Both the soprano singing Maria (Olga Guryakova) and Gorbunova sang their parts with all their force in the very first rehearsals, and moved and gesticulated accordingly. Dodin guided them to reduce everything that they had delivered with such gusto to more intimate sounds, movements and proxemics. Thus, for example, Lyubov's opening line, 'Maria, my daughter', which Gorbunova initially sang imperiously, was re-sung quietly and reworked until the voice was able to communicate a number of interrelated psycho-emotional and situational factors: how Lyubov had risked life and limb to enter a guarded palace and find her daughter; her timidity (*not* her imperiousness) before this daughter; her fear for her husband, and her fear of Mazepa. All of this can be interpreted from the words of her very next lines (beginning with 'Hush, hush! / Don't betray us'), which is precisely where Dodin found the support for his hearing 'Maria, my daughter' as an intimate line. But the heart of the matter was not in the fact that the interpretation could be textually justified, but in how a singing voice, trained to sing out in an extroverted fashion, was to shed its reflexes so that the sense of what could be justified by subsequent lines was already there, present, at the start.

The rest of the scene followed from the tone set here. Take Maria's 'What father? / What execution?' after Lyubov pleads with her to save her father. Guryakova initially sang these questions with bravura. Dodin, on the other hand, asked her to sing them hesitantly and with bewilderment, thereby stressing Maria's ignorance of the situation and putting the long scene between Maria and Mazepa, which had just happened, in a tragic light. Equally, he anticipated what would be developed during the scene, namely, Maria's inability to react in any way other than a deadened manner. Details such as these worked towards the chamber-piece quality that Dodin sought for the whole sequence, in contrast with the grander sweep of the music.

Dodin's method of reducing performance to oblige singers to focus on the meaning of their song also involved looking for speech inflections that could adequately convey this meaning. Perhaps the best way to describe this process is to say that the singers' task was to 'transfer' or 'translate' these inflections into singing. To help them grasp his purpose, Dodin twice took the opportunity in the first week of rehearsals to read verses from *Poltava* to them in a conversational manner, as an actor might do in comfortable, small-scale surroundings. He paraphrased and glossed the verses, and suggested a range of interpretative possibilities, especially for intonation and cadence.

Perhaps the most striking instance of this actorly-analytical approach, which he had brought from his work with the Maly, was the first run through of the opera's conclusion. This consists of Andrey's arioso, 'Maria, I am dying', followed by Maria's lullaby. The singers sang it beautifully, with great feeling and emotional clarity. Even so, Dodin returned to Pushkin to show them a harder edge. He found that they had been 'carried away by sentiment' (18 February 1999) and on this and subsequent runs of the scene, he pared away anything resembling emotional indulgence till the singers found a purity of sound that, on the opening night, was breath-stopping and heart-wrenching all by itself. The process of playing down to find the right measure allowed the singers not only to go through a gamut of variations, layer upon layer, on which they could easily draw (a Maly practice), but perhaps more importantly to know how to build back volume and breath, for example, and deliver more powerfully without losing sight of the nuances that they had discovered. These rehearsals were accompanied by a piano. The litmus test for the singers concerning how they had changed tack and whether they would revert to old ways was when they rehearsed with the orchestra. It was satisfying to observe, when the time came, how few readjustments they had to make to the interpretative principles established with them by Dodin.

The singers were obliged as well to deal with a difficulty that Badri Maisur-adze, who alternates the role of Andrey with Kirov soloist Viktor Lutsyuk, describes as a particularity of Russian opera, one especially striking when the latter is compared with Italian opera. This is its verbal density, which is satu-rated with meaning and virtually prevents the repetition of simple words, phrases, musical refrains and melodies that in the Italian repertoire allow singers to 'rest a little' and take breath (20 March 1999). It is worth noting another factor in the creative process. Maisuradze's short, squat physique – the antithesis of Lutsyuk's elegant body – inspired Dodin to make Andrey a hunchback, with the tenor's unqualified approval. Lutsyuk, in the second cast, cuts a more typically dashing figure for the role. Dodin turned a perceived disadvantage in Maisuradze's physique into an opportunity for creating an anti-Romantic hero. Maisuradze's slightly grotesque air, albeit seen with a compassionate eye, picks up the sinister undertones of the production as a whole. This is a good example of how everything on stage conveys meaning, including signs whose reasons for being there are unavailable to spectators.

Scenography and performance

How does the production look and sound? Borovsky's sets comprise a wooden, scaffold-like structure which has a floor and four rows of pillars making three 'corridors'. A platform cuts across the top half of the structure. Its central piece is crowned by an M-shape rather like the skeleton of a roof. This M motif is repeated upside down on the front and back of the left and right 'corridors' below. The whole suggests the foundations and frame of a house being built or abandoned, with just a touch of a cathedral about its upper part – not unlike, in fact, the top of the Duomo in Milan. (Is this Borovsky's 'intertextual' reference to the cathedral, which is as iconic of the city as La Scala itself? Certainly, the visual allusion to a place of worship echoes Mazepa's depiction of his struggle for Ukraine's independence as a 'sacred task'.) This 'house' is inside walls of uneven height, which are not as high as the building itself. There is ample space between the building and the walls, along which run wooden benches. Lying on the ground are several cornices and curly-shaped objects meant to be stones.

One large, almost harp-like piece standing at the back looks particularly like a shape from Picasso's *Guernica*, which is consistent with the opera's war theme. There are two unobtrusive openings in the walls – 'doors' – opposite each other. The whole construction is in white to suggest limewash, as is typical of old rural houses in Ukraine. For all its allusions to recognisable features – including hints of eighteenth-century Ukrainian palaces – the construction is curiously abstract.

The platform of this classically proportioned construction moves up or down according to events. Dodin describes the design as a 'living phenomenon, which changes like the story itself' (20 March 1999), and it is functional and theatrical rather than decorative. It moves up, for instance, at the end of the first tableau in Act I to open out space for the scene in Kochubey's house. It moves down again for Act II to indicate a shift in place, time, mood and circumstances. It is now a symbol of oppression: the dungeon where Kochubey is tortured; the Ukrainian night of Mazepa's monologue ('How still is the Ukrainian night' – virtually straight Pushkin), which Dodin desentimentalises since it is full of blood, not stars; Mazepa's terror-filled palace, to which Maria appears oblivious. Prisoners are tied to the pillars. The extras used for these roles walk on at the beginning of Act II and take ropes hidden in the pillars to tie themselves up in different positions, one at each pillar, leaning, lying, as if locked in. They hold their positions until they are taken away in twos and threes during the course of the act (in Dodin's imagination, to be executed elsewhere in the cavernous palace). This activity, although discreetly done, gives the act a certain choreographic flow and some counterpoint to its series of long, textually-dense duets in which movement is restrained. Once again, as in *Lady Macbeth*, the extras were prepared by Khamutyansky.

The upper construction moves up a little and then comes down again, lower than before, for the execution scene. A low, box-like shape on the upper construction (from which Maria sings to her girlfriends in Act I) lifts up perpendicularly as Kochubey (Anatoly Kotsherga) is made to kneel with his back against it. A trapdoor flies open to suggest a guillotine when, concurrently, one of the two hooded executioners brings down an axe on Kochubey's neck. Kochubey slides down the chute that had just been created, his fall screened from view by the chorus grouped along the front pillars supporting the platform. A barely noticeable ladder going from the floor to the platform at the back is used for entrances and exits in the execution scene. Maria and Lyubov also run up it, virtually unseen by the audience, appearing suddenly out of the crowd just at the moment when Kochubey shoots down. Timing is of the essence here, as is co-ordination between the 'living' decor and the performers, especially as the tension generated by the whole relies, as well, on the *enchaînement* of the scene's micro-units of action.

Borovsky extends the sheer theatricality of his scenography to the see-saws hidden among the wooden supporting pillars in the front sections of the construction. The see-saw is exclusively Andrey and Maria's space. Andrey slides his way up and walks along it in Act I. A good part of his duet with Maria occurs on it, as she balances his weight with hers. Andrey is shot on it in Act III, falls, slides and lies there unnoticed during the dialogue between Maria, Mazepa and Orlik before the men depart in haste. He sings his concluding aria on it as he crawls upwards towards its tip, where Maria takes her balance as she sings. Dodin rehearsed these sequences with great care, since everything happening on the see-saw had to look effortless, and the closing moments had to follow on without a trace of melodrama or sentimentality. The emotional power, as Dodin saw it, of Tchaikovsky's finale had to come from the transparency of acting, singing and orchestral music combined. The very act of performing on see-saws becomes, by the end of the performance, a metaphor for the precariousness of love, friendship and life itself, which can tip, all too quickly, into war.

Although Dodin presents Mazepa's destructiveness quite ruthlessly, he avoids turning him into a one-dimensional character by stressing Maria's relationship with him. Dodin observed during rehearsals that Maria loves Mazepa for his energy, will-power, decisiveness and virility, all of which drive his political ambitions and would, Dodin believes, attract a spirited young woman. These qualities were not to be expressed so much as *embodied*, which is why Dodin encouraged Alfred Muff in the role to show Mazepa's firmness and presence of mind. Again and again, Dodin's adverbs for Mazepa's movements and gestures were 'quietly', 'calmly', 'gently', 'tenderly', and much the same adverbs were used for Maria's responses. They not only 'corrected' the tendencies of both tenor and soprano to deliver in an agitated, even heroic, mode. They also showed Dodin's desire to 'correct' both Pushkin, where Mazepa is nothing short of a brazen villain, and Tchaikovsky, where Mazepa's motivations largely seem crude and/or rendered insignificant by the mellifluous music, as occurs, particularly, in his love aria 'Oh, Maria, Maria'. Doing things quietly meant going behind the obvious and the rhetorical and drawing Maria and Mazepa as three-dimensional personalities whose love is not only believable, but also inextricably bound up with politics.

Indeed, the production quite clearly overlays the Maria–Mazepa story with the story of the battle of Poltava. Dodin asked Muff to think of Mazepa's big 'Ukrainian night' aria in Act II as similar to Hamlet's great soliloquy: Mazepa, like Hamlet, was asking questions about life, love, death, the motives for action or lack of it, and the consequences of personal and political betrayal, and was doing so in the same thoughtful way. Occasionally, when guiding Muff to find suitable inflections and intonations, Dodin spoke of the aria metaphorically, saying that the 'Ukrainian night' was the 'night of Mazepa's heart'. In this way, the aria was turned into an exploration of Mazepa's conscience, pain, foreboding and awareness that to choose to go to battle, which Kochubey's murder presages, is to destroy Maria and his life with her. Very similar explorations extend the aria 'Oh, Maria, Maria' beyond its love theme.

For these reasons, Dodin works on associations so that kinesic, proxemic, visual and sonic semiotics continually interlink to construct meaning. For instance, Mazepa is positioned during the 'Maria' aria at the pillar where Kochubey had been tied up previously. He lifts the noosed rope that now hangs loose at the pillar, or leans his back against it, as if to put himself in Kochubey's place. (Lyubov, when she comes in, will lift up the same bit of rope as if to rub it, with the truth, into her daughter's face.) In the duet with Maria that follows, he is positioned against this pillar when he asks about the extent of her love, knowing already, as she does not, that Kochubey is condemned. Later in the duet, when Mazepa hints at his political plans, they sing beside this pillar. He imagines freedom behind the power he hopes to acquire, she glory, as the personal and the political intertwine. It is here, too, towards the end of the duet, that Mazepa unfastens Maria's skirt so as to make it drop to the floor. His discreet action elliptically suggests love-making – another example of Dodin's procedure by understatement which here has an after-effect, like shock, since Lyubov enters immediately afterwards and Maria, who is barely out of Mazepa's arms, discovers how deeply he has betrayed her. What also emerges from the Maria–Mazepa duet is the immense sincerity of the characters' emotions. This is precisely why Act III is so devastating. Mazepa's abandonment of Maria and her descent into madness seem unthinkable in the light of the earlier scenes between them. Similarly, the battle of Poltava looks like a gratuitous event.

The chorus of tragedy

The process of cumulative effect typical of Dodin's work with his own company has a good deal to do with how he utilises the chorus. Act I opens with a chorus of women who come in through the 'doors' in the walls during the overture and sit on the benches, waiting to begin. Maria blends in with the chorus until she slowly makes her way up to the platform from which she will sing. It becomes apparent very quickly that the chorus, which maintains its hieratic position throughout the first tableau, dialogues with the protagonist and fulfils a narrative purpose exactly as occurs in Greek tragedy. In the second tableau, small groups of the male chorus (Mazepa's and Kochubey's respective guards) are concentrated in the 'house' area and move minimally, although deliberately, so as not to scatter the gaze. Since the Scala chorus is made up of some 100 singers, Dodin solved the problem of overcrowding without losing vocal power by having the rest of the chorus sing from the orchestra pit. This ingenious solution to problems not only of space and visual configuration but also of dramatic sense was used again for the execution scene so that a mass of people could be implied without clutter.

However, the most extraordinary use of the chorus is in the transition from Act II to Act III when, during a musical interlude, the execution scene flows into a scene of war. The preparatory movements of this cantilena occur before the execution, when the chorus sings passages based on Russian Orthodox liturgy in 'reply' to Kochubey's and Iskra's prayers, bass and tenor (Renato Cazzaniga) in translucent harmony. Dodin and Rostropovich have the brass band required by the score playing from loges to the left of the stage. The music coming from the loges in 'reply' to the orchestra brings an element of surprise, even a touch of kitsch, to what musically begins to be a whirl of sound and, dramatically, a major shift in tempo and scale. The music narrates the battle – wind, cavalry, weapons, clash, fight, flight – while Tchaikovsky quotes his own compositions, notably the *1812 Overture*, signalling Russia's victory over Napoleon, and uses this anachronism to indicate Charles XII's imminent defeat. Dodin rejects any nationalistic interpretation of *Mazepa* which, he believes, is intrinsic to folkloric views of Ukraine of the kind encouraged by Imperial Russia (reflected in Tchaikovsky's music) and, similarly, during the Soviet period. Hence, besides the demands of tragedy, his deletion of the opera's folk scenes.

Meanwhile, in terms of dramatic action, the choral singers, who had faced the execution, now turn towards the audience as the rest file in silently through the 'doors'. After circling the 'house' ceremoniously, they take their places on the benches. Simultaneously, a hooded figure climbs to the top of the platform, takes off Maria's long coat and, with large, considered gestures, cuts off her braid. Maria is still, expressionless, and anonymous in the flow of people moving off and around the platform. The act of cutting off hair acquires symbolic force in this pageant: it signifies the violation of a woman's body and the atrocities of war in general. The hooded figure holds the braid high, like a trophy, for spectators to see. As it passes across the front of the stage, followed by a somnambulistic Maria, its resemblance to Death-the-Reaper is unmistakable. Dodin names this mime character Fate.

The 'living' construction, as Dodin describes it, also enters the fray. The walls turn the yellow colour of the light before a storm. Some lights are dimmed to flatten the dimensions of the performers and show only black silhouettes. This surrealistic image is compounded as the walls part and lift up or slide away to reveal lower walls behind them with black edges, like burnt paper – a fantastic ellipsis for the ravaging fire of war. Small pieces of paper fall from the flies like black snow. They began to fall when Maria's hair was cut off, early in the transition. However, not until the burnt walls are visible do spectators realise that they are to be taken as flakes of ash. The chorus sits silently along the front and the sides and, by its very presence, asserts the narrative function that Dodin has assigned to it from the very beginning. It represents the common people – an image of the citizens of Greek tragedy – who endure, witness and relate disaster. Then, in what Dodin describes as a 'ritualistic manner', they get up and, together, facing the audience, let their costumes drop. Underneath, they are wearing black-edged, black-streaked clothing – clothes that have been burnt like the walls around them. They stand still. Then, they step out of the spot where their costumes have fallen and begin a procession that circumscribes the 'house'. One by one, they exit swiftly out of the 'door' at stage left. With this, Dodin captures superbly, allegorically rather than realistically, historical memories of long lines of refugees from war.

The whole has a strong epic quality that contrasts sharply with the intimacies of Act II. History overwhelms domesticity and leaves in its wake a field strewn with corpses, for the heavy costumes sculpted by the light look exactly like corpses. While the last people in the chorus file out, a veiled figure joins their tail end and comes forward to sit on a bench to the left. Another figure, its mirror image, takes its place on the right. Maria, who has been left behind by the circular procession, drags the discarded clothes/bodies out of the way from the front of the stage. (Guryakova hit on this effective idea late in the piece, thus assuming the responsibility for collaborative creativity which Dodin calls co-authorship.)

Act III begins with Andrey appearing from the back in search of Mazepa (Figure 16). As he sings of the sound of horses, the figures lift their veils. They are Mazepa and Orlik. The music gallops while, in contradiction, Mazepa and Orlik sit still. This is a pithy example of Dodin's discussion with Gorbunova about the superfluity of vocal and gestural 'expressiveness' when the music is performative and does what it says. Dodin's highly stylised, poeticised way of presenting Mazepa's and Orlik's arrival is in the vein of the war scene. From here, the more realistic aspect sustained by Andrey takes over. Orlik (Giancarlo Boldrini), for example, puts a pistol to Maria's head to suggest that he will shoot her unless Mazepa leaves her behind. This is not indicated in Tchaikovsky but is consistent with Dodin's conception of Orlik as Mazepa's foil. Orlik could, in fact, be described as doing Mazepa's dirtiest work for him. Dodin also reconstructs the end. Maria, when she sings her lullaby, does not cradle Andrey's head. She stands and then sits alone, a solitary figure in the devastated landscape.

Costumes and light as dramatic devices

Spinatelli's costumes are a blend of numerous shades of off-white, beige and grey. Her subtle palette is complemented by the fine textures of the fabrics: linens for Maria and the chorus, male and female; silks and cashmeres for Lyubov; fine leathers for the male soloists, which are doubled in a charred version for the war. As regards the chorus's black-edged clothing, Spinatelli explained how she had experimented with burning paper to see exactly how the fire marked it in order to capture its effects in cloth (18 March 1999).

The costumes do not belong to a clearly defined historical period. They have touches of many times and cultures: Ancient Greece; the Italian Renaissance; medieval Europe (Fate, the monks' habits); seventeenth- and eighteenth-century Europe, including Ukraine and Russia, where fashions were western (flared coats, high boots, three-cornered hats, drawstring sleeves); modern shifts. This fine tapestry seeks an indeterminate European quality so as to sustain the generalising power of Dodin's *mise en scène* – he did not want, as we remember, a piece of Ukrainian folklore. Woven into the tapestry are hard, cruel details such as the masks, like terrorists' balaclavas, worn by Mazepa's guards; the pants, like under-clothes, worn by Kochubey, Iskra and the prisoners, and the long butchers' aprons in dark leather worn by the executioners over their bare, heavy torsos.

Kalman's lights capture a central image or idea from scenes and articulate it through colour or shading, flatness or depth. For instance, the light on Borovsky's construction, before the chorus enters, is pearl grey – a mysterious, though soft

Figure 16 *Mazepa* at the Teatro alla Scala, Milan, 1998. B. Maisuradze as Andrey with costumes as corpses and the veiled figures of Mazepa and Orlik.

Photograph by Andrea Tamoni, courtesy of Teatro all Scala, Archivio Fotografico.

light which is associated with Maria as well as her father's house. Thus it re-appears with touches of blue in the finale of Act I. It reappears again, translucent, for Maria's lullaby. Several different kinds of white light, often coming from the sides of the stage, illuminate climaxes, such as the quarrel scene in Act I, or when Kochubey and Iskra pray in Act II. A flash of brighter light appears from above at the centre when Kochubey is executed, and this also gives a sensation of depth to the picture. The most spectacular lighting, with its play of several different tones and shadows, is in the war scene where Kalman follows Dodin's allegory with extreme sensitivity.

As Dodin rehearsed the opera, the Rambouillet meetings were grinding to a halt, unable to find a political solution for Kosovo and the wars in the Balkan region. Dodin was acutely aware of the cross-connections between these real-life events and the make-believe events that he was preparing to stage. When talking with the singers as to what *Mazepa* might be about, he more than once referred to how older generations pursued their goals, as Mazepa and Kochubey had once done for Ukraine, without considering what the consequences of their actions might be for the young. Given his line of thought, it was no accident that Dodin likened Mazepa's war of independence to that of a Karadzic. This indicates his keen sense of how closely artistic creation is related to the ambient world. For this reason, he treats opera not as an antiquated art, a 'dead museum' as he once put it during rehearsals, but as *theatre* alive to the living. 'The most interesting thing about the theatre', Dodin asserts 'is that what happens there could happen anywhere: people love each other, betray each other, like Kochubey and Mazepa, and can die or go mad, like Maria' (inter-view with Radio Three, Milan, 19 March 1999). The tragedy of it is that what can happen anywhere needs far more than the theatre, opera included, to resolve it, or to bring the curtain down and end it.

7 Anatomy of *The Queen of Spades*
From studio to stage

'Herman went mad.' This dry line from Pushkin's epilogue to his 1833 master-piece must surely have inspired Dodin to imagine that Herman does not, in fact, go mad but *is* mad right from the start. Not only does he set his entire produc-tion in a psychiatric hospital but, by taking Pushkin's ending as his beginning, he is able to organise all events as if they were being seen from Herman's point of view. Dodin's focus on what happened to Herman in the Obukhovsky asylum in St Petersburg, where Pushkin dispassionately leaves him, opens up the possibility of combining two opposing perspectives: the novella's, with its chilling account of Herman's descent into madness, and that of Modest Tchaikovsky's romantic libretto written for his brother Pyotr, in which the love story between Liza and Herman is central.

Pushkin's Herman does not care in the least for Liza who is the poor ward of an imperious Countess. His sole goal is to tear from the Countess the secret of the three cards – three, seven, ace – that can win him a fortune at the gaming tables. Herman, in the libretto, wants to know the secret to be socially worthy of Liza who is no mere ward but the grand-daughter and heiress of the Countess. Modest invents a rival for Herman in Prince Yeletsky, Liza's fiancé. Count Tomsky, who in Pushkin is the Countess's grandson, changes roles and becomes her peer and Yeletsky's friend. As in Pushkin, Tomsky tells how the Countess was an inveterate gambler during her youth in Paris. She had lost a fortune, but had won it back thanks to the secret of the three cards learned from the dis-solute Count Saint-Germain in return for her sexual favours. It was predicted that the third person to seek the secret from her would cause her death. While Dodin is obliged by the musical composition to follow Modest's plot, he is nevertheless especially attentive to the tragic undertow of Pyotr's score which draws the opera back into Pushkin's dark world. Dodin thus recovers through the music Pushkin's tragedy of insanity, which Modest had rejected for the glit-tering success bestowed by the Imperial Theatres of St Petersburg, where *The Queen of Spades* was first performed in 1890.

Pushkin's novella is located in the 1830s. The opera mirrors the idealised image of itself cultivated by St Petersburg high society by going back to the reign of Catherine the Great (1762–96) and the Versailles of Marie-Antoinette. The boy soldiers, governesses and nannies in the Summer Garden built by

Peter I feature in the opening scene of Act I and set the social tone. Act II opens with a masked ball that includes a pastorale called 'The Faithful Shepherdess' – an allusion indeed to Versailles – sung to a pastiche of a melody from Mozart's Piano Concerto in C Major K503. Mozart's orchestration and purity of line are, in any case, echoed in the opera, thereby incorporating in its historical contextualisation Tchaikovsky's tribute to a composer whom he greatly admired (Brown, 1992: 229, 245, 246). The ballroom scene, which is full of potential for spectacular staging, ends with the *coup de théâtre* of the Empress Catherine's grand entrance.

The second scene of Act II focuses on the Countess who reminisces about the beautiful people she knew as a young woman at Marie-Antoinette's court. Tchaikovsky overlooks a glaring anachronism, since the Countess is meant to be 80 years old when the opera's events occur, and introduces another when she sings a Romance, also supposedly from her youth, from André Grétry's 1784 opera *Richard Coeur de Lion (Richard the Lionheart)*. Tchaikovsky was probably aware that this opera was 'received as a fable about liberty' on the eve of the French Revolution (Arblaster, 1992: 47), but quotes the Romance just the same for the royalist sentiments that it affords the Countess, its expression of her melancholy, and its use for building up atmospheric effects, musically and theatrically. The words of the Romance are the last she utters before Herman, who has been lying in wait for her in her bedroom, frightens her to death. Its wistful melody runs counter to the turbulent music for Herman as he agonises over his failure to obtain the Countess's secret.

The Countess's ghost finally reveals the secret to him in Act III. Herman rushes off to the gaming tables, but, instead of an ace, pulls out the wrong card, the Queen of Spades, which ruins him. Act III is played out against the backdrop of another Imperial symbol, the Peter and Paul Fortress on the Neva, visible through the archway of the Winter Canal into which Liza, horrified by Herman's betrayal, throws herself and drowns. The Tchaikovsky brothers ignored Pushkin's crisp statement about how Herman, a 'Russified' German, was an impoverished outsider. They solved the problem of his class status vis-à-vis Liza's milieu by turning Herman into a hussar of the Imperial army. Modest was opposed to Liza's suicide. However, Pyotr believed that spectators would want to know what had happened to her and that a closing act comprised only of men would not hold enough interest for them (Brown, 1992: 242). Liza does not kill herself in Pushkin, who was far too much a man of the Enlightenment to indulge in such victim fantasies of women. She happily marries the son of a former steward in her guardian's service.

The discrepancies between the novella and the opera merit attention because Dodin searches in their interstices for the motor force of his own production. Stanislavsky and Meyerhold had done much the same before him, both having been profoundly affected by Pushkin's portrayal of Herman. The difference between their interpretations of the opera lay in how far they were prepared to push the idea that Herman was mad. Stanislavsky began rehearsals for *The Queen of Spades* in 1928. His collaborator Pavel Rumyantsev, who finished the project, reports that Stanislavsky 'did not pursue the idea of showing Herman as a madman' and 'only tried to create an atmosphere of tension around him thanks to which a man in the grip of a morbid idea would inevitably fall into the abyss of madness' (Stanislavsky and Rumyantsev, 1975: 340). Stanislavsky's production notes show him to be equally preoccupied, for the sake of atmosphere, with such details as the 'wraps, baskets, toys, umbrellas, etc.' carried by the nannies in the Summer Garden and the crowd scenes in the Garden as well as at the ball and in the gambling house, all of it throwing Herman's 'nervous' conduct into relief (341).

Meyerhold staged *The Queen of Spades* in 1935. Unlike Stanislavsky's preparations, which had been in the public domain for some time, the rehearsal transcripts of this famous production were not published until 1993 (Meyerhold, 1993: 99–144). He spoke with irony to his cast: 'We know, of course, that Modest was – Modest', but the crucial thing was that 'Pyotr Ilich knew and loved Pushkin' and 'strove to express with all his music what he had heard while reading *The Queen of Spades*' (109). Meyerhold's intention of 'returning Pushkin to Tchaikovsky' (100) was inspired by Herman's isolation which, in his view, was exacerbated by Herman's obsession with the three cards. Meyerhold wanted Herman to have a rebellious air about him like Hamlet, or Pushkin and Lermontov. He thus set his production in the 1830s (119). Nicholas I was to replace Catherine in the ballroom scene, and the city's atmosphere was to be carefree, as 'in paintings, people walking arm in arm'. There was to be no sign of the Decembrist revolt against tsarist autocracy, Pushkin having narrowly escaped the death or exile imposed by Nicholas I on the Decembrists and those associated with them.

As far as one can tell from the transcripts, Meyerhold linked Herman's feeling of alienation to what might be termed a pathology of outsideness (a state of being he probably felt himself in the growing terror of the 1930s). If true, this would illuminate Meyerhold's claim that 'Herman is demented from the beginning' (103) and explain why he restructured the libretto to make its love story of minor interest. Meyerhold's shift of emphasis provoked vehement protest and debate, responses he appears to have anticipated, judging by the allusions of his 1934 speech to the team at Leningrad's Small State Opera Theatre, which was published with the transcripts of his rehearsals (103–15; Braun, 1998: 248). Meyerhold had also cut out the pretty scenes Tchaikovsky had feared 'might turn out rather like some trivial operetta' (Brown, 1992: 282), notably the governesses and nannies in the Summer Garden. The ball, instead of being an occasion for celebration, became a series of tableaux depicting Herman's torment.

Dodin knew both the Stanislavsky and Meyerhold records, although it was Meyerhold who was his reference in his preliminary discussions with Bychkov. Yet he looked beyond Meyerhold's causes for Herman's madness to what could be called its operations, taking also for comparison Prokofiev's *The Gambler* (1929) derived from Dostoevsky. This meant showing how all the opera's events take place in Herman's mind, the past merging with the present, fantasy with reality, and Herman's delirium with the suffering he inflicts upon Liza. Incarcerating Herman entailed condensing the action and some of the music, to which Bychkov agreed: 'Cuts cannot be arbitrary. There has to be a musical and dramatic justification for them' and the result has to be 'musically seamless' (Amsterdam, 27 October 1998). Several choral sequences in the Summer Garden scene were cut on the grounds that they broke the tension generated by Herman's love for Liza (the aria 'I do not know her name') and by his fascination with Tomsky's story of the cards, the phrase 'three cards' being tossed back and forth between the soloists to great dramatic effect. A similar decision was made for the second scene of Act I where Liza's confidante Polina sings of unfulfilled love. Her sombre Romance is followed by a Russian folk song and dance performed by a chorus of Liza's friends. Dodin deleted this jolly interlude which, he believed, added nothing to the situation. By continuing the scene between Liza and Polina without interruption, he brought Liza's forebodings into focus in anticipation of the tragedy about to befall her. Choral passages for guests and gamblers in the third scene of Act III were cut for similar reasons of focus, this time on Herman.

In order to sustain the drama, Dodin divided the opera into two parts instead of its three acts so that the interval could come after the ball, that is, halfway through Act II. This allowed Dodin to do away with a glamorous scene, which had no place in a psychiatric hospital, and go inside Herman's head by making the patients, doctors and nurses, who are played by the supernumeraries and members of the chorus, 'guests' at the ball. Secondly, he was able to avoid the Empress Catherine – or Nicholas I, or any monarch – for the sake of artistic integrity, especially as regards Herman. He therefore replaced the Empress by the Countess whose appearance is Herman's phantasm which rivets his demented gaze, directing everybody's eyes on stage and in the auditorium to it. Such concerted looking emphasises Herman's derangement, which Borovsky's design reiterates when the set comes asunder as the chorus sings its greetings to the 'Empress', bunched up on a ledge. This ledge moves down as the wall enclosing it moves apart in jagged edges to reveal classically proportioned stairs and columns and the white statues of Venus, Adonis and Perseus, all of which still stand in the Summer Garden today. Dodin has the Countess come down the stairs and move to the centre of the stage quickly so as to catch the closing bars of the music. By the third week of rehearsals, Kirov star Vladimir Galuzin in the role of Herman had turned him into a pitiful wreck, staring and gibbering at this apparition.

The impact of Dodin's structural change was bound up with three musical interventions. The first is in Act I when Tomsky cites lines reputedly spoken by the Countess on losing her fortune ('Oh heaven! Oh heaven!'), whereupon Saint-Germain sees his opportunity to seduce her. Dodin has the Countess sing these lines sitting on Herman's bed. Her position suggests the seduction, while her words are his memory and hallucination merging as one. The second in Act II is the pastorale, 'The Faithful Shepherdess', sung in Tchaikovsky by Daphnis and Chloë, then joined by Pluto. Dodin has it sung by Herman, Liza and the Countess – a demonic love trio mirroring the fateful threesome of the cards. The third intervention is in Act III, which in Tchaikovsky begins with Herman reading a letter from Liza. Dodin thought it would be illogical for Herman to read it in an asylum, out of his mind. Consequently, he has Liza read, thereby implying that she is a glimmer of the past, a piece of the jigsaw jumbled in Herman's head. In Galuzin's words: 'Dodin sees our performance as the last fragment, Herman's last day, so to speak, before the end' (Amsterdam, 27 October 1998). This end, as became clear by the dress rehearsal, follows Herman's final crisis when, reliving his loss at the gambling house, he tears up his mattress in search of money. He thereupon falls into a comatose state, incapable of envisioning anything ever again.

Rehearsals by De Nederlandse Opera at the Muzie-theater in Amsterdam

What follows is my abbreviated log-book of Dodin's rehearsals during the second and last weeks of a six-week rehearsal period. The former was accompanied by a piano, Bychkov conducting the singers. The last week was mostly accompanied by the orchestra and included a semi-dress rehearsal to piano and a full dress rehearsal with orchestra. Rather than weave together rehearsal and production detail, as was the case in preceding chapters, the interest here is to try and get inside Dodin's mind and grasp the *evolution* of his creative thought. The compact rehearsal time, so unlike the Maly's, was propitious for such an attempt in that it made Dodin more directive and quicker to intervene than he is with his actors. This pushed his thinking out into the open for immediate access and, being more immediate, it shed light on the type of thinking, if not on the actual method, that informs his work with the Maly.

Rehearsals: 26–31 October 1998

Rehearsals during the second week focused on Act II, the opening and the close of the first scene of Act I, the last fragments of the second scene of Act I, and the first two scenes of Act III. They involved all soloists except Vasily Gerello from the Kirov (Yeletsky) and Marianna Tarasova (Polina), who had prior engagements. Close attention was given to the relations between Herman, the Countess (Helga Dernesch) and Liza (Tatyana Poluektova alternating with Natalya Ushakova). Less time was devoted to Herman's friends Tomsky (Pavlo Hunka), Surin (Harry Peeters) and Chekalinsky (Marcel Reijans), and to the short duets between Liza and her maid Masha (Janny Zomer). Dodin had asked the 19 supernumeraries, whom he had met at the beginning of the week, to read Pushkin's novella and the libretto (copies provided) so that 'they would not be mere automata and be moved around by me, but know as much as the soloists and be treated with respect by them' (26 October 1998). Various movements for these extras were marked in with the help of Maly dance teacher and choreographer Yury Vasilkov. Dodin referred to what the chorus might be doing, although work with this ensemble of 68 people did not start till the third week. He began soldier-marching with the 18 children requested for the Summer Garden scene. All in all, there were a good number of people to 'move around' in an intelligible fashion. A white iron bed 'on which Herman lies, turning in his head everything that has happened' (Dodin) was a centripetal force for every scene – not a mere rehearsal prop, but intended for the production.

Dernesch is a star of Wagnerian opera with a magnificent Isolde conducted by Herbert von Karajan behind her (recorded in 1972). Now singing in a lower register, she approached Dodin's cuts and corrections to her part with the modesty that comes from immense discipline. Galuzin spent eight years in comic roles in musical theatre before singing Tchaikovsky's *Iolanta* in Moscow, followed by his big break in Verdi's *Otello* at the Mariinsky, conducted by Gergiev. He joked that no one knew what his voice was, let alone whether he would make it to the opera, until he woke up one day as a tenor *and* an opera singer. He occasionally made fun of his role in the short pauses between singing, which helped to sustain a working atmosphere that remained warm despite blow-ups here and there, mostly over practical matters.

Dodin usually asked the singers to sing a scene through quietly before they acted it out with a fuller voice. They reworked it in the light of his commentary, the pattern of suggestion and redoing going through numerous permutations. He generally demonstrated what he was after and, although he glossed his actions, remarked more than once that he was afraid of saying too much: he wanted the singers to find what was comfortable for them, albeit within his framework. Dernesch, Poluektova and Galuzin understood almost instinctively, Galuzin observing that years of musical comedy had taught him how to think with theatre directors. This was not a vain boast, judging by his and Dodin's quick uptake of each other's suggestions. The soloists playing Herman's companions were open and eager, but not always sure of their freedom, and less still of Dodin's expectations of them. It was early days, but Dodin did not appear to have communicated enough to them to activate their creativity. Furthermore, the difficulties of working through an interpreter surfaced as key words were lost in the time lag between utterance and translation. Dodin had asked the management to hire trained actors for extras since he wished to avoid the experience he had had with *Lady Macbeth* of constantly showing non-actors what to do.

Dodin told everybody that part of Borovsky's design would be painted in green, the colour inside Russian psychiatric hospitals. This is an example of a sign whose meaning is restricted to people in the know – not unlike Wilson's green alligator in *A Letter for Queen Victoria*. Who knows the joke, besides New Yorkers, that alligators live in the sewers of New York?

Tomsky, Surin and Chekalinsky: 26 and 27 October

Various performances motivated by the words 'taunt' and 'bait', which Dodin had pulled out of these characters' dialogue in Act I, gave vignettes reminiscent of warring Montagues and Capulets. The men played the fool in Act II, mocking Yeletsky's emotions when he sings of his love for Liza. During the pastorale, they created a sense of disguised menace as they roamed around the bed where Liza and Herman were singing. Dodin, dissatisfied, tended to demonstrate more than usual, which resulted in their imitating him rather than sorting out their own stories. None of it sat well on their bodies, although their voices caught the tone he seemed to be seeking. They seemed most at ease in a card game during the pastorale, followed by a 'dance' with three flowers, which they passed around like cards. Tomsky gathered them up in a bouquet, handing it ceremoniously to the Countess. The men must be a projection of Herman's delusions in which he sees the 'three cards' as flowers. Dodin thought that the cards used in the sequence could be passed to a group of children behind and above the bed. It was impossible to tell just how strong this gambling motif would be in the production.

Dodin was concerned that the movements should be open and measured 'without a full stop in between', particularly when Tomsky leads in the Countess and she and Liza change places in a clever allusion to courtly dance. Borovsky's mock set is a copy of the narrow platform flanked by a wall designed for the production. What was striking was Dodin's brilliant use of this space to create washes of imagery by which all the characters, but especially the Countess and Liza, appeared to be both 'real' people and visitations swarming around Herman's hospital bed. It was not clear whether the three men's antics were meant to resemble those of the 'sick' people played by the extras, nor whether the overlap between their grotesque movements and the graceful 'dance' with the flowers would come off once the scene was out of a studio and in a large auditorium. And what about the blindfolds worn by Herman, the Countess and Liza? Presumably they alluded to a masked ball, as specified in the libretto. Would they be blindfolds or masks in the performance?

Doctors and nurses: 26, 27 and 31 October

The first run through of five doctors and nurses was in the storm scene in the Summer Garden when Herman resolves to win Liza or die. Tchaikovsky's trope – the 'pathetic fallacy' by which the storm inside the hero is identified with the storm in nature ('Storm, lightning, wind!' sings Herman) – is here transformed into the unpoetic, literal event described by psychiatrists as a 'psychotic episode'. Dodin guided these characters to take an impassive rather than empathetic attitude towards their patient, indicating by this that he wanted to counter semantic meaning and the performative function of words: 'You have seen it all before; this is Herman's hundredth attack'. He called one of them 'the Professor' to help the actor find suitable body language for the part. He suggested that another might take out a watch from his waistcoat and count the duration of Herman's attack. A third might just stand there with her arms crossed. It was obvious to all listening that Dodin wanted the storm, lightning and wind to stay in Tchaikovsky's music. The contradiction here between action and music parallels the contradiction between words and music in Yeletsky's love song to Liza in Act II. His love is without hope. Dodin went with the tragic power of Yeletsky's words against the rapturous flow of the music accompanying them.

The extras sustained Dodin's no-frills approach in rehearsals of the end of the ball scene. Herman gives the cue ('Now, not I / but fate decides / and I shall learn the three cards!') and, at the beginning of these lines, runs towards the wings. At the very same time, the Master of Ceremonies, who could be a patient or a nurse, comes menacingly towards him, followed by doctors and nurses. As if pushed back, Herman moves backwards towards his bed, Galuzin's body responding to Dodin's prompt: 'You are tired of looking into the future, so you are now looking into your own thoughts.'

During the second *proba* of this scene, Dodin changed the timing of the entrance so that spectators saw Herman moving backwards for no apparent reason. Dodin: 'It is much more interesting for us *not* to see why Herman is moving back, and understand only later, when we do see them [the doctors and nurses].' This is a principle of delayed reaction because the reason for the doctors' and nurses' entrance is clear only when they tie Herman's arms with ropes to the sides of his bed. Only then is it clear that Herman is having another attack, more violent than the 'storm' attack of Act I. The meaning of these actions is cumulative, and the effect, when it hits home, is one of shock because of Herman's state, the unperturbed manner of his carers and keepers and the barbaric treatment they dispense. In order to stress that this violent attack is routine, Dodin asked a nurse to gesture mechanically – a calming gesture – towards Herman from the platform above his bed. Quite by chance, the woman chosen by Dodin had worked for a number of years in a psychiatric hospital. She resisted the role, saying she would rather play a patient! Dodin replied, with humour, that he had no intention of differentiating between nurses and patients any more than happened in life where 'We all have our sicknesses'. He ended up relying on her expertise, for instance, in Act III, to wrap the Countess's dead body in a sheet and carry it, but this was scrapped, to everybody's relief, as being too awkward. In the next rehearsal, a stretcher appeared for moving her corpse. Dernesch is a tall, solid woman, and all but Dodin had doubts as to whether the men would manage to carry her.

Patients: 26, 27 and 30 October

The patients did not appear to be needed until the Empress's entrance in Act III. The walls were to shift just before the chorus sang the last verse of its hymn to Catherine. Courtiers, in Tchaikovsky, bow and curtsy to her. In Dodin, the patients do this with their backs to the audience ('not an "opera" bow to us'), their bottoms sticking out and their arms in odd positions. Dodin and Vasilkov spent time demonstrating a variety of disfigured movements. Vasilkov took care to show the balletic style embedded in them. How the massive chorus was to fit on the narrow ledge was anybody's guess. Nor could anybody guess what the effect would be when the space was opened out and the chorus and extras mingled. This would be a crucial moment, especially because it could overwhelm the image of Herman tied to his bed. Perhaps Dodin intended to dwarf Herman cruelly, thus accentuating the cruelty of his madness? There was no doubt that he was using the Maly Drama Theatre principle of simultaneous actions here, albeit on a larger scale. All things considered, this hypothetically busy scene risked destroying the intimacy that had begun to take hold in the relations between Herman, the Countess and Liza.

There is no funeral scene in the libretto. Dodin materialises Herman's terrified thoughts by placing a funeral upstage left. The chorus is to sing out of sight in the wings, thus solving the ledge problem. The extras were taught how to cross themselves from right to left in the Russian Orthodox manner, but frequently forgot, reverting to the Catholic left to right. Dodin refrained from saying too much and stifling their initiative. Gestures were ordinary. Perhaps its madhouse dimension would disappear from the scene when it went on stage. There were rumbles from somewhere in the House that a mere two scenes – in the middle of the show, moreover – did not give the extras enough work, or justify the cost of hiring professional actors. These anxieties were ill founded, since Dodin had already begun to use extras for Act I, and was bound to use them elsewhere. Nevertheless, stirs of this kind are a reminder of the expense of mounting operas and of the accountability of administrators to the public for the budgets of national institutions. The financial scandals surrounding Covent Garden in the late 1980s spring to mind. It seems impossible, in the current circumstances of opera making, to be allowed artistic mistakes in the name of research.

The Herman, Countess and Liza trio: 26 and 27 October

Why is 'The Faithful Shepherdess' sung by them? The point of it became clear when Dodin showed Galuzin how to put his arm around Dernesch with extraordinary tenderness and Dernesch how to place her head gently on his shoulder. The trio, in other words, is a triangle of desire, the Countess being Liza's displaced 'Other' as this notion relates to Freud's argument concerning transference (Freud, 1962–75). Liza is desired only through the Countess and the *idea* of fortune signified by the three cards. René Girard's theory (1961), according to which desire between two people occurs when it is mediated by a third, illuminates what Dodin is doing. So too, in a closely Freudian variant, does Jacques Lacan's 'dialectic of desire' (1977). How the Countess and Liza blur in Herman's head, the image of one shadowing the other, is objectified in the three characters sitting together on the bed. Although a hospital bed, it is sexually symbolic. Herman and Liza caress each other on it to conclude Act I, and both characters are still intertwined on it when Yeletsky sings his love song in Act II. Their embrace underscores the futility of his love.

The process of displacement and substitution by which Herman confuses the Countess and Liza was subsequently brought out during rehearsals of the second scene of Act II. (Herman is hiding in the Countess's bedroom. He sings 'Footsteps. People are coming . . .') Dodin had initially asked Dernesch to lead the procession of people coming home from the ball. He then felt this was wrong and asked Poluektova to precede Dernesch slightly. The purpose was to avoid 'piling meaning on meaning' (Herman thinks of the Countess, hears footsteps, enter the Countess) and remind spectators that there were *two* heroines in the plot, Liza *and* the Countess. In actual fact, Dodin constructed a triangle of desire in which there is a *third*, secret heroine, the Queen of Spades, who is the Countess's double and nemesis in one. For Dodin, the Queen of Spades represents Herman's insanity.

Herman and the Countess: 28 and 29 October

'The walls move in Herman's mind', said Dodin, as an abject Galuzin sat on his bed facing the audience. When the decor breaks up, the extras will meander in and bow to the Countess/Catherine while the chorus sings 'Vivat! Vivat!'. One of the most fascinating things about these rehearsals was how layers of interpretative detail visibly transformed the singers physically and emotionally. It was like watching a camera showing the processes of change in the human body, or the growth of a plant, in rapidly merging shots. Dodin's observations were incisive, but his tremendous plasticity had the advantage of conveying nuances that could not be caught quickly linguistically, in Russian let alone in translation. Light, nimble and simple, and with a remarkable command of space, he wove his way through the roles to inspire his performers. Dernesch changed from the stiff harridan that she had been playing to a woman of great subtlety whose memories of youth rejuvenated her before our very eyes. Galuzin became darker, but also softer, as he treated the Countess like a lover and then regressed into infantilism – child-like innocence crossed with lunatic oblivion. Galuzin had an extraordinary facility for contouring his gaze, and Dodin knew how to tap into it. He demonstrated how Innokenty Smoktunovsky, in Dostoevsky's *Idiot*, had gazed at the decorations on a General's lapel with such strange interest that spectators were compelled to look too. That quiet but compelling quality was what Dodin wanted for Herman's relationship with the Countess.

28 October

Dodin talked about the second scene of Act I rather than have the singers try it first. He is indifferent to the social implications of the Countess's switch to French when she sings Grétry's Romance. His emphasis is on her memories. To Dernesch:

> She remembers what beautiful music they had – none of those banging drums and cymbals that we have today. She is immersed in her thoughts. She notices the people around her, but they are not listening. So her gestures say all the words that she might like to use to tell them to go to hell,

though not in an angry way. She becomes immersed in her thoughts again. This is a musical piece. It is night-time. She might want to get up. She knew better times, hundreds of guests. She comes to the statues which are her wealth, but also her friends, who are all in the grave. She will try to sing from here, among the statues, talking with them, and with just a little dance-like movement to '*Je ne sais pas pourquoi*'.

Still to Dernesch after demonstrating Herman's movements before he tells the Countess not to be afraid:

> You know the evaluative accent of the 'three cards', what it means. You slowly understand, feeling in his tenderness, stubbornness, determination, that *he* is the third who would come. She gave her secret to her husband, then to her lover, but she was told precisely that the third man who comes for it will represent her death. He is no stranger; and it seems that death has come for her. She resists: 'I shouldn't be afraid of death. I am old, but it's a pity, just the same'. And, as soon as he persuades her to give in, she moves slowly, slowly to the music [Dodin having now come near the bed], and comes and sits down. She could think a little, and then lie down, very gently, like a child who wants to hide from danger. [Dodin indicates that Dernesch could cover herself with the sheet on the bed.]

Dodin to Galuzin, after showing him how to come gently to the bed and wait before he asks the Countess for her secret again:

> 'Old witch!' [libretto] He pulls off the sheet and sees her dead. There are no banal gestures here. No hands thrown up. No big expressions. He simply feels her cold hand and tenderly touches her face. He sees the secret in her eyes, but did not discover it. 'She is dead'. [libretto] He caresses her, as if this should have been his wealth [Dodin here kneeling at Dernesch's side]. In comes Liza. 'Ssh, Ssh, be quiet, she's dead' [Dodin's words]. Liza asks, 'Did you do this?' [Dodin] And he wants to explain, like a child who doesn't know that a toy breaks, that he just wanted to unscrew the toy. He says, 'She is dead' [libretto], as if no one wants to know that she is dead. [Dodin here suggests that Herman should look at the Countess with Smoktunovsky's gaze.] 'I only came for the three cards' [Dodin, his voice child-like and soft]. He doesn't really remember that he was supposed to come for Liza.

After finishing his overview of the scene, Dodin turned to its beginning. Herman was to walk among the statues as if he had been there 30 times before. Galuzin tried it. Dodin observed that he was singing as if Herman was saying the words for the first time, and asked if he could put an everyday, familiar sound into his voice. Galuzin's reply that he would 'have to get used to it' demonstrated how opera and the theatre could differ in their notions of vocal production. Dodin sought the exposition of character, motivation and situation by means of the voice. Galuzin's instinctive reaction was to give his opening gambit full song – a singer's comprehension of vocal virtuosity and projection by which musical interpretation and rendition take precedence over dramatic meaning. Nevertheless, Galuzin understood perfectly what Dodin was after from a dramatic point of view.

When Galuzin sang the opening bars again, his voice conveyed this dramatic meaning. The entire sequence was then performed, Galuzin reverting here and there to singer-style reflexes until he fully appropriated the dramatic impulse behind his actions. Dodin reminded him, for instance, not to look at the statue of Venus (which was inspired by 'Moscow Venus' in the libretto) 'as if he sees *her* for the first time, but as if he is talking with an old lover'. (At this juncture in the libretto, Herman is looking at a portrait of the Countess and recalls what he was told of her reputation in Paris.) Galuzin captured Dodin's prompt beautifully in the way he gazed up at the sculpture's face and caressed its legs, or held them, or touched its feet. Here, as in his unhurried walk through the Countess's park and interior, where he sometimes hid behind the sculptures or just blended in with them, he played on two levels simultaneously: the sculptures were material objects and, at the same time, emanations of Herman's 'sick spirit' – Herman's phrase early in his soliloquy when he wonders whether the Countess's secret is a figment of his imagination ('delirium').

Work continued on refining gestures, movements and proxemics to clarify what was happening to the characters and how they came together. Dodin suggested that Dernesch, instead of sitting on the bed as she begins the Romance, should lie down on it; also that she should sing more thoughtfully and 'with less voice, if possible'. When among her statue-friends ('What wonderful people', says Dodin), Dernesch produced child-like touches with her fingers to her face, possibly picking up Dodin's comments earlier to Galuzin on how Herman might behave beside the Countess's bed. Dodin liked Dernesch's gestures and the fact that she had not reacted overtly when Herman appeared. He asked her to continue the dance-like movements she had begun before Herman's appearance (whereupon Herman says incongruously 'Don't be frightened' in the softest of voices). The idea was to have Herman pick up her movement. The result was magical, and Galuzin walked with her in the same light way towards the bed. Early in the piece, Galuzin had walked behind Dernesch. The dance motif soon encouraged him to walk beside her, which Dodin corrected, saying that his earlier position had been more dramatically effective. Dodin also felt that the space Galuzin had kept between them gave a more pleasing sense of shape. It was amazing what a difference soft leather slippers had made to Dernesch's movements from the first to the later tries. Dodin had suggested she wear them, and they certainly helped her to find the lightness that his tone of voice and hand gestures had attempted to convey.

29 October

Quite a stunning run, madness in Galuzin's eye and body as he skulks about the statues as if he were wandering about in his mind; such tenderness when he and Dernesch come face to face after her '*Je ne sais pas pourquoi*'. Dodin remarks that Vasilkov would help them stylise the dance movements a little more. He comments to Dernesch that the Countess could have 'a shadow of a smile on her face'; that she is right not to be afraid of Herman because he 'belongs to her past', as if he were one of the people she had known. A second run sets off a chain reaction of details: Galuzin takes one of Dernesch's hand and then the other before the 'dance', which gives the whole thing a natural air; Dernesch's body follows her face to express the Countess's dawning realisation that he has come for her secret; Dernesch hides under the sheet (motivated by Dodin's '"I am not here", like a child') and pulls it over her face. These are small details, but they create intensity, focus and concentration for performers *and* spectators. Dodin to Galuzin: 'Pull down the sheet more gently, as if the secret is being revealed to you' so that 'there is no fear when you say, "She is dead." You are saying, "This isn't how we discussed it. We were going to do it together. You knew it would be alright."' A lover's discourse, one might say, although in an unlikely situation.

Herman and Liza: 26 and 29 October

The aim was to play Herman's and Liza's relationship sincerely. Only then, Dodin believed, would the ambiguities fall into place. Poluektova and Galuzin recapitulated what they had covered in the previous week, giving glimpses of how Herman was to mix and merge love, greed, ambition and obsession. Poluektova indicated (also proxemically from her various positions around the bed) how Liza's mixture of love, openness, commiseration and compassion could be interpreted dually: as emotions Liza could have experienced during the time Herman pursued her; as emotions she could have if she were visiting him in the asylum. For the love scene in Act I, Dodin advised Poluektova to find 'behaviour not quite as lyrical as your singing'. Judging from her modifications, such restraint shifted attention to Herman's 'sick spirit'.

Dodin asked Poluektova to be similarly restrained during the recitative of Liza's letter at the beginning of Act III. Poluektova's movement in the next scene (the Winter Canal) is also minimal. She sits on the edge of the bed, facing the audience. Galuzin is flat on his back, unconscious or asleep. The focus is on Liza, and her aria expresses her acute suffering. Her song leads to a duet with Herman in which they say they are united, but sing on opposite sides of the bed. Dodin stressed that their positions must undercut their words. The dramatic climax comes when Herman, in a fit of lunacy, suddenly no longer recognises Liza and attempts to drag her off to the gambling house. Galuzin drags Poluektova about on her knees, an overblown move which undermines the tragedy of Liza's love.

The children: 31 October

The children were met kindly and told that the girls would also march like soldiers. Some of them would dance a saraband in the ballroom scene. They would wear blindfolds, as in a game of blind man's buff. Dodin's words suddenly shed light on the bandaged eyes of Liza, Herman and the Countess: the trio play their own version of this game. Is blind man's buff a metaphor for Herman's lunacy? For Liza's love? For Herman's rhetorical 'What is our life? A game!' at the end of Act III? Dodin marched lightly beside the children, with his knees up high. Because they were very noisy, they were asked to take off their shoes, and were spaced out and rehearsed to march together and in time. This is Dodin's only chorus-line 'number' so far. In Tchaikovsky, children are drilled by a commander in the Summer Garden. Dodin replaces him with Herman so as to make the event part of Herman's delusions.

Behind the studio

Before the week is out, I read Dodin's note in Russian, which will be published in the programme. This is its most important passage:

> The three cards are not so much about a mystical destiny hanging over human beings as about their vulnerability, which tears them apart, as does the ephemeral nature of happiness and their irresistible desire to catch this happiness by the tail – at last, at once, quickly, now, in one go, at any price and forever. To play with the Almighty and win – win, full stop. In striving to win in life, we do not notice how we lose our life . . . It is no accident that the tragic notes of Tchaikovsky's Sixth Symphony, which he wrote just before his death, come to us through the music – the music of a genius – of *The Queen of Spades*. The further we go, the more we hear them in both the music and the story, which is very simple and terrifying, like our lives, and short, like an impetuous and pitiless illness.

Herman has no chance of winning. This is probably why Dodin decided to deal with Herman's 'pitiless illness' in such a rational way.

Peter Sellars is in the Muziektheater. He is clever and sweet, and his production of *The Rake's Progress*, which was premiered at the Châtelet in Paris, is about to begin its season. Sellars to Dodin: 'You know, we *really are* doing the same opera!' Dodin: 'Change yours!' Friendly, witty banter.

Sellars is sharp because *The Rake's Progress* could *almost* be the same opera, give or take several differences. Tom Rakewell, poor and excluded, needs money and social standing to marry his beloved. He thus makes a pact with Shadow (the devil) to achieve his goal. Sellars sees the pact as a metaphor for Tom's desire to overcome social exclusion. As in Pushkin and Tchaikovsky, you have to guess the secret of three cards or lose your soul. Rakewell, although winning at cards, is condemned to insanity by Shadow and thus loses his soul.

His beloved mourns him. Sellars closes Tom's story by putting him in a padded cell. Stravinsky's elegance is deceptive for, irrespective of its inspiration from Hogarth's prints and *The Beggar's Opera*, it hides what must surely be his cross-references to both Pushkin's and Tchaikovsky's *Queen of Spades*. And this resonance is there, as Sellars's comment to Dodin suggests, whether Stravinsky was conscious of it or not, or hit upon it by osmosis with his Russian culture.

The Rake's Progress as directed by Sellars is well and truly American. It is set in a Californian jail. Tom is cast as a street kid. Gestures come from various sub-cultures (black, Hispanic, ghetto youth) and 'popular' cultures (television, comic strips). Its cultural framing is essentially that of contemporary 'hip' movies. Sellars's production is clean, trim and plastically and visually beautiful. It has none of Dodin's psychological intricacies. Sellars and Dodin are at opposite ends of the world, geographically, socially and emotionally. Even so, the terrors of the end of the twentieth century have brought them together, piercing their consciousness to tell tales of illness in their operas.

Rehearsals: 23–30 November 1998

The last week of rehearsals, which included the full dress rehearsal, was not held in the studio but on the stage. At last, it was possible to see what the production would be like. Dodin was caught up in a myriad of details of timing, especially of group entrances, and of placing and spacing. Bychkov worked the orchestra hard, perfecting pace, rhythm, tone and phrasing. His observations had a dramaturgical colouring all of their own: the strings were to be 'more nervous' for Herman's hiding scene; the woodwinds were to convey a sinister quality; the ensemble was to be 'more stentorian' in the Canal scene. All in all, he was aiming for a crisp, multi-layered sound, as well as for balance with the stage so that the soloists could deliver all the necessary nuances of character. He warned them of how the audience's presence would change the acoustics. It would be 'a little like singing in cotton wool', although they should avoid 'the reflex of singing louder' if they felt there was less sound from the orchestra than there should be: 'I want you to trust the orchestra.' Bychkov's way of seeing the musical dynamics of the work was in concert with Dodin's chamber-opera approach to it.

A number of changes had occurred before these last rehearsals involving the children and the choir. Plans for the children's saraband in the pastorale were dropped, which meant losing the garland movements when Tomsky passed the cards to them. It also meant more dance for Tomsky, Surin and Chekalinsky, as well as for Herman and Liza. This was bound to have repercussions on the whole scene since there was a good deal of music in it. Few members of the choir were to play patients, the onus having been placed on the extras. Part of the choir required for the Empress's entrance was to sing in the wings. This streamlined the scene and kept eyes on its main dramatic areas, the stairs and the bed. Thanks to this staging decision, Herman was not going to be overwhelmed by a mass of people, as I had feared. The number of female singers returning with the Countess from the ball was reduced to nine. By contrast, the male choir acting gamblers in the last scene of Act III filled the space.

Since the platform above Herman's bed was only wide enough to hold two rows of people, the children and the chorus were obliged to close in on each other. This was not a problem for the opening scene, but was awkward for the ball scene when larger groups of men and women had to fit on the ledge. A circular ledge to stage right, which opened out like a revolving door for Yeletsky's entrance, helped to ease the situation. It became suddenly clear, thanks to the delicate tones of Chloé Obolensky's costumes, that, by sticking to the wall, the chorus was doing more than solving a technical problem. It was meant to look like a frieze and, at the same time, indicate that its figures represent *voices* swarming inside Herman's head. This is brought home when Galuzin claps his hands over his ears to drown the voices out. He also brings his hand to his mouth to hush them. The choristers clap their hands lightly and kneel or bend forward, their eyes focused on Herman (which is also convenient for seeing Bychkov's baton).

Dodin's change to the pastorale had radical consequences in so far as the triangle of desire formed by Herman, Liza and the Countess was dislodged. Where it had been relatively still, it now relied on movement. Its protagonists were blindfolded, as before, this image alluding to the ideas of the masked ball and the 'game' of life (Figure 17). However, they now made up for the children's absence by whirling and pushing each other around. Chekalinsky 'shepherded' Liza about. Surin steered Herman. Tomsky led the Countess more than before. When this 'dance' was a duo for Liza and Herman, they felt for each other in the air. Liza occasionally thought she had found Herman when she touched the wall. Herman stumbled into the extras huddled at stage left and held this or that head in his blind search for Liza. When the 'dance' was a trio, it turned into a banal tug-of-war, Herman 'torn' by Liza hanging onto one arm, and the Countess pulling on the other. More disappointing still, from my point of view, was how this dissipated energy deflected attention away from the desires at stake – desire for money, sex, power, success, status – which had been captured in a nutshell during the second week of rehearsals.

Nevertheless, something had remained at the end of the pastorale of Dodin's earlier concentrated version. Herman caresses the Countess in his arms and, as he gazes rapturously – or madly – at her face, Surin removes her blindfold saying 'Look, here is your lover'. The Countess looks at Herman, gets up, drops the three flowers one by one that Herman has given Liza, but which have ended up in her hand, and walks out. She does all this as if sleep-walking. The segment is eerie, and the Countess is meant, of course, to look like an apparition. But it is a fleeting moment at the end of a scene that originally had promised to be entirely in this key. Seeing it undergo such a radical transformation was a reminder of how the creative process can meander towards the stage where the path it takes is not necessarily the best of the pathways covered. When I asked Dodin why he had dropped his earlier version, he said he feared the spectators would become bored with so much sitting.

Figure 17 *The Queen of Spades*. De Nederlandse Opera at the Muziektheater Amsterdam, 1998. Act II (Part I): H. Peeters, V. Galuzin and T. Poluektova.

Photograph by Hans van den Bogaard, courtesy of Hans van den Bogaard.

The last scene of Act III. The change of place to the gambling house is communicated by actions: Surin and Chekalinsky pull a piece of green cloth out of Herman's quilt, which has replaced the sheet used in the first rehearsals, and cover the bed as if it were a table: they throw his mattress down onto the floor. The extras are dotted about unobtrusively. Some listlessly pick up cards as the chorus of gamblers play their games. Others lie flat on their stomachs, as if asleep, with their arms or head dangling over the edge of the top of the stairs. Tomsky sings his drinking song about women and Chekalinsky spins a female patient around. A false note: this was a stereotypical prostitute among dissolute men. Dodin worked on a series of surprises in the scene where Herman rips apart his mattress. At first, Herman's action appeared random. It became clear, when he pulled a packet out from the mattress, that he had been looking for something specific. Herman clutched this innocuous packet greedily to his chest. It turned out that the packet contained 40,000 roubles, which he soon emptied onto the 'table'. Cards were shuffled, dealt and played and bunches of them tossed into the air each time Herman won a game. The purpose was to create an atmosphere of fever and commotion. Herman, as if intoxicated, sang 'What is our life? A game!' standing on the green table-bed.

The closing fragments are spine-chilling. At the very moment Herman realises he is holding a Queen of Spades instead of an ace, the ledge of the decor rises to join up with another piece and make a floor above the table-bed. In that same instant, the Countess enters dead centre from the back. Meanwhile Liza blends completely into the crowd. All stand still as Herman, in a catatonic stupor, gathers up money and cards and curls up on his bed with his back to the audience.

Dress rehearsal: 30 November

The most striking feature of the work is its classical quality: the economy of Dodin's direction; the passion concentrated in the singing; the balance between the scenography, costumes and lighting; dignity, despite the unsettling subject matter. And Dodin's dramaturgy is like that of classical tragedy in its fatality (embedded in the three-card motif), circularity (the end is known at the beginning) and massive catharsis in the closing scene; similarly, in how the protagonist carries the burden of the tragedy, implicating all others in it. Galuzin is *always* on stage. He appears before the overture begins, crosses the stage and curls up on the bed with his back to the audience. Only then does the music start. There is no respite for Galuzin even when he does not sing, for he acts without pause. Moreover, the role requires constant singing in the middle range which, as Bychkov remarked, is extremely demanding on tenors and strains their voices.

The production's classical quality also lies in how the extras function as a chorus. This is especially apparent when they mingle with the actual chorus, their actions complementing theatrically what the chorus does musically. The extras are on stage a great deal, which counters the anxieties expressed during the second week of rehearsals that they would be underemployed. However, they are a silent, choreographic *khoros* and their actions are unobtrusive, which maintains dramatic and visual harmony with the soloists. Occasionally they are a support for the soloists, notably in the scene closing Part I when a bald extra exchanges grimaces and gestures with Galuzin. This cameo of lunatic complicity occurs as the walls come apart and the Countess appears and is so persuasive that it becomes horrifying. Nothing the extras do is open to ridicule. Their respect for their characters commands the audience's respect, exactly as Dodin had wished.

The production's tableau-like stylisation stands out during the dress rehearsal, for example, the scene featuring Tchaikovsky's quintet 'I am afraid' early in Part I. It involves Tomsky, Surin, Chekalinsky, Liza and the Countess, each voicing his/her thoughts about Herman's strangeness. The men are on the narrow ledge above Herman when the Countess takes her place on it, well ahead of the quintet. She stands there like a picture of the Queen of Spades, her arms slightly in front of her and her wrists resting slightly above her gown (Figure 18, overleaf). The soloists are spaced away from each other. Bizarre, triangular shadows are thrown onto the wall behind them. The characters move minimally, as does Yeletsky after he enters. He was always meant to wear a black top hat and carry a cane, but new details have been added. He now wears silver-rimmed glasses of the kind worn by Pushkin (a deliberate evocation?) and, at some point, pulls out a notebook from his pocket to write in it (Pushkin evoked again). These are realistic touches, but their effect is eccentric. There are other new details which Dodin had talked about during the week. Galuzin's hair is now plastered down so that he no longer looks like a dishevelled madman, and the flowers in the trio, which Dodin had wanted to be 'chrysanthemums or asters – autumnal flowers', are red roses (probably for reasons of availability), although their dots of red on the simple colour canvas are pleasing enough.

Three scenes involving Galuzin are especially indicative of the work's power. Several days before the dress rehearsal, Dodin took a different angle on Herman's madness in the closing scene of Part I. Instead of having Herman tied up by four male nurses, as before, he asked Galuzin to break free of his bonds. Galuzin does so, turns towards the stairs as if to escape, has the exchange with the bald inmate noted above, and comes back 'by himself in a conscious act' (Dodin) to the bed. He stretches his arms out in submission to his own madness, laughing towards the audience. The effect is chilling and anticipates the eerie musical motif at the beginning of Part II. A similar sense of eeriness emerges from the sequence where the Countess dies, and is carried through to Herman's duet with Liza. Poluektova demonstrates as much anxiety for Herman as Dodin's restraints on her acting will allow. Meanwhile, Herman is a sorry sight as Galuzin huddles up against her. He repeats this crouching movement in the next duet between Herman and Liza, only now he looks at her through the ironwork at the head of the bed.

The third scene at issue is Herman's soliloquy during the Countess's funeral. Galuzin's performance takes off as never before and something about its grand

Figure 18 *The Queen of Spades.* De Nederlandse Opera at the Muziektheater Amsterdam, 1998. Act I (Part I): V. Galuzin in foreground.

l. to r.: T. Poluektova, H. Peeters, P. Hunka, M. Reijans, H. Dernesch, V. Gerello.

Photograph by Hans van den Bogaard, courtesy of Hans van den Bogaard.

intensity recalls Mussorgsky's *Boris Godunov*. Galuzin seems to pull together a host of ghosts: that of Boris racked by repentance, of Raskolnikov tortured by his crime (the Countess suddenly recalls the old woman in *Crime and Punishment*) and of Dostoevsky's driven gamblers. He holds this pitch in the final scene when Herman tears the mattress apart to find his money. Having found it, he slips the money into his coat against his chest, cowers against the wall at stage right and observes the gambling in full swing. Galuzin plays his character's excesses with such natural ease that Herman's last moments, when he slumps back on the bed, clutching notes of money and cards to his chest, are totally persuasive. The audience of a dress rehearsal is always an in-house audience, but we hoped that its roar of approval would be shared by the public.

Scenography

This is proportion, balance and harmony in a classical mode. The high white walls of the hospital are on a light green base the length of the stage and show cornices, panels and an alcove or two. Their texture suggests that various coats of plaster and paint had been applied at different times, as occurs in old buildings. A patch of brick painted over in white suggests where the plaster had peeled off. The whole is streamlined and airy, and its high gloss catches the light. The floor is of polished wood. The white walls move to create the ledge necessary for the children and the choir. The circular ledge used for Yeletsky's love song and, in the last scene, for his game of cards against Herman, glides in at stage right. Architecturally, it belongs to the slightly protruding wall at stage right. The Countess's ghost goes through this wall; Herman then approaches it to feel its surface and understand how she has vanished. After a lapse of time, which allows the audience to grasp the significance of his groping (my 'principle of delayed reaction' above), he finds what appears to be a secret spring for opening the door.

The scenography for Part II is a more spectacular affair. The walls come apart as the platform goes down with the chorus singing on it. The merging of spaces into one allows a play of perspectives which eventually lead the gaze to an opening at the back. The stairs guide the gaze towards the same focal point. Venus, Adonis and Perseus are in place. A bold sculpture of Ganymede on an eagle, which Borovsky had not found necessary for the mock sets, is now at the top of the stairs. A kneeling Cupid in profile is on the previously bare pedestal close to the bed where Poluektova reads Liza's letter (Figure 19, overleaf). Sculptures and stairs are in pristine white to suggest marble and, together with two Doric columns, create a polyvalent space: the Summer Garden and a neoclassical St Petersburg palace; the exterior of such palaces and their interior, with allusions to their vestibules, hallways and colonnaded ballrooms; the interior of Herman's mind. A large green square near the centre of the floor is the colour of malachite, the stone typically found in the tables and urns of Petersburg palaces. Malachite green is repeated in the opening at the back, surrounded by black walls; again in the green cloth depicting a gaming table. In

Figure 19 *The Queen of Spades*. De Nederlandse Opera at the Muziektheater Amsterdam, 1998. Act III (Part II). Design by D. Borovsky.

Photograph by Hans van den Bogaard, courtesy of Hans van den Bogaard.

the funeral scene, these walls slide to one side when the candle-lit cortège makes its way towards the opening. They reveal a strange, malachite-green jagged shape going up into the flies which disappears just as suddenly as it appeared. It must surely represent another of Herman's hallucinations. The whole space is deep, and looks open. The great paradox of Borovsky's design is that it combines realistic detail with a surrealistic aura in an ensemble of arresting formal beauty.

Costumes

Obolensky had thoroughly researched the clothes of carers and cared-for in nineteenth-century lunatic asylums, among them the famed Charenton asylum in France. Long, loose shirts, trousers and skirts, and collars, caps and aprons reflected her findings. She also discovered that very often there was little to distinguish between the costumes of the inmates and their nurses. Accordingly, both groups wear shifts and smocks in a palette of whites and varying shades of beige. There are, nevertheless, several differentiating markers like the over-long sleeves to be seen in strait-jackets. The male nurse watching Herman's first psychotic episode wears a stark white apron and rolled-up sleeves over an otherwise patient-like smock. The character whom Dodin had called 'the Professor' wears a suit under an apron and a startlingly tall black top hat. More sinister touches are to be seen in the butcher-type white aprons down to the ground worn by the four burly male nurses in the closing scene of Part I. Members of the chorus sometimes combine such clothes as a formal black jacket, which is suitable for a gambling house, with the beige trousers of a patient. This kind of sartorial double coding expresses the confusion in Herman's mind between the past and the present. The nannies wear bonnets and dresses in pastels so delicate that they blend into the wall behind them. Obolensky's wardrobe is extraordinarily subtle in tone, texture and fabric. It is also delightfully inventive since no two costumes in any crowd scene are exactly alike.

The soloists' costumes, that of the Countess excepted, were inspired by the fashions of the 1830s. Tomsky, Surin and Chekalinsky are in black and white. They wear swinging coats in Act I and soft jackets in Act II, which they take off for the blindfolded dance to show the billowing shirts beneath them. (Dodin felt, after the semi-dress rehearsal, that the shirts gave the scene a lighter touch than the jackets.) They carry black top hats close to their chests for the cortège. Yeletsky's garments are in a similar vein. The frocks, silhouettes, composure and placement of Liza and Polina are reminiscent of Russian domestic paintings of the period. Liza's youthful freshness is caught in the light, white embossed fabric – with an impression of pale green – of her dress and its crossed bodice and sash. Polina is sophisticated in subdued purple-toned satin. Both dresses have full sleeves that tighten at the lower arm. Both women's hair is drawn back gently to sit at the nape of the neck. Liza's costume changes only at the end of Act II, when she runs down the stairs to Herman and discovers that the

Countess is dead. She wears what looks like a satin gown whose panel opens to show a skirt beneath it. The gown is muted green, close to the colour of the hospital wall.

The Countess wears sumptuous garments. She appears, in Part I, in a superb low-cut, patterned black and emerald green gown in the style of Marie-Antoinette. At the end of the opera, she wears its black counterpart and looks as if she had walked off the card Herman holds in his hand. The phenomenal, high white wigs Obolensky had designed to go with these gowns are crucial for this effect. The Countess looks like an apparition in another sense as well in that her anachronistic image, from the moment she stands on the platform with Tomsky, Surin, Chekalinsky, Yeletsky and Liza, makes her a ghost from the past. In her death scene she wears a white shift similar, but for its length, to that of the patients.

Masha is dressed in a refined version of the costumes worn by the nurses, which makes her seem half real (as Liza's attendant) and half imaginary (mixed up in Herman's mind with the nurses). Herman, when required, throws a brown army coat as a dressing-gown over the pyjama-like outfit that he wears from beginning to end. When he muses among the statues, he is dressed in a black 1830s military coat with brass buttons at his neck. Obolensky gives period touches to Herman's costumes not for the sake of realism but for that of the hallucinatory world that glimmers through them. Reaching the illusory through the real and the invisible through the visible is the core paradox of Dodin's direction of the opera – as occurs, he agreed, in the films of Fellini, Kurosawa and Tarkovsky.

Lights

It was clear on 30 November which lighting choices from the various technical rehearsals would remain for the production. Kalman's lights are neither atmospheric nor decorative. Nor, although painterly in the manner of Wilson, do they have a Wilsonian non-interpretative function (Shyer, 1989: 191–202; Shevtsova, 1995a: 71; Holmberg, 1996: 126–7). Predominantly in whites and yellows, they discourse on narrative, characters, situations and events. The huge black triangles projected behind the soloists in Part I contrast sharply with the starkly lit white hospital walls and make the characters strange, exactly as they might appear to Herman. Since Kalman's swathes of light brook no sentimentality, scenes are softened by dimming and shading. This happens for such intimate moments as the Liza–Polina duet, Herman's contemplation among the statues, the Countess's death, the Countess's funeral and the scenes foregrounding Liza's solicitude for Herman, notably in her first solo in Part II. Dodin had asked for a 'sickly light' – yellow touched with green – for the Liza–Herman scenes so that it would communicate the unhealthiness of the situation and of the people in it. While the prevailing image of Liza as mother-nurse-lover is uncomfortably close to the patriarchal notion of long-suffering women, Dodin uses the 'sickly light' to critically place Liza's self-effacement. This having been said, she has no alternative in the dead-end context of lunacy, which is a disempowering state, if ever there was one.

Light has an expressionistic character when the shadows of the soloists and the choir are cast on the white wall. This is also true of a bright shaft of light projected from the wings at stage left. A prominent feature of Kalman's design, it frequently accompanies the entries of soloists and extras. It illuminates Herman's hallucinations – the children, the trio, the Countess going through the wall – as well as his violent episodes, the second of which, ending Part I, is in a particularly white, brutal light. It throws Herman's frenetic gambling into relief, thereby emphasising the idea that this is his last grasp on reason. Light functions both as a framing device and as narrative closure when it irradiates the green wall that comes back up to its original place during Herman's final moments. In this way, it visually links the end to the beginning, as Dodin has done dramaturgically.

Kalman's signature shaft of light is used filmically and melodramatically, albeit with a touch of irony, when the Countess's ghost appears from the wings, a blast of snow blowing behind her. During the semi-dress rehearsal, Dernesch had rehearsed the Countess's ghost-walking in a long creamy coat with a military cut. The yellow-toned light used then had harmonised with her coat. It had also intensified the 'Russian winter' sensation generated by the wind and snow. Dodin felt that this combination was picturesque and in conflict with his objectives. Whether on the spur of the moment, or in pursuit of a dormant idea, he asked Obolensky to dress Dernesch in a contemporary doctor's white coat, with a stethoscope hanging around her neck. The shock of her appearance like this in the final rehearsal was palpable in the auditorium. And shock ran through the production team who had followed the vagaries of rehearsals to the very end and felt inevitably, as people do when they have 'seen it all', that nothing could surprise them. The costume change in this scene triggered a change of light to a hot-white glare whose starkness was consistent with the overall tenor of the work.

Coda: opening night, 2 December

Panic in the house in the morning. Galuzin, who has had a cold on and off all week, has bronchitis. He will go on, but a reserve tenor has been flown in to sing from the wings in case Galuzin's voice gives out. Galuzin will act the part, regardless. This is announced to the audience as the performance is about to begin. As it turns out, Galuzin manages to sing, although he drops into the lower register for passages requiring greater strength. The incident adversely affects Poluektova and Dernesch, who neither sing nor act as well as they have done previously. Reijans has a bad cold and his Chekalinsky suffers accordingly. This has a domino effect on the rest of the male soloists who, although well focused, lose some of their bounce and sparkle in the pastorale, making it feel contrived instead of inventive. Compared to the dress rehearsal, the opening night was low-spirited rather than conversational and had lost some of its

dramatic tension. Here was an eloquent example of the truism that no two performances are ever alike, which is why several viewings are essential for gauging
a work.

A gesture of great moment on one night may disappear on another. The
timing of an action may significantly alter its impact and shift the meaning of
the scene in which it occurs. Galuzin, for example, found the money in
Herman's mattress too soon. This weakened his tearing actions and obliged him
to cower against the wall for longer than usual. And this gave him less spring
for his lunge towards the gambling table. Multiple viewings allow spectators to
penetrate a production's conception, organisation, structure and direction and
these are relatively stable irrespective of the vagaries of performances and how
they slant perception. The shaping lines of this production remained, and
despite its not-at-its-best performance on the opening night, compared with
some of the rehearsals, it elicited an openly appreciative response from the audience. This confirms another truism, namely, that a well-crafted piece of work
allows plenty of spectator interaction with it, regardless of whether it is deemed
to have been performed 'at its best'.

Post-scriptum from Paris: the 'life' of the production

The production's critical reception in Amsterdam was generally positive, even
when a critic expressed some reservations as to its guiding idea. This was hardly
the case five months later in Florence, where Dodin and Borovsky received a
bad press while praise for the opera's musical interpretation was superlative. A
change of cast, leaving only Dernesch, Galuzin and Hunka from the original
Amsterdam singers, had manifestly not affected its musicianship. The critics
were especially hostile when they compared Dodin's *mise en scène* – 'shameful',
according to *Corriere della Sera* (17 April 1999) and 'a radical and risky operation'
that bred confusion and boredom (*La Stampa*, 18 April 1999) – with his *Elektra*
and *Lady Macbeth*, which they had unanimously acclaimed. Nor did they stint on
their remarks about how the audience had whistled and booed its disapproval,
although *La Repubblica* detected in this uproar a division between the 'tradition-
alists' who thought Dodin had betrayed Tchaikovsky and those who had found
the production 'powerful' (17 April 1999).

Six months later, when *The Queen of Spades* was performed in Paris, the theme
of betrayal returned, notably in *Le Figaro*, which is nothing if not a tradition-
ists' newspaper (14 October 1999). Meanwhile, half of the other dailies that
had recorded the audience's shouts and boos supported the production. For
Le Monde, for example, it was 'convincing' and 'provocative but in no way
gratuitous' (19 October 1999). The weeklies also entered the fray. *L'Express* (con-
servative) noted that Dodin's conception was 'very original and intellectually
attractive' but did not endorse the result (21 October 1999). *Le Nouvel Observateur*
(leftish) gave a strong defence. Its reviewer, prize-winning novelist Dominique
Fernandez, wrote: 'Intelligence of the project; coherence and beauty of the production; musical splendour: a great success' (28 October 1999). According to

Fernandez, Dodin had accurately perceived Herman to be mad since Herman was in conflict over his love for Liza and his passion for gambling, which was a metaphor for 'a love that dare not say its name'. This had been embraced by the production, also because the statues of Perseus and Ganymede quite evidently alluded to Tchaikovsky's own homosexuality.

Karita Mattila as Liza had now joined Galuzin and Dernesch in the triangle of desire that I had spotted during rehearsals and on which Fernandez's interpretation had shed a new light (Figure 20, overleaf). Fernandez found her performance as deeply moving (contrary to *L'Express* which found it 'overplayed'), as Galuzin's portrayal of Herman's 'existential bewilderment'. Elena Zaremba was now singing Polina, Simon Keenlyside was Yeletsky, Gerello had replaced Hunka as Tomsky, and the remaining male soloists were all new. All in all, the critics of Paris were less severe than their Florentine colleagues. Are conventional attitudes towards opera more deeply ingrained in Florence than in Paris? What part did a change of soloists play in the chemistry of Dodin's production and, consequently, in its interaction with spectators? A similar question could be asked of Obolensky's costume alterations. While these cannot be easily answered, it was clear that further cast changes for its second Paris season in February 2001 modulated the 'chemical' reaction within the production once again. Sergey Larin now replaced Galuzin and Alexandrina Milcheva replaced Dernesch. Vladimir Jurovsky conducted in both seasons and was admired both times.

The production had undergone several shifts up to and including its second edition in Paris, notably concerning its principal interpreters. Poluektova's Liza had been a compassionate and devoted woman mired in an impossible situation with a powerful Galuzin-Herman. Mattila, on the other hand, was a much stronger personality who seemed incapable of playing abnegation of any kind, let alone the submissiveness of a character bowing to an implacable destiny. Consequently, her sense of struggle was greater than Poluektova's and closer to that of Galuzin for Herman – so much so that at times she appeared to be in competition with him, vying for the dramatic spotlight by her large gestures, highlighted mimicry and rather ostentatious falls on the bed or the floor. Falling was a feature of Dodin's direction of her character, but Mattila's movements exaggerated it, giving the production a brusqueness that it had not had before.

Mattila's attempt to create a more forceful, more independent woman was fully successful when she performed with Larin. By then she had absorbed the intended equivocations of the role (Liza as a 'real' person contra the Liza of Herman's hallucinations – the ministering angel performed by Poluektova). As a result, Mattila softened her gestures, refined her movements and trusted her splendid voice to lift and carry her role. Also, Larin helped her in that, less compelling than Galuzin from a dramatic point of view, his restraint provided her with a balance. Their Liza–Herman couple captured the emotional force that Dodin was after without diving into melodrama, as had occurred with Mattila and Galuzin – for example, in the scene where Herman abandons Liza for the gambling den. Here Mattila had fallen backwards and downwards on

Figure 20 *The Queen of Spades* at the Opéra National de Paris-Bastille, 1999. Act II (Part II) after the death of the Countess: K. Mattila, H. Dernesch, V. Galuzin.

Photograph by Eric Mahoudeau, courtesy of Eric Mahoudeau.

the bed with her face to the audience and her body sprawled out in an ungainly way. What had looked forced in the first season seemed at ease in the second and a logical consequence of Liza's loss of control: Liza was beside herself, pure and simple.

In short, the changes in Mattila's performance had to do with her reliance on her voice and her growing confidence in her body's ability to say more with less. Thus, in the Winter Canal scene, which is something of a litmus test, she *sang* Liza's intense anxiety as she waits for Herman without reinforcing her point with agitated movements. The second decisive factor was in the symmetry between the singers. Neither of them placed their character in a relationship of submission-domination, nor, as singers, did they try to outdo or dominate one another. The emotional equality between their characters, both *in extremis*, carried the scene on such a 'high' that a potentially deflating moment like Mattila's ugly sprawl on the bed did not bring it down. The continuing 'life' of a production depends on living people, all with their singular qualities, who do not merely reproduce a blueprint left by a director. That Dodin was able to renew his production through them for its second Paris edition also indicates how important it is to treat each performance in the theatre – not least any reprise – as unique, as though performed for the first time.

Rare are the occasions that allow designers to inject new life into their work with a change of cast. Obolensky seized the opportunity for the production's first edition in Paris to redesign its costumes according to the new singers' physique and her sense of them as people, which is her usual practice. She changed the costumes for all the soloists except Polina and Herman, while those for the chorus, patients and doctors stayed much the same. Obolensky argued that some of the garments were 'not right' for these singers, which meant that others had to be modified for the visual harmony of the whole (Paris, 8 October 1999). Mattila, for instance, wore a less elegant, more homespun dress than the one crafted for Poluektova, although it still picked up the green of Borovsky's walls. The Countess no longer wore emerald green satin for her first appearance. She wore a shimmering pearl grey gown of silk (although her second gown remained black). The effect was nowhere near as striking as that of the Amsterdam gown. Nor did it suggest the image of the Queen of Spades on the card in the pack, a loss due as well to the less imposing wig on the Countess's head. Obolensky had certainly created a subtler image, but had exchanged chills along the spine for chic.

The change to the Countess's costume was necessary, she believed, because of her redesigned garments for Tomsky, Yeletsky, Surin and Chekalinsky beside whom the Countess appears on the ledge. These men were now in beiges and soft browns which harmonised with the tones of the patients' costumes instead of being in contrast with them, as had been the case in Amsterdam. The canvas was now softer and Kalman appeared to have dimmed his lights here and there accordingly. It was surprising to see the difference made by the changes to the costumes. They toned down the production's visual impact which, in turn, diminished Herman's plight to some extent, making it seem more ordinary, more domestic, than before. The strongest singing casts were probably the two in Paris and Obolensky may well have calculated the soaring power of their voices in her decision to make more discreet costumes for them. The press in 2001 was quite jubilant. It referred to the 'scandal' that had surrounded Dodin in 1999 ('one of the greatest directors of our time' – *Le Monde*, 8 February 2001) and, this time, recognised the production's tragic vision, connecting it to Tchaikovsky's tragic music. *Le Figaro* observed that 'great productions are like good wine: they need to age for the sediment to settle' (8 February 2001). It listened to the great applause and pronounced *The Queen of Spades* a public success.

Notes

1 From Leningrad to St Petersburg

1 Harrison Salisbury writes in the *New York Times Book Review*, 10 May 1962: 'This was the greatest and longest siege ever endured by a modern city, a time of trial, suffering and heroism that reached peaks of tragedy and bravery almost beyond our power to comprehend . . . Even in the Soviet Union the epic of Leningrad has received only modest attention, compared with that devoted to Stalingrad and the battle of Moscow. And in the west not one person in fifty who thrilled to the courage of the Londoners in the battle of Britain is cognizant of that of the Leningraders.' Quoted by Alexander Werth in his remarkable *Russia at War, 1941–1945* (1964: 297–8). Werth shows that it did not suit Stalin to recognise the extraordinary bravery of the Leningraders since the siege came about largely because of his and Communist Party blunders regarding the true situation of the German invasion and their own response to the situation. In reply to the question of why the Leningraders 'took it' (given, also, the government's appalling record on the eve of the siege) Werth observes: 'The question of declaring Leningrad an open city could never arise, as it did, for example, in Paris in 1940; this was a war of extermination, and the Germans never made a secret of it. Secondly, the local pride of Leningrad had a quality of its own – it was composed of a great love of the city itself, of its historical past, its extraordinary literary associations (this was particularly true of the *intelligentsia*) and also of a great proletarian and revolutionary tradition amongst its working class: nothing could have so blended these two great loves for Leningrad into one thing as the threat of the annihilation of the city . . . The whole problem of evacuation, especially of children, had been grossly mishandled, and little or nothing had been done to lay in food reserves. But once the Germans had been stopped outside Leningrad, and once the decision had been taken to fight for every house and every street, the faults of the army and the civilian authorities were readily forgotten; for now it was a case of defending Leningrad at any price.' (Ibid.: 356–7.)

2 Vilar's Théâtre National Populaire, which he founded in 1951 after founding, in 1947, the Avignon Festival, on whose principles it was modelled, was 'national' because it relied exclusively on government backing and funding in order to fulfil its objective of '*service public*'. This phrase referred to a theatre accessible to all social classes by dint of lower ticket prices, no charges for cloakrooms, transport (for example, chartered buses taking working people from factories and offices to the theatre), low-cost food on the premises for people coming straight from work, and so

on, including pre- and after-show talks to edify spectators. It was 'popular' in so far as it attempted to democratise the theatre, but did so without forsaking its art-theatre credentials, as Vilar's programming shows: primarily classics, notably French, although foreign classics including Shakespeare also made their appearance, and some emphasis on contemporary plays. It could be described as an art-theatre 'for everyone' – in late twentieth-century jargon. See Vilar's collection of essays and notes, *Le Théâtre, service public* (1975). The Maly Drama Theatre in its early days would not have been able to claim the high-calibre projects staked out for the Théâtre National Populaire by Vilar, but both were underpinned by the idea that the theatre should not be the preserve of a select few.

The Théâtre National Populaire, although caught up in post-war progressive ideologies, was not driven by a socialist policy as such. Thus, the political profile of the Maly Drama Theatre is best compared with the socialist one – also with 'public service' as its mission – of the Piccolo Teatro di Milano founded by Giorgio Strehler and his manager-associate Paolo Grassi in 1946. What is especially significant in the comparison between the Maly Drama Theatre and these (and other) western models of 'public service' is not so much the influence of socialist thinking on these models as the fact that they superseded their Soviet homologues both by the scale of their ambitions and the flexibility they enjoyed from operating in democratic structures – a far cry from the rigid state apparatus of the type that controlled the USSR.

3   The authors of 'village prose' (*derevenshchiki*) were the foremost literary group of the Brezhnev years (1964–82) and especially of the 1970s. See Hosking, 1980: 50–83.

4   MKhAT is the acronym for the Moscow Art Theatre after 1920 when the adjective 'Academic' (the 'A' of the acronym) was added to its previous name MKhT.

5   My vocabulary echoes, of course, Pierre Bourdieu whose notions of cultural and symbolic capital are extremely useful for this discussion. See especially Bourdieu, 1979a and b.

6   The four productions are *Alive* by Boris Mozhayev (1968), *Protect your Faces*, a montage based on poems by Andrey Voznesensky (1970), *Vladimir Vysotsky* (1981) and *Boris Godunov* (1982). *Vladimir Vysotsky* was a homage to the great actor, songwriter and singer who had played the title role in Lyubimov's legendary *Hamlet*. Vysotsky died in 1980; the show, by invitation only and in the presence of the police, opened on 25 July 1981 and was banned three days later. Pushkin's *Boris Godunov*, whose principal idea is that a change of leadership simply means a repetition of the same tyranny, fell foul of the Communist Party censors and was banned after the dress rehearsal on 10 December 1982. As for *The Devils*, the production had its first production abroad in 1985, in Paris at the Odéon-Théâtre de l'Europe, in London at the Almeida, then in Milan at the Piccolo Teatro and in Bologna. For further factual details regarding these and other productions by Lyubimov, see the appendix in Picon-Vallin, 1997: 415–28.

7   Dmitrevskaya went on to found and edit *Peterburgsky teatralny zhurnal* (*The Petersburg Theatre Journal*), the first theatre journal in 55 years to be published in the city. Number 0, its test run, appeared in 1992, a good part of it devoted to the Maly. Dmitrevskaya (1986) had championed the company in a highly regarded article in Moscow's *Teatr*, but after 1992 became one of Dodin's (rather than the company's) most severe critics, as will be clear in chapter 4 of this book.

8   Vysotsky's legendary fame as an actor, poet, songwriter and singer together with such widely known facts about him as his compassion for his fellow citizens, his

alcohol dependency – bound up with the conflict he recognised between his ideals and the country's realities – and the harassment he had endured as a citizen and an artist were the potent sub-text of the Vysotsky segment of *Stars in the Morning Sky*. Neither Dodin and the Maly nor their spectators would have forgotten that Vysotsky's funeral in 1980 had occurred at about the time of the Olympic Games. Performances of *Stars* in Moscow in 1988 were additionally resonant because of the mountain of publications, seminars, memorial meetings and television films and programmes which had celebrated Vysotsky's fiftieth anniversary nationally in January of that year.

9   In the words of John Freedman: 'This international icon of theater, then approaching its 90th birthday, was the first to let its internal squabbles go public when it split into two independent troupes, both of which retained the right to use the prestigious Art Theater symbols and name. The company which moved into a newly constructed building on Tverskoy Boulevard kept the Soviet-era name of the Gorky Moscow Art Theater. The one which remained the "house that Stanislavski built" on Kamersgy Lane soon took the name of the Chekhov Moscow Art Theater' (1997: xv). Anatoly Smeliansky (1999: 147–8) states that 'it was not Yefremov, or Doronina, or a conspiracy of grave diggers that split MKhAT, but the times'; further, its division 'anticipated the collapse of the USSR', and both were 'finished'.

10   Birgit Beumers indicates that the catalyst for the Taganka split was a divergence of opinion in the artistic council 'as to whether a contract system should be introduced'. The Moscow Art Theatre, on the other hand, split after Yefremov proposed 'to reduce the rather lethargic troupe of the Moscow Arts company, catering for and working on three stages simultaneously, in order to allow for a more creative and less managerial approach to the performing arts'. See Beumers, 1996: 1407. Beumers correctly points out that the issue of control over the theatres (which gave rise to artistic councils of the kind at the Taganka referred to above) had been debated as early as 1985, that is, before Gorbachev called a meeting with the artistic community in December 1986 'during which he encouraged a process of liberalization in the arts'. This debate, she argues, was initiated by an article by Mark Zakharov, the artistic director of Moscow's Lenin Komsomol Theatre, in *Literaturnaya gazeta*, 31 July 1985. Zakharov 'outlined the main areas needing reform: he challenged the repertoire; the fixed number of actors in a company and the form of their payment; petty bureaucratic control of the theatres; and the absence of responsibility of the theatres for their budget. All these challenges, which were raised in the form of questions, were answered by the statutes for the reform experiment of 1987' which 'was gradually transformed into a new law on theatre organisation. The new statutes were finalised in the Council of Ministers' resolution of May 1991, which allowed the theatres to find private sponsors and open foreign currency accounts, and which enabled theatres to let premises and retain the rent' (ibid.: 1405 and 1410).

11   Vasilyev founded his School of Dramatic Art in 1987 – a studio in the sense of a research group whose explorations do not necessarily lead to public performance. It has been reconstituted several times. None of Vasilyev's collaborators from the 1980s has survived the discords that appear to have plagued his relations with co-workers. Fomenko, who taught at GITIS (the State Institute of Theatre Art, renamed the Russian Institute of Theatre Art) founded the Fomenko Studio in 1993 by bringing together the students whom he had trained at the Institute. This group first performed *Guilty Without Guilt*, to which I refer in my text below, but does not have the status of a company as such. For insight into the notion of the 'pedagogue-director'

exemplified by Vasilyev and Fomenko (which differs from the case of Dodin, a director who is a pedagogue) see Picon-Vallin, 1994: 43–51.

12 See Bharucha, 1991 and Carlson, 1996.

13 Lavaudant succeeded Pasqual as director of the Odéon-Théâtre de l'Europe which stipulated, after it had become a theatre with a European mission in 1983, that the position had a five-year term of office; 'Théâtre de l'Europe' was attached to 'Odéon' at that time.

14 The Union des Théâtres de l'Europe, whose administrative seat is the Odéon-Théâtre de l'Europe in Paris, was founded in 1990 largely on the initiative of Giorgio Strehler, its first president, and Jack Lang, who was François Mitterrand's Minister of Culture for a period during Mitterrand's first seven-year term of office 1981–8. Subsidised by the French Ministry of Culture and aided by the Kaleidoscope programme of the European Commission, the Union's mission is to develop cultural interchange between nations in the form of co-productions and exchange programmes between actors, directors and scenographers for the purposes of creating work and running workshops, debates and exhibitions related to the theatre, as well as annual theatre festivals. The Union's activities have not been confined to the European Union, since one of its most important briefs is to support theatre from the former Eastern European bloc. Apart from the Maly, members of the Union from this defunct bloc include the Berliner Ensemble, the Krakow Stary Teatr and the Teatrul Lucia Sturdza Bulandra in Bucharest. The Helsinki Suomen Kansallisteattetri is also a member of the Union.

2 The work process

1 It is still within this (misleading) perspective that Christopher Innes frames his discussion of Stanislavsky's 'theory of naturalistic acting' and, in relation to Stanislavsky, of Chekhov as 'a major naturalistic playwright'. See Innes, 2000: 53 for these quotations. An attempt to reconsider these terms, without reference to Innes, underlies Allen, 2000: 53–5 and 214. What is singular about Stanislavsky's approach is his idea of unforced play or what his student, Evgeny Vakhtangov, so accurately described as his 'special theatrical sense founded on an internal, natural basis', quoted on p. 72 in Allen, 2000. The confusion between 'natural' and 'naturalistic' continues, whereas, to my mind, Stanislavsky's emphasis on effortless communication of that which has an 'internal' basis – in other words, 'natural' acting – distances him from naturalism, especially as Emile Zola, founding theorist of naturalism in the theatre, understood the concept.

2 This notion is pervasive in the work of Stanislavsky, but *On the Art of the Stage* (1967: 151) provides a succinct formulation. The collected works of Stanislavsky in Russian consulted by me are the nine-volume *Sobraniye sochineny v devyati tomakh*, edited by a team led by Anatoly Smeliansky (1988–99).

3 See Richards, 1995, and Grotowski's essay in that volume: 113–35.

4 These are constant issues in Nietzsche, but see especially *Thus Spake Zarathustra*; *Twilight of the Idols* and *The Anti-Christ; Beyond Good and Evil* and *The Gay Science* (Nietzsche, 1963, 1990, 1966, 1974).

5 Thus Brecht's famous table on the distinctions between dramatic and epic theatre in Brecht, 1965: 37 and notes on the corresponding spectator for each theatre, p. 71.

6 The classic reference, in English translation, is Stanislavsky, 1988. For an account of

how Stanislavsky worked on the actor's creativity from 1927 to 1938, see Toporkov, 1998.

7 See Grotowski, 1997 and Barba, 1999: 53, 67–8, 99 and 105 for Grotowski's early interest in shamanism. The whole of Richards, 1995, could well be taken as a demonstration of Grotowski's mutation.

8 See Sartre, 1943 and, for a coupling of existentialism with humanism, which is fully appropriate for Dodin's perspective, 1970; Kaufmann, 1956; Merleau-Ponty, 1964 and 1997. It should be clear that acknowledging philosophical antecedents is not a matter of somehow 'legitimating' a director, but of indicating his/her intellectual backbone.

3 Dodin's 'theatre of prose'

1 As is well known, Bakhtin's theory of dialogism concerns verbal signs and, above all else, utterances and what he calls 'speech genres'. Verbal signs are dialogical because they are made by speakers to their interlocutors and vice versa. The communication between speakers and interlocutors relies on the shared meanings they attribute to signs, the ways in which speakers anticipate the engagement of their interlocutors in this process of interaction, and the way interlocutors return the meanings of the signs of speakers to them. This whole dynamic is one of reciprocal relations in which the signs being used and understood also undergo modification according to the context and purpose of interchange. See, especially, Bakhtin, 1981 (original Russian publication 1934–5); 1986 (original Russian essays predominantly of the 1950s and early 1970s); and Voloshinov [Bakhtin], 1986 (original Russian publication 1929).

   In the context of my discussion regarding Dodin, his productions are dialogical in so far as they 'talk' with each other by cross-referring to one another. The process of cross-reference integral to Dodin's work as a director not only influences how the performers understand what they play as well as the way they play it, but also how the spectators perceive production X after they have seen production Y, and vice versa. This process of cross-reference operates laterally across the body and corpus (*oeuvre*) of the works made by Dodin with the Maly. Bakhtin's idea of 'intertextuality' for written texts could be used to clarify this idea of cross-reference between productions and between them and spectators' interaction with them. Of course, Bakhtin elaborated his theory with respect to the novel, ignoring the theatre entirely, which does not mean his theory cannot be appropriated fruitfully for the study of performance genres, including non-verbal genres such as dance. See Shevtsova 1989, 1992, 1997a, 2001.

2 *Desire under the Elms* and *The Broken Jug* cited in chapter 2 are the only productions by Dodin with the Maly not studied in this book. Logistics made it impossible to see them while they were available, and *Desire* subsequently suffered a number of programming difficulties which prevented me from analysing it adequately for my purposes. Since these productions formed a pair, a 'foreign' repertoire predating Donnellan's *Winter's Tale* with the company, they would in any case have needed to be grouped together, as are, for different reasons, *Gaudeamus* and *Claustrophobia* in chapter 4.

3 Archie Brown (1997: 167) reminds us that Gorbachev proposed political reform in the 1987 January plenary session of the Central Committee: 'Gorbachev was thus already in early 1987 beginning to think about the need for liberalising or democratising measures that would go beyond simply greater intra-party democracy,

although he was also conscious of the necessity for further change within the party itself.' Brown also notes that the January plenary was followed by 'the most important domestic political events [which] were the June 1987 plenum . . . which radicalised economic reform'. This was more cause for the dissent and apparent confusion that marked the end of the 1980s and wearied people. Hence Kuryshev's allusion to a prevailing negative attitude towards the 'political'.

4 Given the points above, it is nevertheless imperative to note that what Dodin sceptically thinks of as the 'speechifying' tenor of politics during the years of preparation for *The Devils* is bound up with the *necessary* debate and even chatter of what Brown (1997) defines as 'democratization' (p. 182) in a country in the 'throes of systemic transformation' between 'the spring of 1989 and the summer of 1991' (p. 15). The 'first contested all-union elections in the Soviet Union' (p. 187) in May–June 1989 are integral to this democratisation, and the upside of the political rhetoric inspired by such practices as elections is the opportunity for pluralism, which Soviet autarchy had previously prevented. While Dodin fully supported the transformation, his mistrust of current rhetoric reflected the widespread anxiety that the Soviet-style habits of 'double-talk' would carry the day.

4 The student ensemble

1 Thomas Epstein claims, with justification, that 'Russian postmodernism presents a concentrated, intellectualized, and accelerated form of the phenomenon.' Further: 'Always taken with extremes, Russia has once again 'caught up', and with a vengeance, producing a body of challenging, sophisticated, and sometimes extremely radical postmodern texts.' Introduction to Mikhaïl Epstein *et al.*, 1999: vii. All the essays in this volume virtually demonstrate, or attempt to demonstrate, Thomas Epstein's contention.

2 See Bauman, 1992 where Bauman essentially uses the term 'postmodernity' so as to distinguish the *societal* conjuncture that can be used to explain the intellectual-cultural products covered by the notion of postmodernism (as generally conceived by writers on culture) from these very products. However, although Bauman makes this distinction, he nevertheless also uses the term 'postmodernity' (or the adjective 'postmodern') for these postmodern*ist* intellectual-cultural phenomena. The fundamental premise of Bauman's argument goes as follows: 'Most current concepts of postmodernity refer solely to intellectual phenomena. In some cases, they focus narrowly on the arts. In some others, they spill over to include a wider spectrum of cultural forms and precepts. In a few cases they reach deeper, into the fundamental preconceptions of contemporary consciousness. Rarely, if at all, they step beyond the boundary of the spiritual, into the changing social configuration which the artistic, cultural and cognitive developments, bracketed as postmodern, may reflect.' (p. 26). How to formulate the 'social configuration' is the task, as he sees it, of contemporary sociology. I am using 'postmodernism' and 'postmodernist' above to refer to both the 'social configuration' *and* the artistic and cultural developments that are coterminous with the former. See also Harvey, 1989; Featherstone, 1991; Bauman, 1995.

3 The playtext of *Gaudeamus* has been so brilliantly translated by Martin Dewhurst (Maly Drama Theatre, 1992) that there is no need for me to translate myself. All quotations from *Gaudeamus* are from Dewhurst. Lines translated by me from *Claustrophobia* are from Dodin's working text.

4 However, in another English-speaking country, Australia, they were not so sure.

Thus, on the occasion of *Claustrophobia*'s showing at the prestigious Adelaide Festival of 1996, the critic of the *Adelaide Review* (March 1996) writes: 'It is reasonable to ask what the production is signing to us, what it is endorsing and what rejecting. This may be clear to audiences closer to recent events in Eastern Europe but when we bring to *Claustrophobia* our garbled CNN-distorted notions of contemporary Russian life, we are likely to find ourselves at sea.' Further: '*Claustrophobia* is a majestic work but an unresolved one . . . Maybe *Claustrophobia* is just like Russia itself at present – all over the place.'(!)

5 This is a tricky issue since all kinds of stereotypes are involved in any assessment of the differences between the two cultures and their history. Thus, for example, Peter Brook (1988: 153) falls into some fairly trite distinctions when explaining his own move to Paris: 'In England artistic experiment is always viewed with suspicion while in France it is a natural part of artistic life . . . Paris has a long tradition of being a melting pot for artists from all over the world.' That said, there *are* some important differences which have to do with an openness, in France, to non-textual artistic experiment, some of it tied to the seminal work of Jacques Lecoq which was disseminated as 'physical theatre' by his disciples, who had come to him from all over the world, not least from Britain (for instance, Simon McBurney, who founded the Theatre de Complicité in London). Some of it was due to Jean-Louis Barrault's explorations in 'total theatre', particularly in the 1960s and 1970s when he also opened up key new work from across the globe to French practitioners and the theatre-going public through the Théâtre des Nations, under his direction. In addition, the French Ministry of Culture subsidised all kinds of international exploratory work in theatre and dance – the latter particularly after 1981 – which caught on quickly and stimulated local culture, notably contemporary dance.

6 Dodin directs opera

1 I had already submitted the typescript of this book and thus was unable to include *The Demon* and *Salomé* in the present discussion.

Bibliography

Note: The newspapers and magazines quoted have been documented in the text. Numerous additional newspapers were also consulted but are not listed. Nor are various reviews in *Peterburgsky teatralny zhurnal* (1993) 2, (1993) 4, (1994) 6, (1996) 10, (1998) 14, (1998) 15.

Abramov, Fyodor (1977) *Pryasliny*, Leningrad: Sovetsky Pisatel
Allen, David (2000) *Performing Chekhov*, London: Routledge
Arblaster, Anthony (1992) *Viva la Libertà: Politics in Opera*, London and New York: Verso
Autant-Mathieu, Marie-Christine (1993) *Le Théâtre soviétique durant le dégel, 1953–1964*, Paris: CNRS Editions
—— (1994) 'Le Théâtre russe après l'URSS: Le Prix de la liberté', *Théâtre/Public* 116, pp. 21–39
Bakhtin, Mikhaïl (1981) 'Forms of Time and of the Chronotope in the Novel' and 'Discourse in the Novel' in *The Dialogic Imagination*, ed. Michael Holquist, trans. Michael Holquist and Caryl Emerson, Austin: University of Texas Press, pp. 84–258 and 259–422
—— (1986a) *Speech Genres and Other Late Essays*, ed. Caryl Emerson and Michael Holquist, trans. Vern W. McGee, Austin: University of Texas Press
—— (1986b) *Literaturno-kriticheskiye stati*, Moscow: Khudozhestvennaya Literatura
Barany, Zoltan and Robert G. Moser (eds) (2001) *Russian Politics: Challenges of Democratization*, Cambridge: Cambridge University Press
Barba, Eugenio (1999) *Land of Ashes and Diamonds: My Apprenticeship in Poland*, Aberystwyth: Black Mountain Press
Bauman, Zygmunt (1992) *Intimations of Postmodernity*, London and New York: Routledge
—— (1995) *Life in Fragments: Essays in Postmodern Morality*, Oxford: Blackwell
—— (2000) *Liquid Modernity*, Cambridge: Polity Press
Benedetti, Jean (ed. and trans.) (1991) *The Moscow Art Theatre Letters*, London: Methuen
—— (ed. and trans.) (1996) *Dear Writer . . . Dear Actress. . .: The Love Letters of Olga Knipper and Anton Chekhov*, London: Methuen
—— (1999) *Stanislavski: His Life and Art*, London: Methuen
Beumers, Birgit (1996) 'Commercial Enterprise on the Stage: Changes in Russian Theatre Management between 1986 and 1996', *Europe-Asia Studies* 48: 8, pp. 1,403–16
Bharucha, Rustom (1991) 'A View from India' in *Peter Brook and* The Mahabharata: *Critical Perspectives*, ed. David Williams, London: Routledge, pp. 228–52
Borovsky, Victor (1988) *Chaliapin*, London: Hamish Hamilton

Bourdieu, Pierre (1979a) *La Distinction: critique sociale du jugement*, Paris: Les Editions de Minuit

—— (1979b) 'Les trois états du capital culturel', *Actes de la recherche en sciences sociales* 30, pp. 3–6

—— (1980) *Le sens pratique*, Paris: Les Editions de Minuit

—— (1998) *Contre-feux*, Paris: Liber-Raisons d'agir

—— (2000 [1972]) *Esquisse d'une théorie de la pratique*, Paris: Editions du Seuil

—— (2001) *Contre-feux 2*, Paris: Liber-Raisons d'agir

Bourdieu, Pierre and Loïc J. D. Waquant (1992) *Réponses: Pour une anthropologie réflexive*, Paris: Editions du Seuil

Boykova, Irina (1992) 'Poteryany ray', *Peterburgsky teatralny zhyrnal* 0, pp. 26–31

Braun, Edward (ed. and trans.) (1998) *Meyerhold on Theatre*, London: Methuen

Brecht, Bertolt (1965) *Brecht on Theatre*, trans. John Willett, London: Methuen

Brook, Peter (1998) *Threads of Time: A Memoir*, London: Methuen

Brown, Archie (1997) *The Gorbachev Factor*, Oxford: Oxford University Press

Brown, David (1992) *Tchaikovsky: A Biographical and Critical Study*, vol. IV: *The Final Years 1885–1893*, London: Victor Gollancz

Carlson, Marvin (1996) 'Brook and Mnouchkine: Passages to India?' in *The Intercultural Performance Reader*, ed. Patrice Pavis, London: Routledge, pp. 79–92

Castells, Manuel (1996–8) *The Information Age: Economy, Society and Culture*, vols. 1–3, Oxford: Blackwell

Chekhov, Anton (1978) *Polnoye sobraniye sochineny i pisem*, vols 11 and 13 (plays), Moscow: Nauka

—— (1992) *Platonov* in *Twelve Plays*, trans. Ronald Hingley, Oxford and New York: Oxford University Press

—— (1994) *Chayka, Dyadya Vanya, Tri sestry, Vishnevy sad*, Paris: Bookking International

—— (1996) *Plays*, trans. Michael Frayn, London: Methuen

Dmitrevskaya, Marina (1986) 'Ishchem my sol, ishchem my bol etoy zemli', *Teatr* 4, pp. 89–101

—— (1988) 'O miloserdii, pravde i Olimpiyskom ogne', *Teatr* 4, pp. 47–52

—— (1992) 'Dlya veselya nam dany molodye gody . . .', *Peterburgsky teatralny zhurnal* 0, pp. 6–10

Dostoevsky, Fyodor (1965) *The Devils*, trans. David Magarshack, Harmondsworth: Penguin Books

Efros, Anatoly (1993) *Repetitsiya – lyubov moya*, Moscow: Panas

Epstein, Mikhaïl, Alexander Genis and Slobodanka Vladiv-Glover (eds) (1999) *Russian Postmodernism: New Perspectives on Post-Soviet Culture*, Oxford: Berghahn Books

Fanning, David (1995) 'Leitmotif in *Lady Macbeth*' in *Shostakovich Studies*, ed. David Fanning, Cambridge: Cambridge University Press, pp. 137–59

Fay, Laurel E. (2000) *Shostakovich: A Life*, Oxford: Oxford University Press

Featherstone, Michael (1991) *Consumer Culture and Postmodernism*, London: Sage

Freedman, John (1997) *Moscow Performances: The New Russian Theater 1991–1996*, Amsterdam: Harwood Academic Publishers

Freud, Sigmund (1962–75) *The Standard Edition of the Complete Psychological Works of Sigmund Freud*, vols 4–5: *The Interpretation of Dreams*, trans. and ed. James Strachey in collaboration with Anna Freud, assisted by Alix Strachey and Alan Tyson, London: Hogarth Press

Gill, Graeme and Roger D. Markwick (2000) *Russia's Stillborn Democracy? From Gorbachev to Yeltsin*, Oxford: Oxford University Press

Girard, René (1961) *Mensonge romantique et vérité romanesque*, Paris: Grasset

Gladkov, Aleksandr (1997) *Meyerhold Speaks, Meyerhold Rehearses*, ed. and trans. Alma Law, Amsterdam: Harwood Academic Publishers

Golding, William (1999 [1954]) *Lord of the Flies*, London: Faber and Faber

Grotowski, Jerzy (1995) 'From the Theatre Company to Art as Vehicle' in Thomas Richards, *At Work with Grotowski on Physical Actions*, London: Routledge, pp. 113–35

—— (1997) 'Art as Vehicle, 1986' in *The Grotowski Sourcebook*, ed. Richard Schechner and Lisa Wolford, London: Routledge, pp. 367–462

Harvey, David (1989) *The Condition of Postmodernity: An Enquiry into the Origins of Cultural Change*, Oxford: Blackwell

Hingley, Ronald (1992) 'Introduction' in Anton Chekhov, *Twelve Plays*, trans. Ronald Hingley, Oxford and New York: Oxford University Press, pp. vii–xiii

Holmberg, Arthur (1996) *The Theatre of Robert Wilson*, Cambridge: Cambridge University Press

Hosking, Geoffrey (1980) *Beyond Socialist Realism: Soviet Fiction since Ivan Denisovich*, London: Granada

Innes, Christopher (ed.) (2000) *A Sourcebook on Naturalist Theatre*, London: Routledge

Kaufmann, Walter (ed.) (1956) *Existentialism: From Dostoevsky to Sartre*, New York: Meridian Books

Lacan, Jacques (1973) *Le Séminaire: Livre XX, Encore*, Paris: Editions du Seuil

—— (1977) 'The Subversion of the Subject and the Dialectic of Desire in the Freudian Unconscious', in *Ecrits: A Selection*, trans. Alan Sheridan, London: Tavistock, pp. 294–324

Lampert, E. (1965) *Sons Against Fathers: Studies in Russian Radicalism and Revolution*, Oxford: Oxford University Press

Leach, Robert and Victor Borovsky (eds) (1999) *A History of Russian Theatre*, Cambridge: Cambridge University Press

Leskov, Nikolay (1966) 'Ledi Makbet Mtsenskogo uyezda' in *Povesty i rasskazy*, Moscow and Leningrad: Khudozhestvennaya Literatura, pp. 27–73

Lyotard, Jean-François (1979) *La Condition postmoderne*, Paris: Les Editions de Minuit

McFaul, Michael (2001) *Russia's Unfinished Revolution: Changes from Gorbachev to Putin*, Ithaca, NY: Cornell University Press

Maly Drama Theatre (1992) 'Gaudeamus', trans. Martin Dewhurst, *TheatreForum* 1, pp. 63–80

Merleau-Ponty, Maurice (1964) *Le Visible et l'invisible*, Paris: Gallimard

—— (1997) *La Phénoménologie de la perception*, Paris: Gallimard

Meyerhold, Vsevolod (1968a) *Stati, pisma, rechi, besedy: 1891–1917*, Moscow: Iskusstvo

—— (1968b) *Stati, pisma, rechi, besedy: 1917–1939*, Moscow: Iskusstvo

—— (1993) *Meyerhold repetiruyet: spektakli 30-kh godov*, Moscow: Artist. Rezhissyor. Teatr

Nietzsche, Friedrich (1963) *Thus Spake Zarathustra: A Book for Everyone and No One*, trans. R. J. Hollingworth, Harmondsworth: Penguin Books

—— (1966) *Beyond Good and Evil: Prelude to a Philosophy of the Future*, trans. Walter Kaufmann, New York: Vintage Books

—— (1974) *The Gay Science*, trans. Walter Kaufmann, New York: Vintage Books

—— (1990) *Twilight of the Idols* and *The Anti-Christ*, trans. R. J. Hollingworth, Harmondsworth: Penguin Books

Ostrovsky, A. (1992) 'Bes Dostoyevskogo', *Teatr* 10, pp. 31–8

Picon-Vallin, Béatrice (1994) 'Enseigner, former, créer', *Théâtre/Public* 116, pp. 43–51

—— (ed.) (1997) *Lioubimov: La Taganka*, Paris: CNRS Editions

Platonov, Andrey (1988) *Chevengur*, Moscow: Khudozhestvennaya Literatura

Pushkin, Aleksandr (1948) 'Poltava' in *Pushkin: Polnoye sobraniye sochineny*, vol. 5, Moscow: Akademiya Nauk, pp. 15–67

—— (1968) 'Pikovaya Dama' in *Romany i povesti*, Moscow: Mosovsky Rabochy, pp. 193–218

Rayfield, Donald (1997) *Anton Chekhov: A Life*, London: HarperCollins

Richards, Thomas (1995) *At Work with Grotowski on Physical Actions*, London: Routledge

Sartre, Jean-Paul (1943) *L'Etre et le néant: essai d'ontologie phénoménologique*, Paris: Gallimard

—— (1970) *L'Existentialisme est un humanisme*, Paris: Les Editions Nagel

Segel, Harold B. (1993) *Twentieth-century Russian Drama: From Gorky to the Present*, Baltimore, MD, and London: Johns Hopkins University Press

Semenovsky, Valery (1994a) 'Lev Dodin kak zerkolo pucckoy revolyutsii', *Moskovsky nablyudatel* 7–8, pp. 5–6

—— 'Na derevnye Lyevushki', *Moskovsky nablyudatel* 7–8, pp. 19–30

Senelick, Laurence (1997) *The Chekhov Theatre: A Century of the Plays in Performance*, Cambridge: Cambridge University Press

Service, Robert (1997) *A History of Twentieth-century Russia*, London: Penguin Books

Shevtsova, Maria (1978) *The Theatre Practice of Anatoly Efros*, Theatre Papers no. 6, Devon: Dartington College of the Arts

—— (1983) 'Chekhov in France, 1976–9: Productions by Strehler, Miquel and Pintilié' in *Transformations in Modern European Drama*, ed. Ian Donaldson, London: Macmillan, pp. 82–98

—— (1989) 'The Sociology of the Theatre, Part Three: Performance', *New Theatre Quarterly* 5: 19, August 1989, pp. 282–300

—— (1992) 'Dialogism in the Novel and Bakhtin's Theory of Culture', *New Literary History: A Journal of Theory and Interpretation* 23: 3, pp. 747–63

—— (1993) *Theatre and Cultural Interaction*, Sydney: Sydney Studies

—— (1994) 'The Art of Stillness: Brook's *Impressions de Pelléas*', *New Theatre Quarterly* 10: 40, pp. 358–65

—— (1995a) 'Isabelle Huppert Becomes Orlando', *TheatreForum* 6, pp. 69–75

—— (1995b) 'Of "Butterfly" and Men: Robert Wilson Directs Diana Soviero at the Paris Opéra', *New Theatre Quarterly* 10: 41, pp. 3–11

—— (1997a) 'Sociocultural Analysis: National and Cross-cultural Performance', *Theatre Research International* 22: 1, pp. 4–18

—— (1997b) 'Resistance and Resilience: An Overview of the Maly Theatre of St Petersburg', *New Theatre Quarterly* 13: 52, pp. 299–317

—— (1998) 'Drowning in Dixie: The Maly Drama Theatre Plays Chekhov Untitled', *TheatreForum* 13, pp. 46–53

—— (2000) 'War and Ash at La Scala: Lev Dodin Rehearses *Mazepa*', *TheatreForum* 16, pp. 95–104

—— (2001) 'Sociocultural Performance Analysis' in *New Approaches to Theatre Studies and Performance Analysis*, ed. Günter Berghaus, Tübingen: Max Niemeyer Verlag, pp. 45–60

Shyer, Laurence (1989) *Robert Wilson and his Collaborators*, New York: Theatre Communications Group

Smeliansky, Anatoly (1994) 'Strana kotoraya', *Moskovsky nablyudatel* 7–8, pp. 9–11

—— (1999) *The Russian Theatre after Stalin*, Cambridge: Cambridge University Press

Stanislavsky, Konstantin (1967) *On the Art of the Stage*, trans. David Magarshack, London and Boston, MA: Faber and Faber

—— (1988) 'On the Threshold of the Subconscious' in *An Actor Prepares*, London: Methuen, pp. 281–313

—— (1988–99) *Sobraniye sochineny v devyati tomakh*, ed. Anatoly Smeliansky, I. N. Salovyova, I. N. Vinogradskaya, V. S. Davydov, O. N. Yefremov, O. A. Radishcheva and M. N. Ulyanov, 9 vols, Moscow: Issukstvo

Stanislavsky, Konstantin and Pavel Rumyantsev (1975) *Stanislavski on Opera*, ed. and trans. Elizabeth Reynolds Hapgood, New York: Theatre Arts Books

Steele, Jonathan (1996) 'Why Gorbachev Failed', *New Left Review* 216, pp. 141–52

Strehler, Giorgio (1974) *Per un teatro umano*, Milan: Feltrinelli

Toporkov, Vasily Osipovich (1998) *Stanislavsky in Rehearsal: The Final Years*, trans. Christine Edwards, New York and London: Routledge

Vilar, Jean (1975) *Le Théâtre, service public*, Paris: Gallimard

Voloshinov, V. N. [Bakhtin] (1986) *Marxism and the Philosophy of Language*, trans. Ladislav Matejka and I. R. Titunik, Cambridge, MA: Harvard University Press

Werth, Alexander (1964) *Russia at War, 1941–1945*, London: Barrie and Rockliffs

White, Stephen (1995) *After Gorbachev*, Cambridge: Cambridge University Press

Index

eBooks – at www.eBookstore.tandf.co.uk

A library at your fingertips!

eBooks are electronic versions of printed books. You can store them on your PC/laptop or browse them online.

They have advantages for anyone needing rapid access to a wide variety of published, copyright information.

eBooks can help your research by enabling you to bookmark chapters, annotate text and use instant searches to find specific words or phrases. Several eBook files would fit on even a small laptop or PDA.

NEW: Save money by eSubscribing: cheap, online access to any eBook for as long as you need it.

Annual subscription packages

We now offer special low-cost bulk subscriptions to packages of eBooks in certain subject areas. These are available to libraries or to individuals.

For more information please contact webmaster.ebooks@tandf.co.uk

We're continually developing the eBook concept, so keep up to date by visiting the website.

www.eBookstore.tandf.co.uk